AN AFRICAN SCHOOL
A RECORD OF EXPERIENCE

For
Constance
and the children
Nicholas, Elizabeth, Sarah, and
Catherine

KIT ELLIOTT

AN AFRICAN SCHOOL

A Record of Experience

CAMBRIDGE
AT THE UNIVERSITY PRESS
1970

373.11
E46

Published by the Syndics of the Cambridge University Press
Bentley House, 200 Euston Road, London, N.W.1
American Branch: 32 East 57th Street, New York, N.Y. 10022

© Cambridge University Press 1970

Library of Congress Catalogue Card Number: 78–111128
Standard Book Number: 521 07722 2

Printed in Great Britain
by W. & J. Mackay & Co Ltd, Chatham

Contents

Preface

For five and a half years my wife and I taught at a small Roman Catholic secondary school run by an Irish missionary order in West Africa. It was near Jos on the Plateau which stands at the heart of Federal Nigeria, a refuge for innumerable pagan tribes over thousands of years, and now the centre of a prosperous tin-mining industry and a large immigrant population. It is about our experience that this book has been written. Many people have taught in such schools, particularly in the last twenty years of independence and upheaval for so much of Africa. The European secondary-school teacher was the last in the line of explorer, merchant, soldier, administrator, and missionary who have taken part in modern African history. For this reason I thought our experience worth recording; out of the classroom have come the citizens and leaders of modern Africa.

This is a record and examination of experience, and the book carries with it the limitations of this experience. It is humiliating for a teacher to confess that after so many years the children he taught were still strangers to him. Mea culpa. Much of the fault must lie in myself. A warmer and more sympathetic person would have got much closer much sooner. Yet all expatriates in Africa are to some extent the prisoners of their own authority, upbringing and privileges. If we could divest ourselves of that authority, of the need to supervise our classrooms, to arbitrate in school affairs, to direct children through their school work, we could approach our pupils on equal terms; if we and they could expunge the oppressive legacy of military conquest, political power, economic exploitation, and cultural arrogance, we could approach the children we teach with proper humility; if we could abandon our standard of living, the income, the servants and the accommodation that preserve us from the realities of African life, how much we could learn. Then we could begin to overcome those divisions of language and culture that mean so much more than the colour of our skins.

vii

The fact remains that I know more about English children I teach now, after a few months, than I knew about the Nigerian boys I taught for five years. If, occasionally, there is a detachment in my description of these Nigerian children, the reasons must be sought, partly in my own personality, and partly in the social and historical context within which the expatriate teacher works.

As it was, we were strangers in Africa, privileged, and treated with the courtesy and respect due to guests and strangers, but only occasionally admitted to the warmth of personal contact which imbues the complex relationships of African society. We remember with deep gratitude what we were allowed to see. We guess at and try to understand what we did not see and could not understand. We remain strangers.

But even lack of comprehension is important if it can be recognised. Those who are familiar with Africa may not recognise our part of Africa, or our particular type of school with its particular problems. Nevertheless, behind the misleading façade that makes an African school seem so much like its European counterpart there are problems and assumptions which face all African pupils and all their teachers. All African schools and all African classrooms will be more like each other than they are like anything which we know in Europe or America. So little is known about these schools and their children that any record must have value, even if it does no more than explain what it looked like and felt like to be there. This, then, is a record and tentative examination of what we saw and felt, of experience that we found absorbing, dramatic, disturbing, and entertaining, an experience peculiar to a particular place, and a particular period of history.

In conclusion I should like to thank Mrs E. Amechi, who knew and understood far more than I, and who, with her family, has undergone far more than I can properly comprehend in beleaguered Biafra. Her suggestions have enabled me more properly to understand the shortcomings of my book and do something to rectify them. Above all I am more grateful than I can easily say to Miss Jacqueline Reynolds and Mr David Holbrook, without whom this particular record of experience would never have seen the light of day. K.E.

PART ONE

RECONNAISSANCE

1
Arrival

At three o'clock on a January morning I was alone in Kano Airport, rather deaf from eight hours' engine noise. I had spent the night wide awake peering into the darkness over Africa. I was without most of the necessary papers for entry into Nigeria, and half my luggage, the half I had stuffed into the canvas hold-all with the side split open, had gone to Japan with Air India. It was 1960, the year of Africa, according to the Liberal Press. I sat waiting for the dawn, while a turbaned figure, veiled in black, and carrying a spear, paced up and down outside the windows of the airport lounge.

My soul, as the phrase has it, was catching up with me. I was a drop-out from the Cambridge generation that was, about that time, making its name in the satirical revues, in *Private Eye*, and late at night on the B.B.C. I had been on *Varsity*, had the running of the Diary, the features page, the critics' columns, remembered the parties, the gossip, the rivalries of that fierce, egotistic little world, and had once had the prospect of continuing in it, being on the inside, knowing what was going on, what it was all about. Something had gone wrong. I had proved an abominable journalist, and when they fired me in Bristol I had become an almost equally bad teacher in Birmingham. As a further aberration I had become a Roman Catholic in the Oratory on the Hagley Road a month before. I had moved a great way off the beaten track.

Nor could I explain to myself why I was in that empty lounge in Northern Nigeria not far from the edge of the desert. I could not, when I thought about it, even describe what it was I was going to. I had turned down a perfectly respectable job for the Northern Nigerian Government to teach at a boys' secondary school, only two years old, for the Roman Catholic Prefect of Northern Nigeria.

3

This dignitary had written to the Canon at St Edmund's House in Cambridge, a very distant acquaintance of his indeed, to say that he needed two teachers, preferably with English degrees, but any subject would do; preferably Catholic, but upright heathens would satisfy. So I was going to his school with my history degree, and in six months' time my fiancée would also graduate with a history degree, and she would join me. He had sent me a glowing report of the natural beauties of the Jos Plateau—'People come here on holiday from all over Nigeria.' He had referred to the Principal's bungalow 'which would shortly be vacant', and he had sent a specimen contract, and the information that if I accepted he would send me an airline ticket booked open to Jos, a letter to the immigration authorities in Kano accepting responsibility, and that I would receive a kit allowance of sixty pounds. I had written my acceptance, resigned my Birmingham post, and in return received my open booking and nothing more. A series of urgent letters had produced no further response. I had caught the plane from London that January night, leaving Constance behind me, and there I was, with no one in Africa aware of my existence.

After three hours the sun came up over Africa to reveal a dusty flower-bed in front of the airport, and in it a black man in khaki shorts with a hose in his hand. A B.O.A.C. girl arrived with the daylight. She found me a mini-bus and a friendly driver who drove me into Kano, into Africa, along the tarred road which wound jet-black through a flat dusty countryside of coarse grass, scrub, and low bushes, past occasional farms with brown mud-walled huts, and small dry fields of hard brown earth. Against this dun background the people we passed stood out in bright white robes, the occasional farmer with a hoe over his shoulder, a gowned woman with a huge basket on her head, black men in trousers pedalling bicycles, gangs of labourers, stripped and sweating, pushing trolleys made of old lorry chassis.

A friendly European from West African Airways looked after me that day, discovered that I was booked through to Jos after all, and drove me round Kano that afternoon, with its mud walls, mysterious alleyways, robed crowds, its occasional camel, and a little girl with a beer bottle balanced on her head. He took me to his house for tea and that evening escorted me on a tour of Kano bars. The following morning, about two, I fell asleep in my hotel room which I shared with a soft-spoken South African.

The next morning that kindly employee of West African Airways put me on a plane, a little four-engined Heron, so small that it remains the only aircraft I have ever travelled on whose wings and tail are both visible at the same time from the passengers' windows. The little machine taxied away from the airport buildings, then rushed back down the runway, and we droned slowly up over the plains of Hausaland which stretched endlessly into the haze in all directions, flat, brown, parched, dotted with myriads of trees, crossed by an occasional river, of sand rather than water. Here and there were groups of rectangular huts round rectangular compounds. Sometimes a slab of rock heaved its smooth surface out of the laterite. Across the plain stretched a dusty road, one or two tiny cars speeding down it, and an empty railway.

Gradually the infrequent slabs of rock that rose out of the plains of Northern Nigeria became more common, became great domes of granite, fractured and multiplied into ridges and peaks. The landscape became jagged, almost lunar, but for the brush and scrub covering the rocky slopes, the harshly eroded stream-beds, and the nests of minute circular huts that clustered on the hillsides. The notice inside the aircraft flashed for us to fasten our seat belts. The hills below sloped towards us under the wing-tip, and there was a glimpse of many roofs away to our left as the machine banked. This was the Jos Plateau. I had read about it in the Birmingham Reference Library. Its forbidding rocks, its scrubland, and its harsh, gritty soil had defended the survivors of scores of refugee tribes throughout centuries of invasion and warfare. It was the Christianised children of these pagan tribes whom I was to teach for the next five and a half years.

A road, huts, a drainage channel, another road flashed beneath us and the Heron settled on the runway, before taxiing slowly towards the little airport building. Once more I made for a telephone. This time I contacted the mission, and a puzzled voice said:

'No, the Prefect hadn't told us to expect you, Mr Elliott. But if you wait there I'll send the Principal out to pick you up.'

A quarter of an hour later I met my first Irish missionary. He was small, plump and dark. His jet-black hair was greased well back, his eyes were sharp, and against his unusually white skin his chin showed acute, prominent, and rather shadowy. A packet of cigarettes protruded from his shirt pocket. His shorts were enormous, far wider at the knee than the waist. He was very charming, pumped my hand vigorously and offered me a cigarette. He was to be my Principal, and was obviously not expecting me any time within the next fortnight.

He drove me into Jos along a road that passed through rocky, grass-covered country like the heaths on the edge of the Lake District, past tree-covered compounds set among rocks, and into a shady enclosure behind a large white church. A large bungalow on one side of that enclosure was the Jos Catholic Mission, and inside they were drinking tea. Around a long living-room, in solid wooden armchairs, sat about a dozen priests and nuns with teacups at their elbows. The nuns in their white habits wore strange rectangular head-dresses which enclosed their faces like medieval helmets. The priests were in shirts and the same enormous shorts as the Principal which I soon came to recognise as the priestly uniform. There was one lady in the room who was not a nun. With something surprisingly like a leer in my direction, the Principal said to her: 'Our first lay teacher. Ye'll be changing your mind now, Kate, and wish to be staying.' Introductions were made, of which I remembered not a name. I was handed a cup of tea, khaki-coloured and very strong. The milk was condensed, and the jug veiled in a neat little net whose beaded edges hung over the sides.

We drank tea, and the lady left, apparently to drive to Kano, where she was teaching. Then the Principal stood. 'We'll be going. Mr Elliott, ye'll sleep at Vwang tonight and we'll see what we can do with you after that. Ye'd like to see the place, I'd expect.' He struck an attitude of farewell in the doorway, palm upraised—'Be seeing ye'—and led the way out on to the verandah, across the compound to his pick-up.

This was a Morris of indeterminate age, coated inside and out with dust. I took my place beside the Principal, kicking away several bits of dirty machinery and an empty cigarette packet that lay by my feet. A little picture of the Virgin was stuck to the roof, just above the mirror with a prayer for safety underneath it. There was a strange rattle from behind the dashboard. The ignition was being switched on. Instantaneously the engine roared, the gear was thrust down, the clutch let out, the throttle pushed in, a match struck, a cigarette lit, and with dramatic effect we were propelled out of the compound with a whiz of flying gravel into the main road. The Principal's chin was poised, teeth clenched, a few inches above the wheel, eyes glaring at cyclists and children in the road before us, an expired match between the fingers of his left hand, and a glowing cigarette between the fingers of the right. Somehow a green packet of cigarettes with a picture of a galleon on it was thrust at me. Rattling at every hinge, in a crescendo of engine noise, the pick-up surged up the hill out of Jos, doing every bit of forty. We bounced and swayed, lurched and clattered. The cab filled with cigarette smoke.

Outside Jos the pick-up settled down to a steady clatter. The Principal relaxed his grip on the wheel slightly. 'I'd have written to ye before,' he confided, 'but I did not want to frighten ye off. Thought it would be better if the Prefect dealt with ye.' Another cigarette passed over to me. 'Compound's still a bit bush,' he shouted above the engine. 'Ye'll soon settle down.' We were passing through the main street of a town. The Principal's brow was creased, as he tensed himself over the wheel. 'Bukuru. Ye never know what ye're going to meet. They've been living with cars for thirty years, and still they step into the road without so much as a look sideways. Ye bastard!' We lurched into the middle of the road. A boy on a bicycle wobbled beside us. I glimpsed briefly the title 'Onwegbu's Healthy Bread' advertised on the front of it, and a broad grin on the boy's face. 'Bastards,' observed the Principal. 'There's a priest in Kuduna. What he said was, just missing one of them, "Africa'd be a splendid place if it wasn't for the bloody Africans".'

7

We had left Bukuru behind us, and turned off right. 'Five more miles, soon be there. What do they call you?'

'Kit,' I shouted. He seemed very friendly, was quite young, and clearly I was going to know him and work with him for a long period. 'What do they call you?'

There was a second of hesitation. 'I'm a lay brother. My Christian name's Sheamus. Ye can call me Hall Sullivan, if ye like.' I held my peace. Clearly it was safer to rely on the term 'brother'.

'There now,' he said, easing himself back in his seat, 'ye can see the compound, there, beyond the wood. Those hills are the Vet., the Veterinary Research Station. Those roofs in front, that's Vwang. I could make out little but a few patches of grey, presumably corrugated iron, when these vanished behind the trees. It was not for a few minutes that we were out of the wood, a large plantation on both sides of the road, across a bridge—'Dangerous place, that,' he observed—down a long stretch of tarred road that curved suddenly. Then we were slowing down. Something like a ruin stood beside the road on our left. One side of it appeared to be naked concrete wall. A huge emblem in coloured cement stood over the middle in the shape of a shield on which a cross seemed to hover over something like water. We turned abruptly left beside a huge grey building of naked concrete, unfinished and forbidding.

'We're here,' said the Principal. The end of the road was an enormous empty plain. The school compound was in one corner, in front of the low hills, the land belonging to the Veterinary Research Station. Before it and around it the plain seemed endless, sloping to distant jagged rocks and a far-off horizon. 'What d'ye think of it?'

We rattled to a halt in front of two tiny bungalows with a sad effort at flower-beds in front of them. 'Maurice! Danladi!' bawled the Principal. A young good-looking African in a clean white shirt and khaki shorts appeared from one of the bungalows. He bowed towards me. 'Maurice, make you put this master's load for Father Harrington's room. You fit make bed there first thing.' Another Nigerian had appeared at one end of the verandah. He was large, very muscular, rather greasy, was wrapped in a grubby apron sewn out of a salt sack and appeared to be the cook. He scowled at us. 'Danladi, get these things from the back of the pick-up. Quick-quick.' Danladi moved morosely towards us.

I followed Maurice towards the Education Secretary's bungalow. I was to find that the fathers' rooms were much the same everywhere in the mission. The two armchairs were just the same primitive wooden objects I had seen in Jos. The iron bedstead with the dusty mosquito net draped above it, the drab grey blankets, the coarse sheets, the enamelled bowl and soap dish, the mirror in the plastic frame on top of the crude wooden chest of drawers were to be seen in every priest's bedroom I was to see. There was little to tell me much about the Education Secretary. There was nothing on the wall except a crucifix. The reading matter consisted of half a dozen detective novels, Penguin greenbacks, two back numbers of *Time*, a copy of *The Reader's Digest*, a few pamphlets put out by the Catholic Truth Society, and the magazine issued by the missionary society with its sentimental snapshots of Africa and its children's corner. The only other evidence of personal possessions was a cheap suitcase under the bed.

There was some cold water in the enamel bowl, so I sluiced my hands and face before walking across to the other bungalow a few yards away. The little living-room was empty, so I sat down in one of the six big wooden armchairs that were cramped around it and took stock. The walls, bare of any ornament, closed down on me painted in a glum green emulsion to the windows, and a sickly cream above. The floor was uncarpeted concrete, and one or two cigarette ends lay crushed upon it. Now that I had sat down I could no longer see out of the one small window. This was no sacrifice, for the compound, the flower-beds with their few weary marigolds, the occasional beer can, the cook, and the distant buildings were all perfectly visible through the open door. It occurred to me that this was the Principal's bungalow 'which should be vacant' and to which the Prefect was expecting to transfer me when the Principal himself was established in something more commodious.

The Principal reappeared. 'Beer?' to me, and through the door, 'Maurice, bring two beer.'

The young African entered with glasses and two beer cans which he punctured and poured out for us. We drank.

'Shall we eat? Maurice—abinchi.' I understood that lunch had been called for, and followed the Principal into the next room, which turned out to be smaller and darker than the first. Maurice opened an antique refrigerator, at the side of the room, from which most of the white enamel seemed to have disappeared. The interior seemed to be solid with cold-store provisions and ice. A bottle of water was taken out, and our glasses were filled. The food was much as I might have expected from the cook. Like him it lacked grace but made up for that in bulk, and like him it was greasy and made little attempt to please. His skills were of the plainest bake, boil and fry variety, and even for these there had been little call, since the soup came out of a tin, the sausages out of the refrigerator, and the sweet out of a packet of blancmange powder.

We moved a little heavily back into the sitting-room, and over tea I began to piece together the origins of the school. Secondary schools were still rather rare in Northern Nigeria, and it had not been until a few years ago that with the approach of independence the Northern Government had woken up to the threat from the much better-educated southern tribes, the Ibo and the Yoruba in particular, and had set about founding its own secondary schools. Even then, in 1960, there were still only fifteen Government-owned institutions. This had provided the opportunity for the missions.

The Prefect had wanted his secondary school for some time. It lent status to a small, poor province, only recently created. Not until 1958 was the Government prepared to let him found one. When permission had been granted the low building away to our right through the open door had been run up in six weeks, and thirty boys had been installed. The Government was now providing the capital for completing the building, and was also paying teachers' salaries on a scale which I already knew to be somewhat less generous than that paid to its own staff. The province, in fact, was deputising for the Government, recruiting staff and running a school for them, and liable to Government inspection and supervision. The school year was just beginning, and the third intake was due to arrive in a week's time, so that there would be nearly ninety boys on the compound. Most of them were from the pagan tribes of the diocese which covered Plateau Province, and parts of Zaria and Bauchi Province to the east and west. A few came from Adamawa, the trust territory on the Cameroon border four hundred miles away, where there was no Catholic secondary school. Another group were children of Ibo parents, some of the thousands of immigrants from the Eastern Region, who had poured into Jos, Bukuru and other Plateau towns during the previous half-century to run the mines, man the offices and make their fortunes in the markets. Soon I was to know them all well. Now the compound was empty.

'Siesta,' said the Principal. We disappeared to our beds. I collapsed in the hot afternoon, and lay unconscious.

2
The First Meeting

It was a week before I first met the boys I was going to teach. Most of this time I seemed to spend in the Principal's pick-up travelling between Vwang, Jos, and Bukuru. Then, one morning I found a row of grey galvanised iron buckets on the verandah in front of the Principal's tiny bungalow. Each one was stuffed with clothing and had a name painted on the side. Beside one or two of them was a tin trunk, a small suitcase, or a bundle wrapped in a towel. The boys were returning to school. The duplicated instructions issued to each, I discovered, demanded that each one bring: 'One khaki knicker, one white knicker, one khaki shirt, one white shirt, one pair of black shoes, one blanket, and one cutlass.' Knicker was normal pidgin for a pair of shorts. The cutlass, a strip of corrugated iron sharpened at one end, was essential if the school were not to disappear in long grass when the rainy season started. The bucket was to carry water from the nearest tap, across the road in the Veterinary Research Station, for there was no running water on the school compound, the well water was undrinkable, and three times a day a train of water carriers had to trudge backwards and forwards in and out of the compound. That very morning, in the distance, small figures could be seen carrying buckets. The clank of bucket handles, and the distant shouts of their owners now took the place of the incessant swish of the dry wind passing through the eucalyptus trees which overlooked the compound.

I saw the little boys first when they came with buckets on their heads to report to the Principal. They hovered in groups of two or three near the end of the verandah whispering to each other and bobbing at every passer-by. Some of them were children of eleven or twelve with faces like angels, round-cheeked, large-eyed,

delicate-featured, completely tongue-tied with awe and embarrass-
ment. Others in the same form were adolescents with enormous
hands and feet, voices somewhere in their bellies, and wide grins.
They were apparently both very nervous and very willing to please.
Usually a senior boy would be called, more often than not from
their own tribe, and given instructions to find the children a bed,
a mattress, and a meal.

A week or so after the rest came the latecomers. The last was
called Mathias. He might have been thirteen. He was thin and tired,
covered with dust from the lorry, which made him look grey, old,
and ill. He stood just off the verandah late one afternoon, with a
cheap tin trunk and no bucket. One of his legs was bandaged.

'Too late,' said the Principal.

'I was sick,' pleaded the child in a low voice, looking at the
ground rather than the Principal. 'The lorry it was too slow.'

'You have come too late.'

'Brother?'

'You are too late. You should have been here a week ago. Your
place has been taken.'

'Brother?'

'We can't wait for ever. You take next year's exam. Maybe
there will be a place at Kafanchan.'

Without looking up, the boy turned round and limped away.
'What will happen to him?' I asked.

'He'll hang about for a while. He'll find a relation to send him
home in the end. We've usually got to tell one or two extra to
come in case some don't arrive. If they're late, they've only themselves to blame.'

I said nothing. A sick child had been turned away with no
return for his suffering. I had done nothing to help him.

I soon met the older boys. 'I have to collect the fees from Form
III,' the Principal said on the first Monday after term started.
'Would ye like to come? It'd give ye a chance to see them all.' I
followed him to the main classroom block, the unfinished building
with the huge concrete badge on it I had seen when I first arrived.
We sat in his office, which was a concrete cell furnished only

with a desk, two chairs, and a filing cabinet. A group of boys was waiting at the entrance. 'Which of ye's first. Mr Nongo, in ye come.'

A sturdy lad of about fifteen stood before the desk with his feet apart. He glanced curiously from under his eyelids at where I sat at the side of the room.

'And how did ye leave Father Smith, Gabriel?'

'Well, Brother Sheamus.' He smiled broadly, and crossed his legs nervously.

'And did ye see your parents during the break, Gabriel?'

'Yes brother, small, before Christmas.'

'And have ye any fees for me, Gabriel?'

'No, brother.'

'All right—you go and write your parents you must have fees soon.'

'Yes, brother.'

With a last glance in my direction he went out, to be replaced by a lanky youth of about the same age, rather fairer in complexion, who stood uneasily in the same place.

'Well, Benedict, do I find ye well?'

'Well, Brother Sheamus.'

'And how are things down at Kagoro?'

'Well, brother.'

'Ye have some fees?'

'No, Brother Sheamus. My uncle said let you wait small till it come harvest.'

'Ah, Benedict, that won't do. Your uncle has more money than that. You write him soon.'

'Yes, brother.'

A thin boy with a long face replaced him. He had very long hands and seemed not to know what to do with them.

'Well, Gabriel, and do you have any fees?'

'No, brother.'

'All right, Gabriel.'

As he went out the Principal said: 'Ye can't help having a weakness for them. That boy, now. His uncle came in last year.

"Father," he said, "I have been paid. Take Gabriel's fee now or for sure I will drink it."'

The process went on all morning. It served mainly to show the boys their new expatriate teacher, and to display the Principal's knowledge of their homes, their tribes, their relations, and their personal circumstances. No fees were collected. An annual charge of twelve pounds was either out of their reach or their relations simply had no intention of paying it.

I watched them come in. Many of them were as old as I was, but few were particularly tall. Almost all were barefooted, and on their legs, which frequently seemed remarkably thin, were the scars of childhood sores. Their names startled me. There were three Gabriels in the class, a Hyacinth with a slight moustache on his upper lip, an Aloysius, an Augustine, and an Anacletus. Later I was to come across a Remigius, a Lazarus, a Claver, a Theophilus, and a Sabinus, while I also heard of a Polycarp. Their parents made a close study of the martyrology before the christening. Their places of origin sounded as strange to my ears: Shendam, Pankshin, Kafanchan, Kwa, Kwalla, Kwande, Akwanga, Zawan, and Du.

The last boy left shortly before breakfast. As we returned to the bungalow the Principal, evidently in a good mood, said: 'Would ye not like to see them in class. We'll call them after breakfast, and ye can take them for a period. They're fine to teach, just fine.'

So my first Nigerian class was waiting for me an hour later. For the first time I entered one of those gloomy classrooms, with walls of unpainted grey concrete, and five rows of heavy, clumsily carpentered desks. The boys rose to their feet as I came in. There was a tense silence, full of curiosity and anticipation. 'Sit down,' I said. Without a murmur they sat. They waited. Their clothes were a ragged assortment of jerseys, tattered shirts, torn gowns, and frayed shorts, for they had been working in the dormitories that morning, but their faces all seemed identical, all black, all grave, concerned, and intense. No one smiled. There was not a murmur of comment. They were waiting for me to teach them.

'Form II?' I asked. No one answered.

'My name is Mr Elliott,' I said. 'This is how you spell it.' I wrote it on the board in block capitals, turned, and fell off the edge of the tiny cement platform in front of the blackboard. Not a muscle moved as I tottered in front of them.

'I shall be teaching you English and history,' I said. 'I am going to give you a lesson today. Take out your history exercise books, please.' Perhaps, at last there was an isolated mutter as desk lids rose, books taken out, and lids banged shut again, but it was extinguished as they sat with the exercise books open in front of them, pen in hand, waiting. 'Oh, and your textbooks.' No one said anything. Then a boy in the right-hand rank stood, stooping slightly and submissively over his desk. His complexion was olive, his hair curly, not a negro at all, but a half-caste.

'Father—sir,' he said slowly, with a slight lilt to his voice, 'we have not textbooks given us.' Forty minutes stretched ahead of me, with little to do but talk. I knew what this meant in Birmingham.

'This term,' I started as brightly as I could, 'I am going to teach you about the Middle Ages.' This appeared to be what the syllabus required. 'This period I am going to talk about the crusades.' This happened to be a topic I knew well, and I had to talk about something for nearly three-quarters of an hour. I talked volubly for the next ten minutes, spattering the blackboard with names, dates, places, a map. No questions were asked, no noise made. The boys sat with pens poised, waiting for something. Then the light-skinned boy raised his hand a little timidly. 'Father—sir, may we take this down?'

'Well'—I was a little puzzled—'you may, if you want.' The tension eased as every pen set to work. For the next ten minutes everything I said went down in their exercise books. My words appeared to be golden. I was quite flattered. Only later did I realise that no one understood a word.

Then something most unexpected happened. A boy in the middle of the classroom suddenly stood up. He was stocky, rather grubby from his work earlier that morning, his hair matted, and his gown, a loose, unwashed affair, hung over his shoulders exposing a worn vest and his chest. He look frightened, and waved his hand uncertainly near his forehead.

I brightened. Somebody was going to ask a question. 'Well?'

'Sir,' he said, with a frown on his face, 'I want to shit.'

I think my jaw fell open. A disciplinary crisis so soon. Where were the crusades now?

'What?' I said feebly.

'I want to shit,' he said, a little more urgently, 'sir.'

I pulled myself together, and prepared to sustain my authority. 'What,' I said sternly, 'did I hear you say?'

The boy looked even more concerned. Aware that something had gone wrong, he tried to be more explicit. 'I need,' he said, and then thought of the word, 'to excrete.'

Suddenly I realised that this was not a crisis after all. The class was obviously alarmed that something had gone wrong. They looked concerned and bewildered, waiting anxiously to see what would happen next. The olive-skinned boy did his best to help. 'He says, sir, he wishes to go for latrine.' There was a movement of agreement through the class—a satisfactory explanation had been made. The feeling seemed to be that I did not understand English.

'I have pain for belly, this morning, sir,' said the boy in the middle of the class, frowning more intently than ever. 'Gabriel Zi done give me purge. I beg you let me go latrine, sir.'

'Yes, yes, by all means,' I said hastily, and then rather feebly as the boy rushed for the door, 'And never let me hear you use that word again.' The door closed, the tension eased, and the class returned to its exercise books. I had ten minutes left, so I made up some notes which I wrote on the board. The class copied in silence. This was evidently what they wanted. I looked at their black woolly heads, all now bent over their desks. One or two had pencils thrust into their crinkly hair. How long, I thought, before I know them? How long before they know me?

3

A Day in the Classroom

Not until the second Monday of the term did we really settle down to a full daily timetable. I had, some time before, seen posted to the Principal's bedroom door his personal timetable, approved and signed by someone termed the Provincial, whom I understood to be the society's representative in the district. This piece of typed paper told the Principal when to get up, what time his breakfast should be, and what hours of the day should be spent at Mass, teaching, eating, having his siesta, or reading his breviary. It ended by telling him when to go to bed.

At six o'clock, half an hour later than this timetable specified, the hand bell tolled from the nearest dormitory. It was still grey and gloomy at that time. Silence fell again. The eucalyptus trees whispered quietly outside the window. I allowed five minutes, as, I imagine, did the rest of the school, then groped my way to the bowl of water left on the washstand by Maurice the previous night and, like the rest of the school, douched myself with cold water. Through the bedroom window I spat green chlorophyll toothpaste on to the dry grass below.

The gravel crunched on the other side of the bungalow as the Principal, struggling into his soutane, made his way to the nearest dormitory. The priest from near-by Zawan had just arrived. Mass was to be said in the room which was still being used as a classroom during the day. Doing up my tie, I hurried out after him. Hyacinth, the third-year boy with the moustache, was still setting up the altar on the big table which was to be used by the teacher later in the day, while through the door came a queue of sleepy boys wrapped in scarves, second-hand jackets, coarse grey jackets, and motley robes and rags of all descriptions. I recognised Gabriel Nongo, draped in a large towelling dressing-gown. The priest moved swiftly through the Mass. A few children took communion with devout intense faces. When Mass finished Hyacinth extinguished the candles, while the Principal waited as the parish priest disrobed before driving back to Zawan. As the boys shuffled out I made my way hastily to the Principal's living-room.

The aluminium teapot was on the table by the Czechoslovakian teacups with the flowers transferred on to the sides. I poured out rich brown tea, laced it with yellow condensed milk from the tin and tossed in sugar lumps. The gravel crunched outside.

'Morning, brother. Tea?'

'Morning, Kit.' The Principal collapsed in an armchair opposite, a cigarette half-smoked in his hand, threw the green packet with the galleon on the arm beside him, undid his soutane, and flung out his legs before him. A perspective of heavy black shoes, worsted socks, white knees, khaki shorts, aertex singlet, and hairy chest rose to the bristles on his chin and the pearly halo of smoke wafting above his head to the ceiling. He lent forward, up-ended the milk tin over his cup, threw in sugar, stirred, lifted and drank.

'That's better.'

He inhaled again, stubbed out the end, and shook another cigarette out of the packet. Then he winced, got up, and disappeared. The day had begun.

Outside the boys were clanking their buckets backwards and forwards to the tap in the Veterinary Research Station across the road. Loud voices sounded, and somebody whistled. A little motor cycle stuttered along the road. In the dormitories the beds were being made, while other boys were sweeping out the classrooms.

By eight the other European teacher, a lady, had arrived from Kuru, five miles away, in her red and black Vauxhall, visible a mile down the road before it came on to the compound. Boys were wandering in twos and threes towards the classrooms. The hand bell tolled once more, just visible through one of the classroom windows, swinging up and down. There was a little more activity around the dormitories as a few more boys began to trot towards the classrooms. Then we tucked our books under our arms and moved towards our classes.

As I entered Form II I heard a prayer being intoned next door. The Principal was starting his lesson in the approved manner. My own class moved abruptly to attention behind their desks, a mark of respect I was only just getting used to.

'Sit down, boys.'

They sat down quietly. How different from my Birmingham classes.

'English this morning.' I went through the rigmarole. 'You will need your readers, your reading notebooks, and something with which to write. Get them out, please.' I articulated with exaggerated clarity, as I had begun to realise that a number of boys could not understand spoken English. The desks opened and there was a rustle of papers.

'Chapter nine, page thirty. Chapter nine, page thirty.' I was already getting into the habit of repeating instructions like an announcer in a railway station.

The reader was *A Journey to the Moon*, by Jules Verne. This was printed in a booklet about ninety pages long in a text based on a 400-word vocabulary, with all the new items listed in the back. The method used by my predecessor, which I cautiously followed, was to go through the book chapter by chapter, answering the questions on each chapter at the back of the book. An average lesson covered four pages, a rate of progress which would bring us to Easter before we completed the book. Then another reader incorporating a hundred new words would be embarked on. The process was boring to the last degree.

'Ibrahim Pwajok, would you start, please.'

The boy stood up, and we worked our way jerkily through the text for the next quarter of an hour.

Quite suddenly there was an eruption next door. A voice raged on the other side of the partition wall.

'No-o-o-o!'

The reader on our side of the wall fell silent. We all waited.

'An alternate angle, ye eejit. Why can ye never recognise an alternate angle when ye see it? How many times do I have to tell ye? What is it? What is it?'

A voice mumbled.

The first voice rose to a crescendo. 'No! No! No! What d'ye say? D'ye dare repeat it again? D'ye value your life?'

My class sat in rapt silence.

'No-o-o-o-o!'

Somebody in my class giggled. The Principal was having difficulty with a geometry lesson. Silence ensued next door, and once more we droned on with our own work.

Forty minutes passed. The grave little boy on the left-hand side of the classroom consulted the pocket watch which lay on the window-sill, an odd little object made in Austria with a picture of a steam-engine on its face. With no change in his expression he lifted the hand bell from beside it, opened the window next to him, leant out and tolled the bell with much deliberation four times. He closed the window and sat down again.

I moved next door. The Principal slipped out of the door on the opposite side, leaving a mutter of comment behind him which extinguished abruptly as I entered and Form III stood up. 'You will need your readers, your reading notebooks and something with which to write, please.' Form III's reader was not a success, and there was an impatient edge to the boys' questions by the time the bell went.

The boys streamed across the compound to the first meal of the day, while we went to the Principal's bungalow for our breakfast. My arrival had accomplished a revolution in the staff breakfasting arrangements. Mrs Waldron could now safely eat with the Principal. Formerly she had brought with her an egg which Danladi had boiled, and then she and the Principal had proceeded to eat their boiled eggs in entirely separate rooms. In his seminary the Principal had been warned to safeguard jealously both his virtue and his reputation. Though any threat to the former from Mrs Waldron seemed hardly credible, he feared that a daily tête-à-tête over the boiled eggs and marmalade might be rumoured to the Prefect's disapproving ear.

We ate in silence. The Principal, however, refused his boiled egg, and consoled himself with cigarettes and strong tea. He left the table, his face pale, and his forehead furrowed. Mrs Waldron and I smoked a cigarette. The Principal had disappeared. On the other side of the compound the boys were reappearing from the dining-hall. Some already sat on the verandah outside the classrooms. Others were drifting lazily towards them, weighed down by half a pound of boiled rice spiced with peppery sauce. The bell rang again. I had a free period. While Mrs Waldron walked off towards the school I lit another cigarette.

'Hey! Hey! What d'ye think ye're doing?' The Principal had emerged from his bedroom. 'Where d'ye think ye're going?'

He was bellowing across the compound at a line of four women who had appeared from the main road. They were stark naked, but that was not the reason for his wrath. He leapt from the verandah waving his arms with his open soutane streaming behind him.

'Ba hanya! Ba hanya! Tafi! Tafi!'

He reached the path and stood dramatically in their way, arms outstretched and feet apart. One sock had flopped down over his ankle. There sprang into my mind a picture I had once seen of St Pius V turning the Huns back from Rome. 'Ba hanya,' he was shouting. 'You no fit come this way.'

Maurice was now shouting from the end of the verandah a stream of more fluent Hausa. The four women had halted. A high-pitched babble of indignant voices rose from them. They turned round and went back the way they had come. They were pagan women come in from Myango, about five miles off beyond the great rock that stood in the plain opposite the school. They were on their way to the market in Vwang by the shortest route, which led across the school compound. The Principal did not regard them as an amenity. As they stalked back to the road with their huge baskets of yams on their heads, chattering indignantly, the bunches of leaves tied between their thighs swung self-righteously.

The Principal watched them go with one hand on his hip, pulled at his cigarette, and then, with a shrug of satisfaction he strode back to the house, buttoning up his soutane with one hand.

'Can't have them come across like this. I'll let them know this isn't a public highway. Maurice, if these people come again, make you tell them go back. This no proper path to Vwang. Toh!'

'Toh,' said Maurice, grinning.

The Principal disappeared once more, and I turned to a pile of Form III's essays written for me over the week-end. I had done a comprehension with them about a hospital and they had written about the same topic. I resolved never to set it again. The essays all described the same tour of the wards, the operating theatre, and the maternity section, and they all ended up in the mortuary having a good look at the corpses. The general preoccupation with mortality and corruption was even more depressing than the English. I ploughed my way through improper tenses, disappearing punctuation, adjectives that did not agree, verbs that did not correspond and idioms that never crossed the lips of any Englishman. I achieved fifty-two corrections in one essay.

The bell was ringing again. Off I went with the essay books for Form III, who looked at them glumly while I wrote up a selection of errors on the blackboard. I was already making the distinction between English that was grammatically wrong and English which, although it broke no grammatical rules I had ever heard of, was still something different from the English spoken by an Englishman. 'What is wrong with "I went visit"? Why can't I write "He was making much noise that I could not hear?" What is the mistake in "I walked in a bush"?' Form III did not seem to take my point.

I went on to enlighten Form II about the affairs of Byzantium in the sixth century. The topic was related to the conversion of Europe to Christianity, which seemed at least vaguely appropriate to a similar process in contemporary West Africa. The boys did not understand much, but they were happy to draw Santa Sophia. They were still busy at this when the bell rang for them to put their pencils away and wander out on to the school verandah. While we walked back under the hot midday sun for our cup of tea the boys sunned themselves and talked soberly. Nobody was running about or shouting, or kicking a ball, or scuffling, or calling names, or behaving in any other way like an English boy released from class.

As the Principal drank his tea in preoccupied silence a figure darkened the doorway. 'Brudda,' it said. The Principal took no notice. 'Brudda,' it said again. The Principal scowled. 'Brudda,' it said insistently, 'what thing for chop?'

'Danladi,' shrieked the Principal suddenly, 'it be your job make chop. Why you always come to me? Go 'way! Go 'way!'

'Brudda, what thing for chop?'

'Did I not get sausages for cold store Saturday?'

'Yes, brudda.'

'Make you fry them, sir. But not in this ground-nut oil. Not in this ground-nut oil. You remember that. And make you not always be coming to me to ask what thing for chop. You be cook. What thing do I pay you for? You choose chop—you cook 'im.'

'Yes, brudda.'

'Get out.'

'Yes, brudda.'

The great expanse of Danladi's belly with the word salt in block capitals across the middle revolved into his grubby khaki shorts filled out by massive buttocks. He tramped heavily back to his kitchen. The Principal sipped his tea irritably. 'He wants to leave. They always do this when they want to go—they never tell you—just get worse and worse. I'm just waiting, giving him a little rope, then he'll be sorry for himself. Just let him put a foot wrong'—his voice trailed blood-curdlingly away into the cigarette smoke—'just let him try me. He'll see.'

After tea I had two periods of art with Form III. It was the Principal's belief that examination passes in art were a formality, granted after regular attendance at some form of drawing class for five years. He had equipped them with a drawing book, of the type usually bought in Woolworths, and a pencil, then given them to me. Almost all I remembered about my own art at school was the theory of perspective, about which I spent most of a period trying to explain, indicating the road which dwindled into the distance toward the rock, but to no great effect. Abandoning the effort, I took the class into the compound, where they sat in the grass, sketching the angular lines of the new Fathers' House from which the scaffolding was just being removed. I wandered from group to group as they pencilled. One centred around Gabriel Nongo appeared to be discussing theology. At the beginning of the period the question was whether Adam was in Hell, at the end Gabriel Nongo was asking whether daily communion was really enough.

The complete recipe for sanctity, in his opinion, was to take it as a condiment with every meal. The sun was strong, the boys drowsy, and I failed to discern any artistic talent in any of them, nor any at all in me.

As the bell announced the end of the last period I wandered about collecting in pencils and papers. Mrs Waldron was already accelerating down the road. The sun was now at its zenith in a clear sky and the dry heat lit up from the pathways and reflected from the concrete walls. The little living-room in the Fathers' House was hot and airless.

The Principal arrived soon afterwards, stripped off his soutane, threw it across an armchair and then sat on it. 'Maurice!' he roared, 'beer.' He appeared with two tins of Dutch lager, and we drank. 'Ready, Kit? Maurice, abinchi!'

Lunch was predictable. Pea soup made from a dehydrated Swiss brand was followed by the sausages swimming in fat which the Principal identified as ground-nut oil and in which lay boiled potatoes and a few beans drained of colour and taste. A steam pudding of much the same colour as Danladi's shorts ended the meal. Preoccupation settled about the Principal like a cloud, so heavily that even the tea failed to wash it away.

'Bed!' he said.

We went for our siesta. I slept, the perspiration soaking into my pillow, till about half-past three I was woken by a daily drama. The Principal's footsteps crunched past the house toward the pick-up. I heard the ignition turn, followed by that strange clicking and the explosion of the engine, the clash of gears and the scurry of gravel as the machine sprang out of its shed, only to be followed by a squeal of brakes, a grate of tyres on the path outside, and silence. A voice could be heard.

'Brudda!'

'What thing, Danladi?' A hint of barely restrained anger.

'Flour done finish! Fat done finish! Beer done finish!'

'What?'

'Flour done finish! Fat . . .'

'I get you these things only two days ago. What you . . .'

'Flour done . . .'

The pick-up exploded once more in a fury of flying gravel and I heard it skidding round the corner on to the path, out to the main road, and the sound of its engine accelerated noisily into the distance.

I got up. On the far side of the compound the boys could be seen very distantly. They were not expected to need a siesta, and I understood that they had been given some grass to cut under the supervision of the school captain. From my vantage-point it appeared that quite a lot were seated on the grass they were supposed to be cutting.

I drank a cup of tea. Without that fluid the school could not possibly survive. A bell was ringing to tell the boys that they were now off duty, and could go to the football field, or sit over a draughts board, or just doze. I left the compound with the Principal's dog prancing ahead of me to walk out along the road to the distant rock. Not a single teacher now remained on the compound, for the two Nigerians lived in the village.

On this particular day, however, one of the teachers was due to come in. I wanted to learn Hausa, and for that reason I had bought a rather formidable grammar at Foyles which I had since studied to little purpose. The Principal had proposed that one of the Nigerian teachers, Patrick Ohadike, should coach me, which was a well-meaning suggestion but not entirely a sensible one, since Patrick was Ibo and his Hausa was of a colloquial market kind. Patrick was very helpful. He found me a little booklet hopefully entitled *Hausa in Forty-eight Hours* which told me that Scotsmen usually spoke the language very well. I had about half a dozen lessons, but never proceeded beyond the greetings. These were astonishingly complex. A fist waved in the air and the term 'Sannu' had seemed to suffice,

26

together with the response, 'Yawa', but in addition there were appropriate greetings for every time of day, for every place, for greetings at work, on the road, in the market, in the sunshine, on a rainy day, greetings to equals, greetings to superiors, greetings to strangers, and greetings to intimates. They seemed to express a formal, static, hierarchial society in which the exact position, activity and circumstances of any stranger had to be immediately determined before any further social contact could be made. Taken with the correct responses, the process of hailing an acquaintance could be interminable. 'Sannu, sannu, sannu d'aiki. Yawa, yawa. Barka, barka, barka. Madalla, madalla, madalla.' The terms would echo on for minutes after travellers had passed each other. In the end I gave it up. Communication in the school was entirely in English. Only one of the boys claimed to be Hausa, and though the rest all spoke the language after a bush fashion they agreed that their English was better, and what that implied about their Hausa I knew too well. The language was a useful means for getting about the countryside, but as a means of understanding the people I taught its function was limited.

The Principal clattered home just before dark. While Maurice unloaded the bottles of beer, the cans of margarine, the bags of flour from the back of the pick-up, he collapsed in an armchair, rather pleased with a pair of shoes he had bought. 'In the market-place,' he said. 'Would you like to guess how much they cost?'

I feared that I had no idea.

'Twenty-five shillings. There! Not at all bad. Czechoslovakian. Never know what ye can find in the market. Saved me any amount of money.' He admired the black objects, of solid construction but little grace, but apart from this pleasure he looked all in. 'Hate Jos,' he said; 'hot, dusty, never get anything done, complete waste of time. Don't know why I have to go there so often. Maurice!'

'Brudda.'

'Millik.'

'Brudda.'

The Principal was obviously in a bad way. A half-pint mug of a chalky solvent of powdered milk was placed beside him with a small tin of condensed milk we used for the tea. He poured the yellow stuff in and looked at it reflectively. 'Horrible! Have to take it, though. Can't go on with this beer. My tummy's been terrible. Must see that German doctor.'

'You'll have to give up smoking, brother.'

'No, no. Can't do that. Don't know how I'd get to school. No, it's the beer and the seminary food. Terrible the number of priests who suffer from their stomachs all their lives.' He sipped without pleasure. The soup was pea again. The ribs of an obscure animal, possibly goat, had been produced for us. At the end of each was a knobbly piece of gristle which was intended to be eaten. The potatoes had been crudely mashed and a few yellow peas lay beside them. Danladi had made up a fruit salad by hacking a paw-paw into pieces and mixing it with bananas and orange. The Principal avoided it. We both drank some more tea, then left to do some marking.

The boys were having their meal at much the same time; then they had one and a half hours in the classrooms doing what was termed 'homework'. During this time the little boys unfeignedly laid their heads on the desks and slept. The bigger boys all found something to do. They worked unsupervised, but a tour of the classrooms always found silent industry, the boys working to the light of petrol lamps which gave out enough heat to convey a considerable fug to the classroom block. At nine the bell rang once more. Through the bungalow window I could see the lights bobbing back across the compound to the dormitories. Now that the work was over for the day the racket was amazing as the boys laughed and shouted at each other in strident voices. The lights dispersed to the dormitory windows and the noise diminished a little as the boys prepared for bed. The last bell rang at half-past nine, and gradually the voices faded, the lights went out, and there was quiet. In the village a drum was beating.

Shortly afterwards I went to bed, only to wake, rather alarmed, a couple of hours later. I could hear a loud noise of voices, drums beating, pieces of metal clashing, a horn blowing, people shouting and singing. I wondered, muzzily, if there was a riot, rose, and looked anxiously round the compound. It was absolutely still in the moonlight. In the village they were drinking.

For the first fortnight of this routine my classes were anonymous, five rows of heads bowed silently over their exercise books as they attempted to write down everything I said. A few boys in the older forms I knew by sight out of class, but the rest were nameless, alien, indistinguishable one from another. They made no noise, broke no rules, and asked no questions. I wondered if I would ever get to know them at all as I watched them at work in those quiet gloomy classrooms.

Then I took a drama lesson. I was never any good at drama. In Birmingham one attempt had almost ended in a free fight with a cricket stump, while on another occasion a crowd scene had needed the headmaster himself to quell it. Perhaps, I thought, these obedient children will be safer. I felt I ought to try. Those attentive, soulless lessons taught so little. The first comprehension passage in Form II's English books provided the stimulus. An African witch doctor, his name was Ndoku, was described diagnosing a sickness with the help of a gourd which he made to speak. We had read it and the boys had answered the questions on it.

Then, in a lesson before breakfast, I read the passage to them again. Obedient heads bowed down to the textbook as I went through it. 'Now,' I said, 'we will act it.' Every head in the room lifted. Thirty pairs of eyes looked blank. 'First we will move the desk. You, and you, help me, will you?' I picked on two boys in the front row and we dragged the desk over to one side to block the glass Crittall door. 'Now, the front desks, we must move those back. The front two rows can get up and pull their desks back. You'll have to stand for a while.' They did so. The heavy desks scraped across the concrete, the bare feet scuffled, and for the first time there was a murmur, whether puzzled or amused I could not tell. Now the whole classroom was disarrayed, the boys out of their desks, the desks out of order, the spell of formality broken.

I did not really know what to do next, but I began by choosing a boy to take the part of the witch doctor. I asked who would like

The Classroom

An African classroom looks like a re-enactment of educational history. The dungeon-like classrooms, the oppressive masonry walls, the straight rows of primitive furniture—their precise position marked on the floor by a principal with a mania for straight lines, the blackboard screwed to the wall, the teacher in front of it, barricaded behind his massive table, chalk in hand and in full pedagogic spate, the boys with their heads down, writing all he says, are all part of education as it was in nineteenth-century England—as it is now in most of Africa. We were luckier than some—we did have electricity, less lucky than others who could afford architects and factory-made furniture, but wherever you went in the continent the atmosphere in each classroom would be very much the same.

to act. No one responded. Looking about, with nothing to guide me in my choice, I noticed a broad grin, and chose the boy behind it. 'What's your name?' I asked.

'Julius,' he said, standing up. He towered over his desk, far too large for it. 'You be Ndoku.' I knew at once that I had made a mistake, for there was a rustle of barely extinguished laughter. I went on; there was nothing else for it. 'Now we've got to have the child who is sick, and someone to be his mother.' A little boy called George became the child. 'The mother?'

'Magaje,' said somebody.

'Yes, Magaje,' said a few subdued voices, and somebody giggled.

'All right, where's Magaje?' A boy who normally sat in the front row grunted. He had a shock of uncombed hair and a torn shirt. He looked at the ground. 'No,' he grunted.

'It's quite easy,' I said.

'Will not! Don't want to!' and he edged back. I submitted, and a slender, well-spoken boy called Athanasius took his place.

I described the actions of each of the characters, the witch doctor waving his calabash, the child complaining of sickness, the anxious mother, the ceremonial waving of the magic gourd, and the voice which came from it. Julius was a dreadful mistake. Delighted with his position, he shambled about the front of the form, grinning, shaking his hands, and mumbling incoherently. He was gigantic, and the whole class seemed in danger from his huge limbs, and his great clumsy hands and feet as he lumbered about, obviously quite unable to comprehend what he was supposed to be doing. The class was delighted.

Then it was time to bring in the crowd, so I gathered all the boys to the front of the room to explain their part. I stood there, surrounded by them. Quite suddenly all my perspectives changed. Never again were they to be docile, anonymous ranks, their woolly black heads bent over their exercise books. For a second I was back in a Birmingham classroom. Around me stood the type of every boy I had ever taught, in every shape and personality, fat and thin, dark and fair, short and tall, bright and lazy, interested, derisive, uncertain, stupid and intelligent, good and bad, cheerful or unresponsive, hemming me in, waiting to see what I was going to do. They were just the children I had known at home; I, their teacher, and at their mercy. It was frightening.

Then the vision vanished. They were harmless again. Amused, puzzled but docile, they did as they were told, and acted out the play. Julius, spluttering but pleased with himself, tripped over one or two people and caused even more delight to the rest of the form. Then they put the desks back and returned to their places. The bell rang, and they left, quiet and well-ordered, to go to breakfast. The old order had reasserted itself, but never as it had been. Perhaps I was beginning to know the boys.

Later that week I set that form to describe themselves to me in their weekly essay. Then I began to discern the physical differences. Thomas Yilzen proudly described himself as the possessor of 'a fine broad nose' and I saw that it spread from cheek to cheek, while Thomas Kaagnan described his as 'rather pointed', and certainly it was long and slender in comparison. Athanasius Chukwu wrote about his 'fair complexion' and it was a light ochre, while Mark Dimka was 'black', and yet another was 'reddish'. Oliver Longkwang was complacent about being 'very fat', and Clement Sati was happy to be thin.

For a long time my picture was based on their fluency in spoken English. Eric Anderson, the half-caste with the European features, olive skin, and wavy hair, was always easy to recognise, and always ready with an answer. So was Athanasius Chukwu, a light-skinned vivacious young Ibo. If I did not take care my lessons easily became a dialogue with these two. Then there were those who were more reticent or more lazy, but who would usually understand what you were saying and proffer an occasional answer. There was a fair-complexioned, slight and rather short-spoken boy called Oliver Longkwang, and George Kwanashe, a cheerful, bright-eyed little tadpole in the front row.

Then there were those who did not understand, but who were always happy to answer: a lanky fellow with a permanent grin in the back row, Thomas Kaagnan, and a glum, heavily built neighbour called Mark Dimka. In the front row, sprawled across his desk, for which he was far too large, always grinning rather vacuously, was Julius Dadiel, who lost control of his English as soon as he stood up, always stuttered out the wrong answer, and always had his hand up to cope with the next question. Finally there was the lump, those who kept themselves to themselves for varying reasons, either because their English was so bad they could not understand a word, like poor goggle-eyed Raymond Dongtoe, or handsome wooden-faced David Dung, or because bitter primary-school experience had taught them to keep their mouths shut, like Fidelis Dung and Gabriel Salla, or, like Jerome Magaje, they bore a grudge against the whole world.

The older boys were easier, since they were in constant attend-ance on the Principal. Fairly quickly I understood that five of them ran the school. Alexander Jibiri was the school captain, assured, frank and good-looking, as valuable for his shortcomings as his virtues, for he could always be relied upon to forget an order that was impossible to carry out. It took me a long while even to begin to understand the tribal politics within the school, but Alexander was the oldest Goemai, the largest tribal contingent in Vom. Much of his authority must have come from that. He had displaced Bernard Ibrahim, the only member of the Marghi tribe from far-off Adamawa, who was now a house prefect, a soured and failing member of the school hierarchy who was soon to leave for good to train as a male nurse. Alexander's two deputies were both from the Katab group of tribes, who between them were almost as strongly represented as the Goemai. Hyacinth Ruwang was the moustachioed sacristan, always trying to behave as if he were five years older than his actual age, which was then about eighteen. Peter Kure, who was older, held his position partly by virtue of his powerful physique, partly because of his exceptional intelligence, and partly also because of a sinister brooding power that was part of his moody personality.

These boys all possessed authority which was more searching than anything possessed by the Principal. In practice it was they who had the interpretation of the school rules. His dependence on them was demonstrated by the position of Kevin Dagai, whose power within the school was limited because he was one of the only two Higi from Adamawa; yet on his efficiency as kitchen prefect depended the peaceful and efficient running of the whole school. He had to supervise the deliveries of food to the kitchen, and the issue of food to the school cook. It was normal for any contractor to attempt a fraud, particularly if he were in the position of Shadrach, the school supplier, trying to supply all the educational institutions in the diocese at cut rates, build a large new hotel in Bukuru, marry his deceased brother's wife according to Ibo custom, and subsidise a host of dependants and relations. A close watch had to be kept on his deliveries for short weight, undersized yams, tainted meat, bad fish and subgrade rice. It was a difficult task for a European who ate none of these things, took time, and would have made the Principal responsible every time a meal proved to be inedible. Kevin held down a key post in a country where most trouble started with a complaint about food.

I was soon to learn how much depended on heeding this hierarchy's opinions. A couple of months after my arrival the Principal had to go round the primary schools to interview the two hundred children who had proved their literacy in the entrance examinations. Having told me where the cane was and presented me with a soap dish of assorted keys the Principal left for the bush. All was peaceful until the week-end, when there was to be a football match. I had then only a glimmering of how seriously the game was taken. Later, when our own school was suspected of witchcraft, and I heard of victorious teams pursued off the pitch by flying rocks and beer bottles, I became wiser. The team in this case was a local one, the Onoks, the protégés of Mr Onokwei, a rising businessman in Vwang, who had his enemies. The referee was to be the school football coach, a pleasant young man called Nelson who was planning to marry a school-teacher not of his own tribe who had already borne him twins. In consequence he also had his enemies, though I was not to know this.

The problem was ostensibly one of boots. Alexander came to me on Sunday morning looking worried and said that the Onoks were going to wear football boots. Our boys had no such things. They played barefoot and regarded boots as weapons of offence. Alexander was not happy and clearly wished to cancel the whole affair. He, the football coach and Mr Onokwei came and went from the verandah all morning. Against Alexander's wishes, I decided that the match should continue and that boots should be worn so long as they were not studded.

That afternoon the crowd round the field was large and there were rather a lot of young men in addition to the hundred or so urchins who usually arrived on the touch-line. I sat on my wooden chair by the side of the field while the referee decided how lethal or otherwise the boots worn by the Onoks actually were. The game started reasonably quietly, though Mr Onokwei's team rather over-powered our boys and showed every intention of using their weight. Penalties were awarded and by half-time both sides were even, both were rather touchy, but not really dangerous. Alexander was still worried, and I ought to have stopped the match then, but in England things were not done like this. The second half pro-ceeded. Boots were clearly swinging more freely, the coach was obviously having more difficulty in keeping control, and there was almost a fist fight between the centre-forwards. Five minutes before the end a richly deserved penalty was awarded to us. Edmund Masaweje took the kick and as the ball went in the right-back jumped on top of him. At once every player on the field seized his man, while the referee seemed to go down between the two centre-halves.

The football field disappeared as the whole crowd rushed on to it to join in, arms and fists waving, first-formers and the ragged children from the town capering and shrieking, dust rising, and me superfluous to it all, trying to find someone to heed my shouted instructions to get back to the school. I was so clearly harmless that the town mob, who had considered beating me up while they were about it, decided to leave me to get on with my own preoccupa-tions. Eventually I persuaded a line of reluctant first-formers to trail back to the school. I found Bernard Ibrahim, and heaved him out of the scrum by main force, protesting, 'It is hard to leave our brothers to be beaten,' and set him, and then the other senior boys, to get the school safely back.

It was over in ten minutes, the whole school, dusty and excited in the main classroom, the mob back in the town, and the referee in jail charged with assault. The next few hours were spent trying to get him out of the police station—his relations eventually bailed him out. The next few days were spent visiting the police with Alexander, trying to verify everyone's statements. It had all blown over by the time the Principal returned. The boys, Nelson's relations, Mr Onokwei, and Mr Onokwei's relations, all settled it among themselves, and I never learnt what happened in the end. After three months in the country I knew nothing about it, or its people, or the boys I had to teach.

4

An African School

First I had to learn about the school itself. It was so difficult at first to understand just how different it was from an English school. Superficially everything was the same; the dormitories and class-rooms, the laboratories and offices, the house system, prefects, and school uniforms, the cricket and football pitches. A visitor to a school like this saw all these similarities. The Bishop from the south, for example, whom I had to show round soon after that strange football match, saw but a fraction of the truth.

He came soon after we had moved into the new Fathers' House. A few days before that Danladi had finally been sacked after reduc-ing a fine piece of imported beef to the colour and consistency of a charred brick, and we settled down with Dennis instead, a withered and deferential Ibo, who was believed to add considerable tone to our new residence.

A week after the move I was passing through the hall downstairs when the telephone rang. The Principal grimaced and picked it up. His expression changed immediately.

'Yes, my lord.' His hand, clutching a cigarette packet, waved at me, thumb downward.

'Oh no, my lord! Is he, my lord?' With one hand he was shak-ing a cigarette on to the table by the telephone. 'Is he really, my lord?' A box of matches appeared. The cigarette was in his mouth, a light was struck and the cigarette glowed. The skill was peculiarly the Principal's own. A cloud of smoke surrounded him and the cigarette was waved in my direction. 'Of course, my lord. I'll be pleased to. Half-past four. This evening. Yes, certainly, my lord—a pleasure.' He put the telephone down.

'Jesus,' he said, and hurried into the sitting-room.

He sat down. 'A bishop, up from the south. The Prefect is sending him here—this very evening. Maurice!'

'Brudda?' He appeared through the door.

'Maurice, make you get ready this house. You make him clean proper. There be two man extra for chop tonight. One be big man, bishop. He dey from south. You sweep down this verandah. Put plenty beer for fridge. We got soda?'

'Yes, brudda.'

'Dennis!'

The new cook's face appeared meekly and enquiringly round the door. 'Was the brudda calling me?'

'Yes, Dennis. We get bishop this evening.'

'Ah-ha-ah, brudda! Oh yes, brudda!' Dennis moved round the doorpost, rubbing his hands vigorously, much as if he was contemplating cooking the bishop himself. 'We fit get small chop first brudda, some small potatoes fried, fried ground-nuts small. We get soup. You like tomato? I fit get two chickens, cockerels, brudda. You like 'em roast? You like queen of puddings, brudda?'

'That's the man, Dennis.'

'A-a-a-ah, brudda!' His smile grew wider and a little insecure. 'I tink, brudda, dis cost small.'

'O-ho, Dennis, I think I give you plenty.' There was a jangle of small change in the back pocket of the Principal's shorts. A handful of silver passed over. 'And make you not come back.' Dennis received the money in cupped hands, and bowed himself out backwards as if he were leaving royalty.

'A fine cook, that Dennis. We did well there. Kit, when this bishop comes, will you take him over the compound? Keep him busy for about an hour.'

I went for my siesta after lunch thinking about that hour. Visitors in Northern Nigeria were always expected to show an interest in schools and hospitals, which were usually new and often the only ones within a hundred miles in any direction. This was particularly the case in the Prefect's new, extensive and poverty-stricken province in which a secondary school was an indication of status and achievement. The problem was what to show such visitors in a school that was still half built and half bush.

I was still cogitating when the Prefect's Peugeot arrived with the Bishop from the south accompanied by his chaplain. 'Not such a figure as our man,' observed the Principal. He did not possess the Prefect's embonpoint, the suspicion of blessing or interdiction imminent under the impeccable soutane. Hands were shaken all round, but no one, I was grateful to see, dived to kiss his ring. The Bishop seemed preoccupied, hardly looking at us, speaking practically not at all, and leaving it to his chaplain to mediate between him and the common world.

'Ye had a good journey, my lord?' enquired the Principal.

'He did, but, och, his lordship is rather tired.' The Bishop and his chaplain were both Scottish.

Maurice brought us tea, and while the Bishop drank it in gloomy silence the Principal went chapter and verse through the early history of the school. The chaplain listened on behalf of his lordship to make the appropriate responses and the occasional 'Is it not so, your lordship?'

The moment arrived.

'Ye'll be wishing to see over the school, my lord.'

'Of course, of course,' said the Bishop to his teacup.

'Mr Elliott will do the honours. Show them over, Kit. You'll excuse me, my lord, I have business small upstairs. I'll see ye this evening.' Under his breath as he passed me, 'An hour, Kit. Keep him going till it gets dark.'

Out on to the back verandah I led them, avoiding Maurice's washing-up left there to dry, and out on to the gravel along which the lorries brought the provisions from the road across the compound to the dining-hall a quarter of a mile away. We formed a procession, with the chaplain a little behind my left shoulder, the Bishop studying the ground thoughtfully a couple of yards behind, and the Principal's dog leaping ahead of all of us.

The first stopping place in the perambulation was the nearest dormitory. 'The beginnings of the school, my lord.' It stood to the right of the path and beyond it were the little bungalows we had once occupied, now empty, waiting for the Nigerian staff to move in. I took them into the dormitory. 'This wing is still used as a classroom.' Thirty heavy wooden desks in six lines, a blackboard screwed to the wall, a low wooden platform beneath it, and a crude wooden table made up the furniture. 'The first form work here.' A small figure wrapped in coloured curtaining stood up uneasily and said 'Good evening, sir. Good evening father,' inclining unsteadily towards us.

'Hullo, Edmund; you shouldn't be here. Get out!' The figure shuffled quickly past us and scurried away along the verandah with the suspicion of a mutter as it passed the nearest dormitory door. We followed him, our leather soles clashing on the concrete.

'The dormitories are all the same, my lord, eight beds in this one—'What are you doing here?' A lump under one of the counterpanes stirred and a gollywog head emerged blinking at one end.

'Fada—er, sir—I mean fada—sir,' it babbled.

'Why are you here, Lazarus? You know quite well nobody is supposed to be in the dormitories at this time. Come along, out on to the football field.' The face blinked at us again, its mouth open. Then it recollected itself.

'Fever, sir.'

'Have you seen Gabriel?' Gabriel Zi was the sick prefect, sometimes glorified by the title infirmarian. All who fell sick were expected to consult him in order to be diagnosed into four classifications: nonsense; have an aspirin; take a purge; go to the Principal for further treatment.

'Yes, sir. He gave me tablet, sir. Said "go to bed", sir.'

'All right, Lazarus.' The face disappeared under the counterpane and the lump reasserted itself.

The 'snap—clump—snap—clap' of a table-tennis game was being tapped out in the next room.

'This is the recreation-room, my lord.'

'And what do they play?' asked the Bishop abstractedly.

'Table-tennis in here, my lord.' There was only that one game to be played in the recreation-room. Four boys clapped their bats down on top of the board which stood on a pair of rickety trestles, while their ball danced away to one corner. They stood sheepishly, one rubbing his left heel with the toe of his right foot.

'That's all right, boys, that's all right boys. I'm sure his lordship won't mind if you carry on,' said the chaplain encouragingly. One of them collected the ball. They glanced at each other, but although all four fidgeted none of them dared to start.

Apart from the table-tennis board the main evidence of recreation was provided by the marks on the wall, which had been mottled by innumerable balls bouncing against it. The white lampshade had been broken. A few stools stood in one corner, and on one a draughts board had been left, with a few crude square wooden counters lying upon it.

'Draughts, I see,' said the chaplain brightly.

'Yes. I don't think the Principal likes it very much. I believe he thinks they gamble.' Patrick Ohadike had recently reported this, and two days later all the boards were called in and formally burnt. The game probably continued. When I tried to teach them chess later on the carved pieces were used instead of draughts counters.

'Ah!' observed the Bishop gloomily, 'they would, they would.'

'All right boys, carry on.' I shepherded the pair along the verandah. 'Four dormitories in each block,' I continued remorselessly. 'Sixteen boys sleep in each wing, eight in each of the smaller rooms. There are two boxrooms.' I flung open the door of one in the corner of the building. There was a smell of dust. Half a dozen old mattresses, some cardboard boxes and a few old hoes could be discerned dimly lying about the floor. A shelf had been run up on the far side and on them waited a row of suitcases and boxes for the end of term. Duty done, I shut the door.

This dormitory block differed from the other two in only two respects. One of the wings was still used as a classroom, and it had a garden. In his first year the Principal had laid down a little brick-edged path leading twenty yards to a gutter. In the exact centre of the lawn on either side he had established a star-shaped flower-bed. His chief concern had been geometry. The star shapes were perfectly regular in form and exactly at the centre of their lawns.

Having achieved this regularity, he seemed to have shown less concern for the contents of his garden. At its lowest level gardening is easy in Nigeria, and having discovered an evergreen bush which produced simple blue and white flowers he had thrust cuttings into his beds, where they had flourished in insipid abundance. The Prefect had probably handed him a packet of zinnia seeds a year or two back, and these had now naturalised and were throwing up their rudimentary carmine blossoms which seemed to survive throughout the year. Among them were tall flowers of the marigold variety which produced a large, fleshy bloom like an overripe orange daisy.

On the steps of the dormitory we stumbled over a child with an algebra textbook. He stood, bowed, watched us go and then turned back to the mysteries of simple equations.

'The washrooms,' I declaimed. A windowless, cement-walled shed ran by the side of the dormitory, with half a dozen buckets outside the open door, which offered a glimpse of concrete partitions running the length of the building inside. I drew no attention to the shed further back which housed the latrines, holes in a concrete slab above a septic tank. Once a day a bucket of water was supposed to be flung down them, but as no one in authority made a habit of going near them there was little assurance that this was ever done.

I indicated the buckets. 'We need the buckets to carry the water.' A drill-hole had been bored to find water, and the cast-iron pipe which indicated its mouth stood in front of the Fathers' House near the road. The drilling company had gone a considerable way down out of pure goodwill to the mission and had then received a contract which had offered cash as well as goodwill. The workers had decamped for a few days never to return. The firm had gone bankrupt and left us with the mouth of the drilling and a number of lengths of cast-iron piping. 'The boys have to carry water across the road from the Vet. every morning, every lunch-time, and every evening.'

'Very sad, very sad,' said the Bishop.

'Another dormitory.' They were all the same with their rows of iron bedsteads, each with its brightly coloured cotton counterpane covering a mattress stuffed with cotton heads whose seed pods and husks could be felt pricking through the fabric. By each bed stood a little wooden cabinet with a cheap padlock, and inside each were each boy's personal possessions: his clothes, a mirror, a piece of soap, a hank of coarse bast with which he scraped his skin when he washed, a small jar of scented pomade with which he rubbed down his skin after washing, a chromium-plated torch for illicit study after dark, a pair of shoes without laces, probably a rosary, perhaps a missal, and normally a photograph of a friend, or of the boy himself, snapped at the most flattering angle. At the end of each room was a cubicle in which two senior boys slept, with the ventilation grid diligently stuffed with old newspaper to keep out the draughts.

The buildings themselves were primitive. The pine rafters were bolted to the tops of the walls, supporting the galvanised zinc roof, with the trade-mark of the manufacturer, a black hand, repeating itself on each sheet above the boys' heads like a cabalistic sign. 'Made in England' it said underneath, again and again and again. The steel Crittall frames which equipped almost every postwar building held greasy panes on which were impressed the occasional palm-print, and on the end window of one of the cubicles the mark of greasy post-prandial lips. The doors, crudely carpentered, hung a little crookedly, painted in the Principal's choice of red. The rafters over one of the verandahs were already spongy with wood-worm.

The second dormitory was quiet, deserted except for a lump in one of the beds which stirred slightly and moaned, 'Purge.' Nor was further enquiry necessary. Once a quarter the boys considered it good medical practice to absent themselves from class, swallow a packet of Epsom salts obtained from Gabriel Zi, and wait for their bowels to do their worst.

I attempted to raise my party's flagging spirits. 'Cigarette, my Lord?'

'Thank you, thank you, smoke my own.' It was an English brand, for he had moved beyond the Nigerian varieties. Mine were the type with the galleon on the green packet, rather sour to the tongue, but at one shilling and sevenpence for twenty I did not feel like grumbling.

'We'll go to the football field.'

'Yes.'

We left the dormitories behind and passed the Senior Primary School, which looked, for the time being, quite smart, as it had just received its last coat of paint for the next five years. We crossed through the vegetable beds beside the school, over the plank which spanned the deep gutter flowing out of the Vet., to reach the field itself. Peter Kure stood on the touch-line beside two shapeless bags of leather, footballs whose seams had been ripped apart on the hard ground. Two more balls bounded about the bare earth of the pitch, which was bald, but for a few strands of creeping grass in the corners. The second form was running about noisily. Beyond the pitch the school ended in a wall of uncut grass four feet high which waved for another quarter of a mile to the eucalyptus trees on the edge of the stock farm, beyond which rocky grass-covered hills walled us in from the south.

'Your boys good at football?' asked the chaplain.

'They're very keen.' I really had no idea how good they were, but they certainly played almost nothing else.

We skirted the edge of the football field. The evening sun was behind us, a soft golden light drew even the furthest hills and the distant lake close. We walked as if on the floor of a sea of light. The yellowing grass glowed gold, and the deep brown of the boys' faces, arms and hands was enriched by the same colour. The light mellowed the concrete walls of the dormitories, revived the faded pasture on the stock farm hills, softened the harshness of the distant rocks. Something Berenson had said about 'a sense of untrammelled but not chaotic spaciousness' seemed appropriate to this desolate countryside.

'It's nice on an evening like this.'

'Yes,' said the Bishop.

We reached the dining-hall. Down one side of the building the deal tables had been set in that long, low, gloomy room. On them stood the tall, white, enamelled pitchers of water, the polythene beakers, the aluminium bowls waiting empty in the middle of each table, the cigarette tins of salt, the metal plates and the cheap cutlery. It was the most decent time to see the dining-hall, for, if the concrete floor was dark and slippery, at least the soggy lumps of yellow garri, made from pounded and boiled cassava roots, did not lie in sticky gobbets on the plates among the greasy fragments of peppered meat or dried fish. Nor were there puddles of water on the tables, or crumbs and fragments scattered about the floor.

At right angles the main recreation-room opened off the dining-hall, equally empty of boys or equipment. A couple of benches stood against one of the walls and there was the same mottled evidence of balls having been bounced in the room that there had been in the smaller recreation-room. Intriguingly, twelve feet up the end wall and three feet below the ceiling was a single large, dusty footprint, whose origin was a mystery.

I did not offer to take them the few yards along the covered way which led to the kitchen. No priest in charge of the Prefect's building had ever been able to contrive a kitchen stove which did not smoke. Therefore all institutional cooking in the diocese went on in an atmosphere like that of a railway tunnel in the days of steam. The school kitchen was black with soot from the rafters to the slippery concrete floor. The large wooden tables in the centre of the room were impregnated with it. It had been absorbed into the pores of the cook's sweaty skin and soaked into the fabric of the stewards' sackcloth aprons. At the back of the kitchen the masonry stove ran along the wall like a bench, inside which the firewood flickered and smoked. Some of the fumes escaped through the chimney shaft that ran up the centre of the wall but most curled out of the front of the stove, or out of the circular holes on top of it on which stood the pots and the great cast-iron cauldron from West Bromwich. The cook and his attendants moved through the murk, glistening with perspiration in an atmosphere compounded of wood smoke and sweat.

Whenever they could the denizens of this cave abandoned it, and had I taken the Bishop to the back he would have found the kitchen staff camped out of doors among peeled yams, mortars, old

The Classroom Block

By 1962 the classroom block was finished, but like so many buildings in Africa it was difficult to tell at first glance if it were still under construction, or already in the process of decay. It stood for a year among its own stony debris. The surfaces of pillars and walls could have been weathered into their irregularity, or could still be waiting for their last coat of cement. The outline of the cement blocks was imperfectly concealed by worn-out grey distemper. Crevices snaked down the portico and the walls. The windows, whose odd pattern was sometimes betrayed where the builder had run out of his original stock of Crittall frames, suggested alterations made by the users over the years. Such buildings always looked prehistoric. Born of cheap labour, relatively cheap cement, and limited technical skill they were reminiscent of an earlier age of monumental architecture. They stand in megalithic splendour all over Africa, as little likely to disappear as Stonehenge.

tin cans, and the washing-up still slimy from its dip in cold water, put out to dry. A couple of well-fed vultures would be eyeing them from the roof, alighting occasionally with a gentle flop and an unfolding of wings to rustle among the filthy wood shavings by the

stacks of firewood for a morsel of rotten meat, bald head on one side, eyes unlidded, and wicked beak probing for carrion. Beyond led the drainage gutter, slimed, rank and overgrown, in which the crabs and the cockroaches bred, and along which the rats crept. Further off still was the rubbish pit, deep enough to accommodate an elephant, with a charred conglomeration of abandoned milk tins, tomato puree cans, bones and smashed beer bottles in the bottom.

From all this I diverted the Bishop along the path to the classroom block, half of it still naked concrete with grass growing in the empty window spaces like a relic from antiquity.

'When we've got our full complement of boys, then it'll be finished. I don't think there was the money to put the whole building up at once, and anyway, I expect that the windows of the unused classrooms would have been broken.'

'For sure,' said the Bishop.

'The building father says that a good soaking in the rains does a lot to improve reinforced concrete.'

Our shoes rang on the concrete verandah, past the shells of the unfinished classrooms, till we stood under the enormous portico which housed the stairway and carried the school emblem.

'This will be the staff-room.' I indicated the cavern behind the portico, empty of everything except one of the bundles of twigs which the boys used as brooms when they swept out the classrooms in the morning.

'This will be where the clerks work.' We had no clerk, nor were we to have one for another two years, when we eventually acquired Christopher; and his clerical career was soon interrupted by a charge of rape, brought against him by his girl-friend, who produced his shirt and trousers at the police station as evidence.

'This is the Principal's office.' It was furnished with a deal table, a chair and a filing cabinet, presumably of great value, for the room was heavily barred across the windows on both sides. The door, however, was fitted with a simple lock of a type for which a master key was easily available in any Nigerian market.

'The third form works here.' The room was an unpainted dungeon containing the same heavy wooden desks we had seen in the dormitory. There was, in addition, a small book-case which contained all the school had to offer as a school library. The Principal particularly recommended Billy Bunter to the boys in his older forms, and several of these books in their yellow dust jackets could be seen there. I was surprised to discover that these had a following, and that the catch phrases of Greyfriars were sometimes bandied about the Vwang compound. The other volumes were less successful: cheap editions of children's classics such as *Little Women*, *What Katy Did*, *Treasure Island,* and *Lamb's Tales from Shakespeare*, printed on coarse absorbent paper and seldom disturbed. At the back of the room a stretch of buff-coloured strawboard had been nailed up with a map of Columbus's voyage pinned to the middle.

Form II's room was similar in all respects. Across the blackboard someone had scrawled in large untidy characters. 'This day Titus have drunk in one breakfast 16 cups of tea. A record, comrades!' At the back of the room was posted my rendering in pen and ink of St Simon Stylites and pillar, an aid to the study of the desert fathers.

'Upstairs, my lord, is the science laboratory.'

All visitors were expected to take a keen interest in the science laboratory. The science subjects in which African rulers detected the secret of European success was also seen by the boys as the highway to affluence as doctors and engineers. Thus the Prefect had decreed that the school should have a 'science bias' and the Principal was the holder of a science degree. I did my best to minister the glories of the laboratory, the bunsen burners, weighing machines, pipettes, acid bottles and so forth, that the Principal had so lovingly ordered and installed.

'The school has a lot of land, has it not?' said the chaplain, looking from the back windows of the laboratory across the compound.

'About sixty acres, I believe.'

'Isn't there a good view of it from here, my lord?'

'The Principal plans to put a cricket pitch in the centre here. You can see the outline marked by those bits of hedge.'

'Does he play cricket?' asked the Bishop.

'Hardly.' He knew as little about the game as I knew about the hurling, of which the priests talked incessantly. Nevertheless cricket seemed to be an appropriate game for a boarding school and a huge oval had been marked out in undernourished lantana hedge. We looked down on it now, entirely covered by long grass under which the hummocks left by local farmers a couple of years before were still visible. From one side to another of the future cricket pitch ran the school's main drain, three feet deep, down which a slimy green fluid from the washhouses oozed in the dry season, and along which in the rains a muddy brown flood rushed from the Vet. to the gutters beside the road. From the three dormitories which stood at equal distances round the perimeter paths had been worn through the grass, winding, like all African paths, toward the classrooms below us.

It was growing dark. I had fulfilled my hour, and over at the dormitories the bell was ringing. There was a slight murmur of voices as the boys began to wander toward the dining-hall. 'Shall we go back to the Fathers' House?' The chaplain's face, I felt sure, brightened.

'Of course, of course,' said the Bishop, a little less gloomily.

We made our way back, passing Hyacinth with a couple of Tilley lamps which would be lit in the classrooms when it became dark in a quarter of an hour's time. The Principal was still not available and we stood briefly on the upper verandah looking across the plain toward the great rock two miles away. The setting sun infused the whole sky with fire. The Vet. hills to our left stood jet black against a blaze of flame-coloured cloud, already deepening into funereal purple.

'Father.' The Bishop was addressing the chaplain. 'You brought the cards with you?'

'Of course, my lord. I expect the Principal will be with us shortly.'

The cares of office cleared from the Bishop's face as the night fell. 'Shall we go downstairs?' he said cheerfully. 'We may soon be able to begin. You play, Mr Elliott?'

'Play?'

'His lordship means bridge, Mr Elliott.'

'Yes, I—er—have done. Not often—but I'll try, though.'

The shadows of the afternoon flitted briefly across the Bishop's face once more.

'Father Harrington comes later, my lord,' pointed out the chaplain.

'Ah, yes!' The Principal was approaching us along the verandah, buttoning up his soutane.

'Greetings, my lord! Ye've seen the compound.'

'Of course, of course, brother. You'll join us for bridge. I took the liberty—I hope you won't mind—of bringing a pack with me. We could have a rubber before dinner.'

Hardly another word did the Bishop speak that night except to make his bids. Though I did not improve that first rubber by revoking twice, Father Harrington arrived in time to save his games for the rest of the evening. He returned to Jos well enough pleased.

5

An African Countryside

I had learnt the grubby secrets of the compound within a month of
arriving, but it was only after the Bishop's visit that I began to look
outside. I had, of course, been into the Vet., where the Principal
had a number of social connections, on many occasions, but this
was not the Plateau, the country from which the boys came. It
was no more than an outpost of suburban England. Its offices,
laboratories, and maintenance yards lay inside the fertile, pumice-
laden walls of an extinct volcano. Round the outside were the
European bungalows almost overwhelmed by flowering shrubs
and trees, white, yellow and pink frangipani, golden tacoma, pink
and yellow hibiscus, and scarlet poinsettia. To the south of the
Veterinary Research Station the neat drystone walls of the stock
farm ran across a range of hills that extended two or three miles
toward the Provincial Secondary School at Kuru. Beyond this I
knew nothing.

Out of the school compound I looked to the north-west across
the great plain; in one corner stood the school buildings, and to the
west were the Vwang hills with their fantastic jagged skyline,
weird, hostile, apparently innaccessible. I was looking into the unknown. It frightened me. It was a dark continent, associated in my
mind with violence, cruelty, wild beasts and savage tribesmen. The
great jagged rock which jutted menacingly out of the plain in
front of the school was the ruin of some ancient geological devasta-
tion, and now looked the haunt of devils and leopard men. It was
several weeks before I ventured out to it with the Principal's dog.
A fat, furry little animal came indignantly out of the boulders at its
foot and barked at me. I think it was a hyrax. I saw no more wild
life around Vwang after that.

The rock lay a mile or two out from the school and around it the Plateau lay like a sea, with the occasional outcrops like ships hull-down on the horizon and the Vet. with its hills like an island. Underneath my feet the soil in the fields grated and crunched, almost pure quartz, granular, like yellow sugar. In the little fields were heaps of knobbly brown stones, each cairn the harvest of a few square feet of land. Yet the area was, by the standards of the high plateau, relatively fertile, for in their little compounds, each with a few eucalyptus trees planted near them, I estimated five or six hundred people made a living on about five square miles of poor farmland.

My first-hand acquaintance with the country was limited for a long period to the immediate vicinity of the compound into which I walked with the Principal's dog and to the two towns, Bukuru and Jos, which the Principal visited almost daily in his dilapidated pick-up.

Bukuru was nearest, to the north of us, shortly after the junction of the main road. Its very existence depended on the great compound belonging to the tin-mining company, a fortification surrounded by stone walls twenty feet high topped by barbed wire. Because of this there had been established along the main road a couple of banks, the offices of an electricity company and an oil depot. Around these had camped every tribe in Nigeria in a town of small stores, rectangular mud-walled compounds and unsurfaced pot-holed streets. Nobody belonged there and the lorries, minibuses, and taxis came and went, taking people to and from their homes in every other part of the Federation.

Jos looked more permanent. The European administration had put up stone bungalows along the road that wound into it from Bukuru and the south. On the hillsides above the town the miners had built expensive homes, and even in the native township down in the valley prosperous Nigerians had built substantial concrete tenements and villas to let to others or to live in themselves. The heart of the town was the main street, the commercial area which ran parallel with the railway line. At one end were the canteens of the great European stores, further down were the Syrians, the

Lebanese, and the Indians with their rolls of cotton cloth, shirting, suit material, twill, drill, poplin, and canvas, their cheap hardware and electrical equipment, their toys and their trinkets. At the bottom of the street, where the railway ended, was Jos market.

This dusty area within its high walls always seemed the busiest place of all. Everything was sold here. In the rows of stalls and sheds were the sections where the Ibo and Yoruba sold their lengths of brightly coloured cotton cloth, the little stalls where the Nigerian housewives bought their pins, wool, mirrors, clothes-pegs, sugar lumps, tins of sardines and corned beef, condensed milk, matches, needles, soap, and other household items. Here you could buy bicycles, here pots and pans, here baskets, here sandals made out of motor tyres. In another part the flies buzzed about the meat-sellers' booths. Elsewhere the stinking black cakes of dawa, fermented locust beans, were offered for sale, and bowls of acha grain, of millet, sesame seed, beans and palm kernels; heaps of yams were piled here for sale, piles of small round coco-yams, huge earthy cassava roots, golden maize cobs, bundles of bitter leaf, headpans of okra, bright red and green peppers, trays of green and yellow kolanuts, paw paws in orange and green, green oranges and bananas, pineapples, plantains, and sugar-cane. There was little that you could not buy. Hippopotamus meat and crocodile tails came up from the lowlands; lorry loads of grey, powdery natron smuggled across the border from Chad was sold here as it had been in West African markets for two thousand years for medicine, purges, and cookery. Monkeys' tails, feathers, dried herbs, bones, skins, and poisons could be bought for magic-making. Charms, aphrodisiacs, stolen antibiotics, pornography, exercise books, the Communist Manifesto, the Bible, Muslim amulets, pools coupons, the latest records were all to be found somewhere in the market-place, while between the booths, up and down the alleys, thronged all the tribes of West Africa, bargaining, gossiping, arguing, complaining, thieving, soliciting, and begging.

Beyond the market-place in the low mud houses on the grid of dirty streets was offered every service the Europeans provided on their side of the market. Mechanics could overhaul a car using replacements from mountains of mechanical junk at the back of the market. Lorries could be equipped for a police inspection, with lights, brakes, and tyres, returnable in forty-eight hours. There were blacksmiths, stonemasons, tailors, native doctors, barbers, printers, bakers, booksellers, carpenters, and cycle mechanics, all in their dark little houses, with the rubbish lying in the streets outside, making their living and hoping for a fortune before they returned home.

For Jos, like Bukuru, was nobody's home. Fifty years before, of course, there had been no town there at all. Even in 1960 it was still only a temporary stopping place. Over 40,000 people of every nation, English, Scottish, Irish, or Welsh, Indian, Syrian, or Lebanese, Hausa, Yoruba, Ibo, Birom, Tiv, or any of a hundred others, were only staying long enough to complete a job or earn some money before they returned to whatever corner of the world they described as home.

Some of our Ibo boys came from families which had settled in Jos and Bukuru. The Birom came from their villages to the south of Jos in the neighbourhood of the school, Zawan, Gyel, Du, Foron, Kuru, Vwang itself, and Ryom. To reach the rest of them you had to start from Jos on the metalled road which led through Bukuru southward on its way toward the Eastern Region and the coast. Two miles south of Bukuru a turning off south-east led down toward the great tin workings at Ropp, past ranges of sterile sand and lakes of lifeless water, into Pankshin Division, where, said one of the boys, God having bestowed all his gifts at the creation had nothing left to give except stones. The little town of Pankshin was 120 miles from Jos, and in the hills around it lived the sixty or so subdivisions of the Angas people. Beyond and to the south of Pankshin was Lowland Division, of which the chief town was Shendam, which had been declining gradually since the days in the last century when it had been the centre of a Goemai kingdom. The Goemai were still there and provided us with nearly a quarter of our boys. Around them lived their ancient feudatories and rivals, remote and isolated from the roads, Kwalla, Kwande, Mirriam, Kwa, Yergam, Gerkawa, Dimmuk, Dorok, and Mentol.

Another group of the boys came from further down the main road to the south. Forty miles from Jos the metalled road came down the edge of the Plateau, winding its way for three miles down the Assob Pass to continue southwards another eighty miles through Akwanga before carrying on, leaving the foothills of the Plateau behind it to move through Lafia down to the River Benue at Makurdi and on toward the Eastern Region and Enugu, its capital. Around Akwanga were the hills in which the Eggon and Mada boys had their homes.

The last important group of boys came from the southern part of Zaria Province. To reach them you had to leave the main road a few miles south of the Assob Pass and drive west along the dusty road, through the high forest that fringes this southern edge of the Plateau. In the distance to your right the edge of Kagoro Massif rises like a wall. All this territory is settled by the different sections of the Katab group of tribes, Kagoro, Kaje, Kagoma, Kachichere, Numana, and many others. Peter Kure and Hyacinth Ruwang were both from here, while a few of our Ibos came from the railway town on the junction at Kafanchan just south of the furthest edge of the Kagoro Massif.

The territory from which the boys I was teaching came was hardly less in area than Wales, and supported a population of little more than a million people. Within the school itself there were already representatives from over twenty different tribes, each with its language and culture as distinct as those of any European nation.

6
The Rains

For six months I learnt little about this kaleidoscopic area of modern Africa outside the school. I lived with the Irish priests, and it was their culture I learnt most about. I had previously believed that the Irish were a species of Englishman with an engaging accent, an attitude calculated to exasperate the Principal, who had made himself the centre of a minor international incident at London Airport by refusing to pass through anything except the gate marked 'Aliens'. The age-old grievances of the Irish were shouted into my right ear on the way into Jos along with the part played by the British in the Second World War, their wicked designs upon Ireland, the fate of Roger Casement, the enthusiasm of all Irishmen for the use of Erse, the achievements of the National University of Ireland which possessed an international expert on the properties of seaweed, all declaimed above the roar of exhaust, the rattle of hinges, and the crash of gears.

Worse still, I was among a subspecies of the Irish, for the missionary society's headquarters was in Cork and the majority of its members seemed to come from either County Cork or County Waterford. Their attitude to natives of other areas was conservative. 'He comes from Dublin, which is rather a different place altogether.' 'Agh! He's a typical Kerry man, if you know what I mean,' which I did not. Cork and Waterford appeared to be embattled city states whose inhabitants had little but ill to say about each other. This impression was partly the result of the hurling season, which was in progress at that period. Hurling seemed to be a sort of frenzied lacrosse played with bats that were half hockey stick and half truncheon, and a wicked leather ball with a lethal seam which travelled, I was gravely told, at up to a hundred miles an hour. Through some unaccountable oversight the Principal, a Waterford man, had chosen the Cork colours, red and white, for the school football team, so to compensate he bought a bath mat in the same colours and made a point of standing on it on his way into and out of his bath.

Irish and English, Lent came upon us in the Fathers' House in March. The weather had been unusually hot, the sun blazed from the zenith out of a sky of blue enamel, and the ground baked hard as brick, the football field offered a surface like asphalt. The boys' lips cracked in the dry air, and in the Fathers' House the ill-made doors warped, and the huge monopitch roof banged and rattled all night as the day's heat went out of it. The Principal's stomach grew worse.

On Ash Wednesday he appeared after breakfast from an early visit to Jos with several bottles of medicine and fifty packets of chewing gum. His Lenten austerity would combine strict attention to Dr Holling's advice on his health and a regime without either cigarettes or beer.

The following morning the compound smelt slightly different on the way to Mass. There was a strong, rather sour scent of dust and dry grass overlaid by damp, and an unexpected dampness clinging to the face and throat before the sun came up. 'When do the rains start?' I asked the Principal.

'Not soon enough,' he said, chewing grimly.

Two nights later, when I looked across the compound in the moonlight, a halo glistened round the moon, and as I looked there was the ghost of a second halo outside that.

> I saw the new moon late yestreen
> Wi' the auld moon in her arm.

'Sure the rains are coming, but not for a few weeks yet. Holy God, but I'm nearly through this chewing gum.'

Even on the school compound I sensed an increasing tension as the rains approached. If the rains came late the early sowings would be impossible: if they came early and the first showers were. followed by drought the priceless seeds would be wasted. The welfare of the boys' families depended on what happened in the next few weeks. As we waited and Lent passed the dry harmattan wind came down once more, bringing with it the fine diatomic dust from the Sahara that closed down on the Plateau in a grey haze.

''Tis no good,' said the Principal. 'I've only three packets left. Won't last me the day.'

The harmattan lifted, but a dry wind passed over the compound in a ceaseless current, flowing endlessly through the eucalyptus that bowed before it at the roadsides. The heat increased mercilessly, stirring up the brown dust devils that moved steadily across the farmland in the distance. Sometimes they stalked us on our way across the compound in the midday break, catching us by surprise, hurling doors shut, slamming windows, spinning dirt, twigs, leaves, paper, madly about us, stinging our eyes, dishevelling our clothes, buffeting our face and arms, and then with a hiss and a roar they had stormed across the compound, into the trees beyond, in a commotion of upflung branches. Then they would be gone, and the heat would be even more silent and oppressive by comparison.

The Principal planted a packet of two hundred Galleon cigarettes on the living-room table. 'I'll have to smoke 'em. I can't go on with that chewing gum.'

In the morning and evening there were clouds, shoal upon shoal of mackerel sky across the tremendous red of the setting sun.

> As if through a dungeon-grate he peered
> With broad and burning face

'Yes, at home, if ye saw that of an evening, ye'd know for sure there'd be rain on the morrow, but not here, not here.'

Then the great cumulus clouds began to build up. At lunchtime a haze over the Shere Hills thirty miles to the east began to solidify, darken and silently fill the eastern sky. Nothing else happened and in the evenings the cloud disappeared.

'How have I done without it for so long?' said the Principal through the cigarette smoke.

The Plateau was full of static electricity. The shirt crackled as I drew it over my head and the comb sparked as I pulled it through my hair.

'Gives you a thirst, this weather,' said the Principal, looking at his beer glass with its half pint of chalky solvent of dried milk.

The lightning had started, just the occasional flash, at first, after dark. Night after night this intensified. In the darkness the great cumulus clouds stood enveloped in mysterious flickering light. Within them the electricity flashed back and forth in sheets, in vivid forks; from time to time the whole great cloud would be luminous with lightning. Hour after hour this went on in the clinging, oppressive evening, quite silently. Very rarely there was a distant, menacing rumble.

dry sterile thunder without rain

'No,' said the Principal, 'nobody ever gets hurt by lightning in this country. You see, although there's such a lot of it, there are two types, wet lightning and dry lightning. It's only the dry lightning that hurts. Fortunately most of the lightning round here is wet —that's why we haven't had a conductor put up since the one on St Mark's dormitory.'

Then spoke the thunder

Late one afternoon the monstrous cloud over the Shere hills changed its shape. Its swollen, rounded crest fanned out gradually above its base, while, below, the colour of the cloud changed to a deep and ominous grey. The southern half of the sky was gradually overcome. There was a distant rumble. Then, quite suddenly, the hill above Kuru a couple of miles away became indistinct. At the same time there was a low murmur round the Fathers' House. The wind was getting up; the dust was stirring; pieces of paper moved and twitched; the trees fidgeted and rustled. Then the far side of the compound, half a mile away, was suddenly obscured by brown dust. The boys on the football field were running toward the dormitory. Maurice was busily shutting doors and windows downstairs, and then the wind swept across, quite dry and laden with dirt, laying the tree-tops horizontal before it, roaring round the Fathers'

59

House, but not carrying a drop of rain. By now the front of the cloud was directly overhead, swirling and seething as if on the boil. The hill above Kuru had been obliterated, then the far side of the compound was sealed off by a grey curtain, then the dining-hall, then a vicious jag of lightning shot down on the school's one lightning conductor just opposite, and as the whip-crack explosion smote the Fathers' House, the first drops clanged on the roof and the rain burst. The countryside disappeared; water crashed against the windowpanes; hail clamoured on the roof; the lightning flashed down again and again, and the thunder seemed to be exploding on top of the house; the land outside was a sheet of water; fingers of rainwater reached under the door. It lasted a quarter of an hour. Then the thunder retreated westward. Outside it was quiet, clammy, surprisingly cold. Water was gurgling away into the gutters. The earth began to steam. The dry season was over.

'Brother Sheamus, Brother Sheamus!' It was Gabriel Zi coming over from the nearest dormitory, followed by a little first-former who was rubbing his arm ruefully. 'This man says he was hit by lightning.'

'Get away with ye!' answered the Principal, and we went indoors.

Two days later Holy Week started. On Easter Sunday the Principal drank two bottles of lager before lunch. 'Wonderful!' he said, and then winced. We were back to normal.

With Easter behind us my main concern for the last half of the term was to nudge the fathers into building me a bungalow, for the day term ended I was going home to get married and there was no evidence at all that I would ever have a house for Constance to live in.

A week after Easter the Principal returned from one of his daily excursions to Jos with a roll of paper. 'The Prefect told me to show this to you. If you think you want any small improvements you're to tell me and I'll give them to him.'

He gave me the blueprint of a rudimentary bungalow, no more than a row of rooms along a verandah, with a kitchen some yards off at the end of a long covered way. I suggested bringing it next to the dining area.

'No, no, I wouldn't, Kit. She won't want to do any cooking in this country. Don't ever go near the kitchen. Keep it is as far away as possible and don't ask any questions. Much better have it that way.'

As I went on to suggest that it was strange that the cooking area should be no larger than the store, that there was no door between the two, and that to get from the main bedroom into the bathroom next door one had to go out on to the verandah, the Principal's face clouded.

'I wouldn't myself like to tell all those changes to the Prefect. He's a bit uncertain. He's doing ye a great favour letting ye see all this. He might be a bit put out if he thinks ye'll be finding fault too much. Why not just leave it that there's a door through to the bathroom?'

I saw the Prefect myself, and he was charming.

'Quite so, quite so, Mr Elliott. Just what I was thinking of myself, what? Your wife should be perfectly happy there. It's a nice little place, don't you think so? What? What?'

That week after Easter the storms were coming regularly. An urgent forking of lightning in the north-east usually presaged a bad storm about midnight, when the whole Plateau seemed to go up in flames. The house felt as if it would take off, while huts in the fields opposite collapsed, and the lightning took bites out of the masonry of the nearest washhouse.

Nothing happened about our bungalow for another month. Then, as we were finishing our breakfast, the Prefect appeared in the far corner of the compound, studying the ground.

'Had we better ask him in for a cup of tea, brother?'

'No need! No need! He'll come over himself if he wants. I wouldn't like to encourage him.'

The Prefect's authority was exercised that morning. I was informed that the site of our bungalow had been chosen. It was to stand opposite the junior staff quarters, which belonged to the Vet. and where loud gramophones played nightly.

The rains were now under way, and the Plateau had suddenly turned green. The strange grey euphorbia whose blunt fingers rose

Boys clearing grass

The boys were the school labour force—a fact that they greatly resented. For much of the school's history there was no money to pay any labourers to clear roads, football pitches, or athletics tracks. Hoes and pangas, strips of sharpened corrugated iron, were essential parts of their school equipment.

from the hillsides suddenly put out leaves. Streams filled, flowers blossomed, birds flashed in dazzling red and yellow plumage, and the earth overflowed with life. Columns of black ants marched along earth-covered paths to find new homes, and the termites sent up clouds of flying ants to float out of the ground and drift round the Tilley lamps in the classrooms during homework, where the boys collected them in hundreds, pulled off their wings and ate them. Sausage flies, beetles of every shape and description, some half as big as a man's fist, mantises six inches long, butted on the window-panes, fell on the tables, crawled on the floor. Mosquitoes whined, crickets shrieked, and on the walls in the darkness the occasional scorpion waited quietly. Toads by the dozen sat complacently on the verandah, fattening themselves on the flying ants, while tiny green and scarlet tree frogs sat on the window-panes, and twice a snake crept in.

Nothing happened about our bungalow for another month. 'Never ye mind! Never ye mind! We'll soon have it started. 'Tis only six weeks to put up a bungalow. There'll be a roof over your head in no time.'

By now it was the end of May and the grass was up, its harsh, broad blades so rough that they could cut the skin. Out on the compound the boys were slashing away with their cutlasses of corrugated iron to keep the paths and the football field from disappearing, but where their cutlasses did not reach the grass grew six or seven feet tall.

Nothing happened about our bungalow for another month. My fare was booked, my marriage arranged. As I left the compound to catch the plane the first spadefuls of earth were being lifted out for the foundations.

PART TWO

BUILDING A SCHOOL

7
Marriage

Constance came back with me to the compound a month later. A new chapter in my life had started. The last six months had been an interlude, a hyphen between my adolescence and my manhood. In the Fathers' House I had been an observer. Now, married, my situation had changed. I was no longer alone in an unknown land, but in my life I was in the uncharted territory of marriage, the setting up of a home, the birth and upbringing of children. Constance and I were seeking to know ourselves in our new situations, just as we were seeking to know our pupils and the land they lived in. The two tasks were the same.

On the face of it little had changed in that month. The grass had grown, and without the boys it was very quiet. Otherwise the only development was a pattern of bricks where our bungalow was supposed to be. The Principal evacuated the Fathers' House.

'I'll leave ye to yourself. I'm sure ye'd not be wishing me around you. Dennis and Maurice'll look after ye. Ye can rely on Dennis.' We said that we would be perfectly happy to have the Principal on the compound with us, and that in any case we expected that there was work to be done about the school. 'No, no. Ye can have just yourselves. I'm sure ye'll be thankful to have just yourselves.' He rattled off to the Vet., where he enjoyed the hospitality of the Director's house for the next few weeks. From time to time he would arrive on the compound fit and sun-tanned, to report on his full and enjoyable social life.

As the pick-up disappeared Dennis's withered face appeared meekly round the corner of the sitting-room door. 'Welcome, sah! Welcome, madam!' He bowed into the room. 'What thing master and madam want for chop? You have mixed grool?'

67

'Mixed grool' arrived out of the fridge, the Principal's purchases from the cold store earlier that morning: sausages, bacon and black pudding, swimming in fat.

The following morning, after we had breakfasted off more of the Principal's cold-store purchases, Dennis's face once more appeared grieving round the doorpost. He rubbed his hands sorrowfully, as if a near relation had died. 'So sorry, sah! Cow killed early for market. Steak gone, sah.' His face then brightened optimistically. 'They have homp, sah. You like homp? Very good meat, sah.'

'Homp, Dennis?'

'Yes, sah. Homp from back of cow, sah, very good meat—very tender.'

'O, hump, Dennis, yes, from the back of the cow, of course; yes, we'll have hump.'

Dennis went on his way rejoicing as if a bereaved relation had indeed been restored to him, and he served 'homp', a colourless rubbery piece of anatomy which arrived on our plates very frequently during the next month. No doubt it was cheap, and certainly Dennis looked very prosperous, and was very friendly towards us.

Meanwhile, with little else to do, we watched the rain fall. Throughout July, August, and September it never seemed to stop. In each of those months as much rain fell as falls on Manchester in a year, not torrentially but incessantly. The whole Plateau was mist-laden, cloud-covered, sodden; flowers extinguished, trees motionless, birds silent, the countryside muted grey and green. In the fields in front of the Fathers' House we watched the farmers hoeing glumly, endlessly hacking out the grass from around their crops. Wood swelled, doors jammed, clothes rotted, books mildewed.

One thing did happen. Three weeks after our installation Constance woke early one morning, looked pale, and fled along the upstairs verandah, down the stairs and into the lavatory, where she was violently sick. The same thing happened the next morning, and the next, and the next. After about a week we realised what was happening. We explained to the Principal that she was pregnant.

'Tis not,' he said. 'Dennis is using too much ground-nut oil. Ye must speak to him.' The Director's wife was shrewder, and sent us a packet of Avomine tablets. The Principal took fright, and for several weeks we were unable to see a doctor because he feared that the pick-up would be too dangerous. His training had taught him to beware of women, and for nine months, I believe, he feared to be found compromised on the main road between Vwang and Jos, delivering a baby in the passenger seat of his vehicle. We were marooned even more effectively than before. Our diet became even more restricted as the sight, let alone the smell, of Northern Nigerian egg was sufficient to send Constance in full flight for the lavatory.

The Zawan sisters rescued us at the end of September. I had met one of them before, Sister Thomas More, a small bird-like figure in a nun's habit perched on the edge of the half-finished septic tank outside the Fathers' House delivering a lecture in a high-pitched voice on the construction and maintenance of cesspits, septic tanks and the like. I understood that she had just finished clearing out the sanitation of her maternity hospital. A few weeks later, at the convent, she had been delighted to learn that I came from Surrey. 'Near Ascot, Mr Elliott! Have you not been there? And Epsom! I'd never missed a Derby in my life.' She was a late vocation who had at some period trained in Birmingham and then nursed on the Elder Dempster ships which served West Africa before deciding to become a nun in a missionary order.

The nun's habit apart, she and the other two Zawan sisters were three elderly ladies who ran between them a convent, a maternity hospital, and a boarding primary school for girls on the edge of one of the more dismal Birom settlements a few miles off the main road. Sister Eta, soft-spoken and bespectacled, had an appearance of open-eyed simplicity and extreme gentleness. Mother Virgilius was tall, heavily built, and grave. Her silences were awe-inspiring and she had a temper. There is a legend that she once called a priest 'a bloody eejit' who had run his car into a ditch to avoid the Zawan Volkswagen.

They were all infinitely kind and charitable. They had to be, I imagine, to live with Sister Thomas, whose energy knew no bounds. She was normally up at five and over to her hospital, disdaining a siesta, and working all day in and out of her little hospital, out to visit her leper settlements, in and out of Jos with her patients, never still, a reproach to all who came near her.

Her domain was the maternity hospital. There she had her office with her 'clerk', a cat, fat, soft, sleepy, and arrogant. To one side of her hospital compound stood the row of tiny wards loaded down with flowers, the verandahs festooned with honeysuckle, and everywhere pots, paint tins, margarine cans and oil drums, painted green, stuffed with soil and exuberant with geraniums, poinsettias, lilies, leaves and blossoms of every shade, hue, and description. Sister Thomas went about with her eye on other folk's gardens, ready always to raid them, or to offer cuttings from her own compound.

Each little ward was quiet and clean, shaded by the flowers crowded outside, a cool relief from the harsh sunlight blazing down on the Plateau which stretched on all sides far beyond the trim euphorbia hedges that bounded Sister Thomas's little kingdom. There were always half a dozen pregnant women, huge and resigned, sitting waiting their time on the verandah with a blanket draped over them. Others would be in their beds with their faces concentrated, moaning occasionally. In the other wards would be a few more women with, swinging from the ends of their beds, cots with their tiny inmates. Sister Thomas would show you round as proud as if she had produced the babies herself, chuckling at the mothers and their babies. The women would smile back, tired and shy.

These were usually straightforward cases. The serious ones were rushed into Jos Maternity Hospital by car for Dr Holling to look after, though there were sometimes differences of opinion about what exactly a serious case was. Occasionally the emergency was too extreme. A woman in the last stages of a delivery, sometimes with the child already arrived, would be brought in by relations. Then Sister Thomas would resort to sugar, water, brandy and hour after hour of unremitting attention to bring back a scrap of humanity to life, carrying with it, more often than not, all the sacraments that could be administered by the parish priest in the hour of its need. There are several Muslim herd boys going about Northern Nigeria alive thanks to Sister Thomas More; and also, though they do not know it, baptised and confirmed Christians carrying the final seal of extreme unction. Many are the canonical puzzles that Sister Thomas must have left to be unravelled in the next world.

She acted first and thought about asking permission afterward. There was a children's ward at the far end of her compound which had been a shed, but somehow Sister Thomas had raised a hundred pounds, painted it, filled it with beds and with sick children before anyone thought of telling the Prefect.

As if a maternity hospital were not enough, and a children's ward, she ran an orphanage into the bargain. There were always three or four infants in her care. For two years there was Thomas, a little Ibo boy. His mother had delivered him on a railway train between Bukuru and Kafanchan, and after her death, his father, a lorry driver, had no home for the child. Sister Thomas looked after him. There were the Fulani twins, slender and fair-complexioned. Their mother was also dead and their family was on the move. Sister Thomas looked after them, too. There was always somebody and always you would be told of the children's first teeth, their walking, their ailments, and their tantrums. You would be invited to come and look at their progress, to play with them. Then, one day, just as they were growing into sturdy little toddlers, they would be gone. Thomas went to his father's new wife, where he died a year later. The twins were carried off to the precarious shelter of a Fulani encampment when their clan caught up with them once more. There was never any security for her in her devotion to her children, nor any end to it, for no sooner had one child gone than another baby was left with her, or a mother died in childbirth, and her infinite affections were engaged once more.

She was neither remarkably strong nor particularly young. If she came out for a meal, she normally fell asleep before it was over. Similarly she frequently dozed off in the chapel when the sisters were saying their rosaries in the evening. Once she did break down. Her arms ceased to move. For forty-eight hours she was at last

brought to her bed. We saw her in her room, which was almost devoid of furniture and possessions. Her thin arms, just recovering their strength, were extended above the coverlet; her face was haggard and lined, her hair straying in white wisps across it; she looked unbearably tiny, old, and tired. Within a week she was as hard at work as ever, bustling, chattering, chuckling, tactless, and indomitable.

The sisters took us to Akwanga for a few days, where the order had a teacher training college which prepared girls for their primary schools. Whatever order the sisters belonged to or wherever they set up a convent they always displayed a genius for civilisation. Zawan itself, overlooking, on one side, the great meadow where the circumcisions took place in a brief nocturnal ceremony once a year, and, on the other side, the great spoil heaps of a large tin working, was a haven with its fruit trees and its shady parlour. Akwanga was equally cool, quiet, and efficient, with a parlour

A Staff House

Ours was a rather miniature version of a normal European bungalow, stowed away in a corner of the school compound, and shielded only by a few eucalyptus trees from empty miles of rocky plateau. We slept in the room at one end, lived worked and ate in the room at the other, and let the children inhabit the middle. The ants swarmed up through the bathroom floor once a year; the dog pushed his way between the burglar-proof bars; the water tank at the back collected the dust in the dry season; at the beginning of the wet it sometimes needed a raincoat to get a meal from the kitchen, or visit the children in their rooms along the verandah. Like most Europeans we planted a garden, with trees whose blossoms we would never stay long enough to see, fruit trees that would never bear any more than half a dozen oranges, and flowers and vegetables which grew amazingly fast but needed enormous quantities of manure. The children benefitted most. Both garden and house were full of evidence of them. For such a small house—it was little more than sixty feet long—it supported a large community: two Europeans and three children, four servants, a dog and a variety of transient cats.

which possessed a table that appeared to spread itself with the most desirable meals, like something out of the Arabian Nights. A couple of hundred yards away the parish priest lived with his cat and a cocker spaniel, munching his way through the remains of the previous night's steamed pudding; and it was with him that I was obliged to stay. After an easeful week-end with a couple of brief expeditions up into the hills where the Akwanga mission had been established only a few years before, we returned to Zawan.

It was the beginning of September and the unending downpour was at last beginning to lift, the sun to appear a little more frequently. As we drove up toward Zawan the rocks, the fields and the sides of the roads were full of masses of small yellow flowers, making the hillsides look like huge rock gardens full of children and goats. It was as though the sunlight had been stored away during the long wet months, to be displayed at last as the rainy season approached its end. We looked forward, now, to seeing the boys.

They returned at the beginning of September. Our bungalow was at last finished and we proceeded to set up house under the eyes of the school. This was a process of colonisation which started in the bedroom at one end of the house, where our monumental four-poster, constructed around two single mattresses because no adequate double mattress was available, stood alone in the middle of the cement floor. The process continued by way of the bathroom, missed out the two tiny intervening bedrooms, and concentrated on the kitchen and the living-room at the other end of the house.

Like the Principal's dog, who followed us from the Fathers' House because we fed him and the Principal's servants did not, and like the cat we had obtained from Zawan, we were, and probably still remain, semi-domesticated. That is not to say that we took no interest in the furnishing of the house. Constance displayed an interest in, and an enthusiasm for, interior decoration which I had never previously suspected. Every Syrian store and commericial warehouse in Jos was ransacked for curtain material for the living-room. A suitable design was finally identified in Jos market-place, a rich combination of black, red and blue. A week's negotiation followed with the suspicious Ibo stallholder before we finally had enough. We then had to turn it into curtains—a difficult matter, for neither of us knew how to use a sewing machine, and it took a whole morning to learn to thread a shuttle. The last curtain was completed at two o'clock one morning. Privacy was ours at last.

We had no carpets, and the straw mats, which were all we could afford, turned up at the edges, a snare for the unwary. Constance proposed to use roofing felt instead. We had seen it nailed to the floor of a house in Jos. As we could not get hold of that either, Constance decided to have the floor painted black instead. The effect was striking. Like the paint, it soon wore off. The final result, coated with mansion polish, was of mottled grey.

Then there was the furniture. I designed it, and the results were more unique than practical. The book-case stretched for twenty feet across one end of the living-room. It sagged in the middle. The chairs were imitated from a design we had seen in Jos. They were rather elegant, and fell over backwards if you touched them carelessly. They also tended to ease the sitter gradually forward on his cushion, till he ended virtually on his back, with his knees level with his head. We remained convinced that they were exceptionally comfortable.

We were less proud of the sideboard. This was very much my own design, had three substantial compartments to it, and four hefty drawers. It weighed about a quarter of a ton. None of the drawers would close. After a month Constance ordered it out of the living-room. Sweating and swearing, the cook, the garden boy, and myself heaved and bashed the monster out of the door and round into the kitchen, where it spent the rest of its working life.

It was the kitchen in which Constance took the greatest pride. As a result of some diplomacy I had managed to get it enlarged from the twelve-foot-square cubicle of the original design. The Prefect's fridge was installed, and the only gas cooker in the district. In went the fine new saucepans, the cast-iron frying pan, the new cutlery, the coffee grinder, the mincing machine, the chip basket, and all the other paraphernalia that made up a good part of Constance's trousseau.

We took on servants, a succession of them, till at last we were left with Bonaventure. Bonaventure had originally been taken on to work as a garden boy and carry water. Having come up from the East he had bribed his way into the army, posing as a Northerner (for the army could never recruit enough of these, and had far too many Ibos). Nobody could have looked more like an Ibo, so when they threw him out of the army Bonaventure seemed to have become a petrol-pump attendant. At all events he appeared grinning on the verandah dressed in a T-shirt and a peaked cap with the Esso sign printed loudly across both of them. It was he whom Constance taught to cook. He was still working for us when we left, despite periodic rows, and by that time he had married a young woman called Grace and had just become the father of twins.

Now that the boys had returned they were fascinated. They were more than usually concerned to run errands which took them to the house, and there they lingered long in doorways, craning their necks to see what they could see. They took the longest way to the post office, marching sideways past the front of our house. With more or less circumspection they made their enquiries. 'How much did madam cost?' enquired one of the first-formers. 'Seven and six,' said Constance. Consternation!

'Madam must be very young,' observed an elderly Beri-beri at the back of the same class. His estimate was seventeen. A little Goemai was rather concerned that Constance did not cook all our meals. 'Madam, you must take care. That man may poison you.' All the children were obsessed with poisoning, as a threat. They declared it was on the increase, and that women were the chief culprits. 'Are you not worried, madam, that Mrs Waldron will run away with your husband,' asked another, apparently concerned that she came over to us for coffee during the break.

The older boys were a little more circumspect. As I prepared to leave the third form at the end of a lesson, a voice behind me said, 'Sir, would you let me ask a question?' I halted.

'What is it?'

The solid, rather overfed form of Ambrose Zamani had risen from the back row. 'The class would like to—you will not be angry, sir?'

'No, I don't expect so.'

'Do Europeans beat their wives?'

'I don't beat mine, if that's what you mean. Most Europeans don't beat theirs. Hardly any of them do.'

'Do they let their wives argue with them?' asked Gabriel Pinukei earnestly from the side of the room.

'They can't usually stop them. I don't think it worries them very much.'

'Do their wives do as they're told if you don't beat them?' asked Ambrose.

'It's not really a question of doing as they're told,' I tried to explain. 'I don't think I expect my wife to do just what I tell her.'

'But how can a European rule his wife?' pursued a worried Gabriel Pinukei.

'I do not understand this European marriage,' observed Kevin Dagai. 'None of us understand it.'

'Well—look—perhaps we'll have a lesson on it. We can do something on it in our next English period.'

Kevin's face brightened. There was a murmur round the form. 'Yes, yes, the boys would like that.'

The following week I put before them a collection of statements on the topic of marriage.

The first was by Edwin Muir, the only statement I could find on married love as distinct from the pre-marital kind.

> Yes, yours, my love, is the right human face.
> I in my mind have waited for this long
> Seeing the false and searching for the true.

We worked out that this man had married because he loved his wife, and that affection was the main, perhaps the only motive.

Gabriel Nongo stood up puzzled and indignant. 'This cannot be so.'

'But it is, Gabriel. Most Englishmen marry because of affection, simply because they love their wives.'

'It costs too much money for that. How much money do you have to pay for your wife?'

'I think I paid seven and sixpence for a licence to get married.' A wave of shock, consternation and laughter. 'I didn't have to pay her father anything for her.' A Nigerian girl, of course, has cash value to her father. According to the amount of education which has been invested in her so the value of her bride-price rises, and has to be paid by her suitor. 'It sometimes happens,' I said, 'that the girl's father will even give her money to take with her to her husband.'

'Then you marry to get money?'

'No, Gabriel. Very few Englishmen get any money from their wives when they marry.'

'You mean an Englishman marries just because he is fond of his wife?'

'Yes, Gabriel.' I was glad that my point had been understood.

'It cannot be so.' He sat down. This seemed to be the general attitude of the form.

We looked at St Paul.

You who are husbands must shew love to your wives as Christ showed love to the Church when he gave himself up on its behalf.

They were all acquainted with the passage, which would be read out as part of the nuptial Mass when they eventually got married.

There was a blank silence. 'I don't know what this means. I don't think it means anything to us,' said Peter Kure.

The bourgeois sees in his wife a mere instrument of production.

The reaction to Karl Marx was prompt enough. Augustine Ebodike, a grave, conscientious, devout, and intelligent Ibo, rose slowly from his seat. 'Yes, among my people this is so. Yes, for us wives are instruments of production.' From various parts of the class there were nods and mutters of agreement.

78

'How do you mean? In what way?'

'They produce children,' said Joseph Ajuji, a Goemai boy. 'What use would they be otherwise?'

'You need wives if you are going to farm,' said another Goemai boy, 'as many as possible, the more wives the more you farm. That is why my people marry so many. That is why they are instruments of production.'

'If you had not come to school, would you have married more than one wife?'

'I expect so,' said the same boy. 'I would need them if I were a farmer. All farmers have many wives.'

'All rich men, too,' said Andrew Gwaza, a quiet thick-set boy from Kagoro. 'Rich men have many wives. It shows that they are rich. They have power. Men respect them.'

'Wouldn't it be easier to hire men to work for you?'

'You can't beat men,' retorted Ambrose. 'They will be lazy.'

'They cost much,' added Joseph Ajuji once more. 'It is much easier to feed a wife. Anyway, she will get a lot of her own food and clothing.'

'What happens in a town?'

'I would marry a teacher,' said John Maigari, son of a Goemai chief, 'then she could earn me money.'

'Yes,' it was Ambrose again; 'a junior primary teacher would be best. It would not be good to have a wife who knew too much. Otherwise she will not do as she is told. She will be unfaithful.'

'Too many are unfaithful,' said another of the Ibos.

'They answer back. They are always quarrelling. There is never peace,' agreed John Maigari.

'It is difficult to beat an educated wife,' Ambrose complained.

The argument went on and there was little for me to do except listen. There existed, often in the same boy, cynicism and sentimentality. That sturdy Angas, Anacletus Tunkuda, for example, was in full agreement with the theory that women were instruments of production, yet the pillow slip on his bed in the dormitory bore a message picked out in pink, 'Ever your sweetheart', and on the other side he was encouraged by another reminder from his

girl-friend, 'I love you for ever', in blue, with flowers embroidered round it. Gabriel Pinukei, full of distrust for womanhood, particularly educated womanhood, was also a reader of
books like *Married for her Beauty*, by Bertha M. Clay, 'a writer',
he said, 'of "books for men".'

However, even by their standards, I had done well out of my
marriage. 'See,' said a little boy in the first form, 'how fortunate
Mr Elliott is. Formerly he had no house and no car. Now he has a
wife, and with her money he has a house, and a car in which he is
able to drive to the dining-hall.' I could drive no further, as I did
not possess a driving licence.

8

'Macbeth', a Baby, and an Athletics Team

That prosperity which the little boy had observed was illusory. That first autumn of our married life was hard as we set about the business of setting up a new home at the same time as we tried to found a new school, encumbered as we were by preconceptions about both. The rains had ended, and on the Plateau outside the compound the last hungry months before the harvest dragged by, with the granaries almost empty, and the grain still unripe. By the end of November the worst was over for the farmers. Their crops were ripe and as the sun came up, on our way to Mass, the children could be heard calling and singing in the fields, driving the birds from the ripening grain. The annual ritual, on which the life of the Plateau depended, was coming to an end. Small groups of women stood in the fields, their backs rising and falling, singing as they flailed the corn.

The general sense of relief that the harvest was now in did not reach our bungalow. We looked gloomily at the uncut grass, the rubbish lying about the compound, the boys unsupervised, the classrooms unequipped, and we quarrelled with the Principal. The harmattan settled across the compound, a grey shroud of dust. Cobwebs hung in the corners of the classrooms. Dirt smeared the uncleaned windows. In this colourless oppressive season the school was a foul, slatternly slum. Rusty beer cans lay among the brown grass. Pieces of rag and scraps of filthy paper drifted across the dormitories, or clung to the withered hedges planted round the ruinous cricket pitch. Nightly Constance vomited as the time for her delivery came nearer. In the Fathers' House the Principal suffered from his stomach.

It was at that unlikely period that we set out on our attempt to remake the school in the image of Arnold's Rugby, seen through the distorting lens of our own experience of maintained English grammar schools. The clichés of a dozen speech days had settled in our subconscious, phrases like 'liberal studies', 'educating the whole man', 'doing your bit' emerged. While Constance continued to be sick I started to run a debating society, produce a school play, and train the athletics team. They provided much of my contact with the boys during the next few years.

The first venture along these lines was the debating society, whose constitution I had drawn up in fantastic detail a month after my arrival in Vwang. It was based on that of the Union Society at Cambridge, ran into twelve pages, innumerable clauses and a couple of appendices; and while appearing to spread responsibility evenly throughout the school, left it squarely in the hands of the Principal. The election of committee members allowed six different choices for each office and needed at least three counts before a decision could be announced. It was intended to develop the boys' powers of self-expression, wit and repartee, after the manner of the Cambridge Union, by debating such motions as 'This house intends to marry four wives' (or 'go back to the land' or 'establish a dictatorship in Nigeria'). By June we had debated that 'This house would prefer to be a school-teacher rather than a farmer', and, with Mark Dimka in the chair threatening to fight individual members of the house, there was a deadly earnest debate that 'This house does not like cutting the grass as a school punishment'. The Principal vetoed a debate on corporal punishment. In September we were debating that 'This house would prefer to attend a teacher training college rather than a secondary school', which turned out to be a purely monetary issue, since both commenced immediately after primary school, but a teacher training course lasted for only three years and the students received pay right from the beginning. In November the Principal invited some of his friends from the Vet. to listen to a debate on 'This house would like to get married at sixteen'. Most of the boys would have been married a great deal earlier than this had they not come to school. The speakers were all uncompromisingly direct and uncensored, culminating in Lawrence Obidieguwu's commentary on his more erotic night-time fantasies, upon which the visitors departed in some consternation.

The following term was a busy one and it was not until the following autumn that the society was revived and started to consider a quantity of proposals, all along the lines that this house would prefer to be a farmer rather than a teacher/civil servant/ politician/stonemason/shopkeeper, etc. Then the Principal intervened and handed the whole thing over to Father Kelly, a young priest who had just joined the staff. He was very keen and envisaged debates in which the chairman's task was to summarise the arguments for both sides at the end of the evening and on his own initiative award the victory to whichever he decided to have excelled in both argument and debating skill. Gradually the society faded. Debates still occurred from time to time. You could hear them half a mile away. The speeches were drowned in thunders of applause or dissent; the chairs and forms were pounded rhythmically; the bell clanged; and the whole affair would end in a disorderly surge across the compound working itself out for the next half-hour before the final bell for lights out.

After the inception of the school debating society we started the school magazine. Magazines, like debating societies, were run by all the best schools, and like the best schools we assembled ours by throwing together the more fluent essays from the boys' exercise books, introducing them with a few words by the Principal and rounding them off with reports on school activities. A title was proposed by Gabriel Zi, *The Pioneer,* which the Principal vetoed, and the project languished till the end of the year, when it was hastily resurrected, entitled prosaically *St Jerome's College School Magazine,* duplicated, and issued free of charge to the boys, who neither could nor would afford to buy it. Various friends of the Principal on the Vet. received copies, and some were scandalised by Gabriel Nongo's attitude to the English as spawn of an indigent society, come to relieve their poverty at home by wallowing in the fleshpots of Africa. The issue was not otherwise notable.

A far more ambitious venture was the school production of *Macbeth*. At first we were all united, the Principal, the boys and ourselves, on the proposition that all the best schools produced school plays. Thereafter the conflict started. The boys did not know what a play was, or a theatre, or footlights, or actors, or any of the other technicalities of European dramatics. The Principal knew all about these, but his vision of a school play was *H.M.S. Pinafore* in full traditional rig-out produced by himself before an audience of admiring fathers and sisters. My own belief was in Shakespeare suitably dressed up for the Nigerian scene. As it happened providence provided us all with *Macbeth*. It was a set book for G.C.E. and every Nigerian schoolboy liked to feel he was starting his School Certificate syllabus half a decade before he went into the examination-room. It was stocked in a reasonably attractive edition on the crowded shelves of the rogue who sold the school its books. There was also a record of the whole play belonging to one of the Principal's friends on the Vet.

One of the first functions, therefore, ever to be performed in the upstairs sitting-room of the Fathers' House was a public hearing of Alec Guinness recorded in the part of *Macbeth*. The third form had been hurriedly instructed in the first two acts which they hardly understood at all, and they assembled respectfully on the upper verandah. Five minutes later the Principal arrived with his soap dish full of keys, tried them all in the lock, mumbled something, and disappeared again. When he returned everybody had climbed in through the window. Finally he made his triumphant entrance through the door and the performance started. At the end of it all the Principal asked various rather sheepish individuals if they understood it. 'Yes,' they answered. 'Right,' said the Principal, 'we shall produce it. There will be a public performance.' We were committed.

Auditions took about a fortnight. Peter Kure, morbid, impressive, and intelligent, became Macbeth. Lady Macbeth was given to Eric Anderson, who was blessed not only with good looks but superb English, something to do with possession of a Scottish grandfather on one side of the family and a Syrian grandfather on the other. The smaller parts were easy enough. Lawrence Obidie-guwu, a confirmed hypochondriac, became the doctor. Anacletus Tunkuda, with a figure like a middle-aged N.C.O., became the wounded soldier who brings the news of Macbeth's victories. The porter was an utterly incoherent but appropriately cheerful Goemai called Thomas Kaagnan from the second year. The big parts were the real difficulty. It is likely that Banquo, Macduff, and Malcolm were still not quite sure what they were saying when the whole production took place after many vicissitudes a year later.

The Principal believed that it was the Principal's duty to do all. It was only in the autumn, when it became clear that it was a physical impossibility for him to produce half the scenes and me to produce the other half that he reluctantly gave up his authority over the production to me. It was my theory that if only the boys repeated their parts often enough and if their actions and movements were prearranged in meticulous detail and also repeated often enough, some of the meaning might eventually get through. Starting in the autumn, for four months the poor fellows were directed round and round one end of the room where Mass was said, draped in the counterpanes from their beds, chanting Shakespeare over and over and over again. Wearily they went through, obediently repeating phrase after phrase, and at the end of each evening I would trudge back through the dusk half asleep and slightly drunk with rhetoric, muttering to myself, 'Blood will have blood, stones have been known to speak, choughs and mag-gotpies brought forth the secret'st man of blood, blood will have blood . . .' over and over again.

It was an obsession. I could not sleep with pondering the details. Every step, every hand movement had to be planned. New ideas on how to produce Shakespeare on a pittance kept on rising. The colour of the supernatural in Africa was white, so dress the witches in sheets. What on earth effects could produce eight kings without laying the audience out in laughter? None, so the scene would have to be cut. What would we do for alarums when we had no trumpets? Use drums instead. How could we deal with the last scenes where Malcolm's army pops on and off the stage in between

Macbeth's speeches? Keep the army off-stage altogether and let disembodied voices speak the commentary on Macbeth's fall without allowing them to be seen at all. Twice a week the poor uncomprehending actors trudged patiently round and round the end of the Mass room, pursued by my utterly incomprehensible instructions, puzzled by my phrenetic enthusiasm for the archaic phrases I made them repeat. Then the Principal arrived with a visitor. He watched the cast plodding through their lines. 'It's no good,' he said. 'I'm going to come and take it over. Don't do anything more.'

Then the baby arrived. I was enduring a homily at the time from the vet to whom I had gone with our cat, who was having kittens. He spoke to me about the Chinese at length for over an hour, and when I finally returned Constance had been suffering from back pains at intervals for over half an hour. I got the car ready. 'Nonsense,' she said, 'it can't be starting. What will they say at the hospital when we arrive so early?' The twinges were coming every five minutes, so to an accompaniment of protests I drove to Jos at a break-neck pace as if I expected twins to arrive within the hour. For all I knew there might well have been twins due for arrival at any moment. I had even taken the precaution of reading what to do in such an eventuality.

I stayed with Constance, which was as well, since no doctor arrived. Rumour had it that he drank heavily. In the small hours of the morning Constance was moved into the labour ward, vomiting for positively the last time as she left the lying-in room. The umbilical cord had wound round the baby's neck, and there was an hour's hard work before Nicholas arrived with a jump. The cord was clamped and cut, his back was clapped smartly, a wooden palette thrust down his throat; he choked, coughed, and bawled vigorously, from a rubbery blue turning pink, healthy and terribly noisy. It was half-past three. After I had seen Constance washed, I drove back to Vwang, and as the light dawned on Good Friday morning I contravened canon law with a huge meal of sausages and bacon.

Five days later I drove Nicholas and Constance home, so reverently that at length Constance lost patience and told me to get a move on. I had prepared an evening meal in celebration, which we ate with a sense of considerable well-being. As the last mouthful disappeared a sound like a cockerel crowing reached us from the bedroom. Nicholas was awake. He remained awake for the next eight hours. As I plodded up and down the verandah in the small hours I reflected that we had a problem on our hands for the next twenty-odd years.

The next two months turned out to be the more immediate crisis. Constance developed an abscess, and it seemed that we gave up sleeping. Worse still these were the last days of the dry season, and we were awake through those long oppressive nights, which shuddered occasionally with lightning, waiting for the weather to break. Often there seemed to be the sound of rushing water outside, but it was only the incessant dry rustle of the dusty wind in the eucalyptus leaves.

In Spock we trusted. There was no one else to consult, for we knew almost no one on the Vet., and there were no relations, friends or women next door who could act as an oracle in emergency. Everything had to be referred to the book: his complexion, moods, the colour of his napkins, and the state of his temper. Night after night he lay in Constance's lap while I flicked nervously through the index, a confusing business when an infant complaint like hiccup was indexed under 'bubble'. Spock was terribly good at technical terms. 'Hyper-tonic' was the term we thought applied to Nicholas, who never slept, and made the most appalling noise while he was awake. For our position, though, Spock was very appropriate. In case of emergency his normal advice was to go to the doctor. Like every other parent in Nigeria, we did this every time his temperature went up. It might just be a cold, but in the tropics it could equally well be malaria, typhoid, or meningitis.

On Constance the arrival of a male child conferred considerable prestige. Interest and approval was displayed to both her and the baby as soon as she returned to the classroom six weeks later. A male heir was the highest boon that could be conferred on a successful marriage, and even the oldest and most gnarled members of the most senior forms occasionally poked their finger at Nicholas and made endearing noises.

The play had come to a stop. It was Easter, so the Principal was equally busy taking part in the elaborate ceremonies that fill Holy Week, in which the holy oil and holy water are blessed, the church stripped and redecorated, the paschal candle lit and the sacrament restored.

Then they came to ask what was happening about *Macbeth*. The Principal transparently lacked the time to do anything about it. So, for the last time, reluctant that so much energy should be wasted, we set to. A stage was built at one end of the dining-hall. At the back and the sides it was screened with dark brown hardboard that nobody thought to whitewash. Lighting consisted of a row of lamp sockets at top and bottom of the proscenium arch in which a number of coloured bulbs could be screwed, thus intensifying the gloom still further. The curtain was transparent to any light behind it, so that the scene-shifters came through in vivid shadow play.

Kuru provided us with two shields and a number of halberds. Somebody had been overtaken by a similar Shakespearian intoxication there, but had been moved on after the preliminary rehearsals. We bought little white cotton caps from the market for sixpence each, sewed flaps into the back, painted them silver and called them helmets. We treated crude canvas jerkins in the same way to produce something like mail. Swords, very blunt and brittle, were sixpence each from a Bukuru blacksmith. Trinkets and Muslim praying beads from the market, and a peacock feather somebody had picked up in the stock farm provided our only ornaments, and when all else failed we took down our curtains and draped half the cast in these. Finally, looking as if we had raided a junk-shop, we were ready for our dress rehearsal.

The Principal, thank God, left us to it. He could hear quite well enough from his house on the other side of the compound. It all started in pitch darkness. Unfortunately my electrician was well beyond anyone's reach with a bundle of switches half-way down the dining-hall. The witches muttered their indistinct incantation according to instruction, accompanied by a roll on the primary school's big drum. The darkness failed to lift. An interested murmur rose to uproar while I sent messengers down to Bernard Ibrahim. The lights came on in all the wrong places to disclose a scrum at all the entrances on to the stage as Duncan and his court struggled to come on through the wrong doors. The stage had been built at precisely the opposite end of the room to the one in which we had been rehearsing. All those involved instructions had now to be carried out the other way round. There was chaos. Five minutes later it subsided with Duncan and his court in approximately the right place, and the wounded sergeant, looking as if he were suffering from severe stomach pains, reciting his speech in a deadly monotone. Each actor then marched to somewhere near his right position on the stage, declaimed and retired. Then they fought their way out of the wrong exits to loud applause, darkness fell once more and the scene-shifters could be heard tumbling over the platform they were supposed to be moving.

The witches came on, three broad grins imperfectly concealed by three white sheets. On a stroke of inspiration their nails were lacquered silver. To roars of laughter they circled through their part, tripping over each other once or twice, before Macbeth and Banquo emerged on to the stage, as usual through the wrong entrances. So we went through the play. Some hint of the story began to dawn, though the first form had to watch three performances before they finally made up their mind what it was all about. The fact that Macbeth was a villain conveyed itself. They greeted him with howls of execration. Lady Macbeth, however, really took them aback. Five years later, to boys about to take the School Certificate, she remained the revelation of the play. She turned upside down every Nigerian relationship, not so much because she was responsible for a murder but because she made her husband do as she told him. For this audience she was the really malevolent character. Macbeth was not really to be blamed with a wife like this. So they listened to Lady Macbeth, played with tremendous verve, with awe and almost in silence.

The grand climax to the evening's entertainment was the last act. Macbeth was in his castle and around him the forces that were to bring him to justice collected, and drums beat, and Birnam Wood marched on Dunsinane. The rebel army was supposed to be invisible in this production. Its heads appeared round every corner of the scenery. Drums were supposed to beat at the end of every brief scene. They had an odd habit of beating at every other moment in the middle of Macbeth's most important speeches. Finally, as the denouement approached, the rebels could be seen making their way from side to side of the stage behind Macbeth's back to reach their appropriate entrance. The delight of the audience was extreme. As each new face appeared it was applauded. As the prospect of battle at the end of the scene came nearer and nearer, they became more and more wildly excited. As battle commenced between Macduff and Macbeth their partisans on each side cheered them on. Their great blunt swords swung round the stage at appalling peril to both actors, the sheet metal shields clattered and dented, and both opponents appeared to forget their parts entirely. According to plan, Macduff retreated, to be seen only a few minutes later, puffing and sweating profusely, shoving his way across the back of the stage to find the entrance he believed he should come in at. A roar of encouragement rose from the audience, drowning my own imprecations in the wings. He disappeared again, to spring once more from the other side of the stage, a little before time, waving the bundle wrapped up in an old stocking that was intended to represent Macbeth's head. His final words were utterly lost in the uproar that ended the performance. I asked a little boy, an hour later, how far he had enjoyed the play. 'I enjoyed it, sir,' he said, 'very much. It was very, very funny.' A beam of pure pleasure spread across his face at the recollection. In the dormitories the sound of the boys' appreciation could be heard dying away.

Oddly, the production was a success. The two invited audiences enjoyed our strange performance, but as far as the boys were concerned the greatest privilege was the arrival, quite unexpectedly, of two dozen real girls from Akwanga Training College.

They were most impressed. Only the very best schools, they wrote to tell the boys, ever produced a real play. The cast was delighted. Fame at last. 'We used to see,' wrote Alexander in an essay, 'this man coming for rehearsals, and we would say to each other, "what is this man coming for, this European, to disturb us?" Then we performed the play. Up to that time I did not really understand it. Then I did, and it was an interesting story. The girls from Akwanga came, and they wrote to say how clever we are. Now we are very pleased with Mr Elliott.' Three years later a boy whose English was not very good was describing the ritual which commemorated an ancient Kwalla war. 'Watching this dancing,' he wrote, 'is as exciting as watching a play like *Macbeth.*'

A process of discovery and self-discovery was going on. Gradually a sort of fellowship was growing up. However little any of the boys had understood about the play, there was a mutual pride in work shared, success and prestige achieved. The formal relationships of the classroom were eased a little further. Then the Principal decided that I should produce no more plays. He had plans for *H.M.S. Pinafore.* Instead I was to look after the athletics team, despite the fact that I knew nothing about athletics. I little realised how serious that responsibility was.

Athletic activity of any sort was a very serious business indeed, far more serious than *Macbeth,* and almost as serious as the G.C.E. This was the case in the boys' homes. The great wrestling tournaments were trials of manhood at which the girls appraised the virility of possible husbands and lovers, and they were also believed to influence the success of the harvest, the potency of kings and the destiny of the State. Games with less ritual significance, like the ball game played by the Katab which so much resembled lacrosse, provided a useful outlet for the rivalries and inhibitions of tiny and impoverished societies in much the same way as village football had once done in England, and by much the same methods:

sometimes their necks are broken, sometimes their backs, sometimes their legs, sometimes their arms, sometime one part thrust out of joint, sometime another, sometimes their noses gush out with blood, sometime their eyes

start out, and sometimes hurt in one place, sometimes in another. But whoso-
ever scapeth away the best goeth not scot-free, but is either sore-wounded,
and bruised so as he dieth of it, or else scapeth very hardly. And no marvel,
for they have sleights to meet one betwixt two, to dash him against the heart
with their elbows, to hit him under the short ribs with their gripped fists,
and with their knees to catch him upon the hip, and to pick him on his neck,
with a hundred such murdering devices.

Stubbs could very well have been describing one of those football matches we fought with St Murumba's, the secondary school
the Prefect had built in Jos whose boys were mainly Ibo, and with
whom our Northern boys fought out on the football field that
terrible cleavage in Nigerian society between the two races.

At the beginning of each match the players sized each other up
like boxers in the ring. The wings eyed each other with insolent
grins. The centre-forwards tried to stare each other out. Such
matches were fought with the savagery of pitched battles, the
elbow in the ribs, the knee raised to the groin, the boot between
the legs, the shoulder in the back, the oath, the indignant challenge,
and the clenched fist. The victims of penalties writhed for minutes
after their assault. Unlucky goalkeepers would lie prostrate with
the ball in the net behind them. The winded and stunned lay
ostentatiously about the pitch. Even without these trimmings the
obstinacy was grim and unrelenting. One of our centre-halves
played a match with a pulled muscle in his ankle. An inside-right
was still on the field at the end of a second half with a broken wrist.

The rivalry surrounding each match knew few limits. The Jos
boys firmly believed that we practised witchcraft. Individually
they were undoubtedly better players and they could think of no
other reason why they should lose every match played against us
on our home ground. Believing that the charm was connected with
the main entrance, their lorry was always instructed to come
another way in. The culprit they identified as our chief supporter
in the town, a Yoruba mechanic of some prestige and strikingly
ugly appearance. One of his four wives, all from different tribes,
was related both to Edmund Masaweje, one of our backs, and to
the Long Koemai, the head of the Goemai Kingdom. This may

have been why his huge figure in its Yoruba gown and baggy trousers, its floppy Yoruba cap, its great feet and hands, was always loping along the touch-line baying encouragement.

The fathers made their own contribution. After dark on the eve of our greatest match, the one which would decide who should be the first winners of the Bishop Ring Cup, the Principal surreptitiously shortened the school pitch in the belief that this might help the team. The game itself was an endless, dusty endurance test during which a team of ten fought for the whole of the second half to hold a lead of one goal from superior opponents. When it was all over the dust cleared from the ensuing riot, and there could be seen, among the jubilant, clamorous mob, the figure of the Principal in his white soutane, dancing with Peter Kure in the middle of the pitch.

Athletics was a less emotional activity, but our prospects in it were not encouraging, for the boys were not strong enough. A lifetime of malnutrition had left them shorter and lighter than most of the competitors.

Despite the boys' courage and obstinacy, for two years the Principal's choice of team colours, bright white singlets and bright red shorts, advertised our position well to the rear in almost every event. Alexander and a skinny little Kagoro lad called Lucas Dangaana did quite well in the jumping events, and not quite so well in the sprints. Our throwers would usually come last. Our long-distance runners started valiantly as if they proposed to sprint round the course. On the far side of the track, ahead of the rest of the field, the rhythm of their pounding feet would falter, the arms would begin to flail, the head jerk backwards, and the runners' pace would falter into a painful, contracted gallop. The rest of the field would pass him, and he would stagger in, gasping, fifty yards behind the last man.

The annual match against the Teacher Training College at Kafanchan was the great privilege of the athletics team, who presented themselves at nine on the Saturday morning of the competition dressed in gleaming white shorts and shirts and were supervised carefully on to the bus to avoid stowaways. The bus was not a great success. It was late, the natural consequence of arranging anything through the priests, who always knew somebody who would oblige and who normally turned up late, if he turned up at all, and broke down an hour or two after setting out. In this case the bus was only an hour late. It was not a remarkably comfortable affair. Such buses were usually made up of a lorry chassis, with a bus-like superstructure attached, and slatted seats run up inside. On the sides, in bright colours, would be painted the name of the proprietor, and very flamboyantly, somewhere on the front, a slogan, either pious such as 'Dominus Vobiscum', or merely fatalistic, 'No telephone to Heaven'.

The bus set off, its bright white-uniformed occupants shouting and singing, their faces grinning through the windows, cheered on by their friends. We left an hour later. Fifteen miles from Kafanchan we caught up with them again. The dusty, corrugated, stony road ran through the forest. At the bottom of a dip in the road the lorry sat crookedly on the grass verge. Its occupants were red ochre in colour from their crinkly hair to their bare feet. The laterite dust lodged in their eyelids, fringed their eyelashes, coated their faces with a dull, soft down. Their carefully washed uniforms appeared to have tarnished. Only their grins remained unfaded. The moment they had reached the laterite the whole bus had filled with dust. You could not, they said, see from one end of the bus to another. Now, they said, there was some small trouble with the engine. The dip was overhung with trees, hemmed in with thick undergrowth. The air was thick and stifling, full of stinging gnats. We were all beaded with perspiration which was beginning to trace pathways down the dusty foreheads of the athletes. Fortunately the engine was already nearly to rights. The bus got on its way once more, howling in bottom gear out of the dip, and then, as it picked up speed, dispersing a swirling cloud of dirt from its wheels which gradually gummed a sticky deposit on our windscreen, half a mile behind.

There was a tumultuous welcome at Kafanchan by cousins and brothers and uncles. While we sipped beer in the fathers' living-room the sound of festivities drifted across to us.

When we got to the field there was a band. It was entitled the

St Peter Claver Primary School Band. Its members stood an average of five feet high and they were equipped with three drums, a number of tin whistles, and a collection of tin cans filled with pebbles. Two little boys were needed to carry the big drum. The larger of the two carried it on his back, while the boy behind beat it. The band knew three tunes which they played to a syncopated dance rhythm in time to which the members shuffled about the field. I was not conscious that these little people ever stopped. As each event started St Peter Claver Primary School Band, puffing at its tin whistles, shaking its tins of pebbles, and tapping its drums, swayed rhythmically towards a better vantage-point.

Around three o'clock the competition started and worked its leisurely way through to dusk. Nobody cared to start any new event till the previous one had finished, and crowds of spectators drifted across the field in the hot afternoon from the athletics track, to the jumping pits, to the throwing areas. The rules of the competition were odd. For Kafanchan the meeting served the purpose of preparing for a national competition. The cup for this competition had been awarded by a retiring education officer who, hoping to encourage traditions of sportsmanship, had specified that all events take place as relays. Even performances in the jumping and throwing events were totted up or averaged.

Almost the last event to take place was a relay with four laps of a quarter of a mile. As we had expected, our place was well down on the scoreboard, and we did not expect anything to be gained from this. Nobody in the school liked running the 440 yards. Those who tried always started at a sprint and ended it last at a painful limp. As no one volunteered for the last lap, Alexander took it over. To our surprise the team held on to the rest of the runners during the first and second laps and only began to fall back in the third lap. Then it was Alexander's turn. There was an eternity as the two other Kafanchan teams passed the baton and their runners tore down the lanes, Alexander hopping from foot to foot on the change-over line, while our last runner hobbled towards him, almost oblivious of the shouts of his supporters trotting beside the track. As he came up Alexander wrenched the baton from him and sped for the bend with clenched jaw and pounding feet. He ran as if he were starting a 220, overhauling the leaders on the bend, overtaking one, then another, reaching the half-way mark well ahead with pandemonium breaking out from every side of the field. We waited for the inevitable to happen. The strain was beginning to tell; the shoulders were tautening; the pace was shorter; the head held further back. Even from the other side of the field you sensed the agony, the taut neck muscles, the contorted face. Still he was holding off the rest of the field, but now on the bend the figures behind him were remorselessly cutting down the gap. The row was growing. I could only see Alexander fitfully for, leaping across the field to join him, the whole team was running beside him, and on the outside of the track a dense mass of spectators shrieked at, and ran with the runners. In the straight all I could see were the heads, Alexander's just in the lead, and the head behind him moving closer and closer. Then they disappeared. Around the runners on both sides, and closing in behind them, the crowds swept them out of sight, a confusion of waving arms. A few minutes later the team emerged, carrying Alexander. He was only just conscious. We had won the race.

There was one more event, of which the last lap was one of half a mile. Our only competitor was Clement Sati, a slightly built Angas boy from the second form. All that we knew about him was that he could finish and win us a point. The tension was over now, the result of the match never in any doubt, the end of the last race a foregone conclusion, the crowd exhausted by its own enthusiasm. Clement looked insignificant beside his huge opponents, but he kept up with them for half the distance before he began to fall behind. At this point runners tended to drop out quietly or collapse conveniently on a distant part of the track. It was not a country were people were kind to the defeated. Clement, however, kept going, dropping further and further behind, and obviously in pain. The field was already emptying by the time he finished, and he had nothing to run against but my stopwatch, but he fought to the very last yard. If Alexander was the hero of the moment, Clement was to be our hope for the future.

We had been beaten, but with honour. That night there was a party, and long after dark the boys were counted back on to the bus for the two-hour journey home. Afterwards when we had a lorry I always travelled with them. The journey home was always pleasant. The heat had gone, and although it was probably quite chilly for the boys seated on planks in the back of the lorry, on the wooden ledge beside the driver a refreshing breeze blew in over the windowless door. The bush on each side of the road moved past, black and impenetrable in the forests below the Plateau, empty and indistinct on the Plateau itself. Over the stones and corrugations of the laterite road the lorry bounced and swayed; on the pass up by Assob the gears groaned and the engine growled; then we would reach the top of the Plateau, and the engine note rose to a monotonous drone as the tarred road spun away beneath us. On the back of the lorry the boys talked or sang, and when they sang it was right through the repertoire of a scout camp from my own childhood, simple tunes, familiar words, high above the growl of the engine, and breaking through the silence of the bush.

9
A Rebellion

On such occasions there was fellowship between us, returning late at night from an athletic meeting, or shuddering on a cold morning through the daily exercises, or watching the team in our kitchen eat their great hunks of bread liberally spread with margarine and Marmite to build up their strength at the end of each day of the season. But in the school as a whole the boys were an enigma. They must have known that it was a bad school, not as bad as some, but squalidly maintained, incompetently run and autocratically administered. Yet there was hardly a hint of complaint. As time went on I tried to work out what underlay their passivity. And once the veil slipped, the confusion of loyalties and emotions was briefly revealed, and I knew them a little better.

Normally the boys' reserve was almost impenetrable. No matter how muddled the administration became they went peaceably to their classes, worked hard, and carried out their homework without supervision. The prefects and senior boys ran their own republic, and overt disorder which threatened their studies, and therefore their examination results, was firmly controlled. So long as Kevin Dagai was able to ensure regular and edible meals there would be no protests, and the only obvious trouble was when a particularly bad breakfast brought the boys out on strike for half an hour one morning. I found the school sitting on the verandah and Alexander came toward me saying: 'They will not go in, sir. The breakfast was too bad.' He turned toward Form III and made a token effort at command. 'Go in there! Get into your classes now.' Nobody paid any attention, so I left them, reported the matter to the Principal, who had already been warned by Alexander, and it was his job to reach an accommodation that got them back into class a short time later.

Though this was the only visible expression of discontent, the boys followed their own inclinations without hindrance. They went into the village. They took taxis to Bukuru. They occasionally got drunk. Uniforms were unwashed, unrepaired, or, in the senior forms, not worn at all. The bigger boys, in particular, slept late in the mornings and stayed up late at night. They set up their own systems of authority, each one a patron, with his own clientele of juniors who washed for him, copied up his notes and received his protection. Such systems were built up within each tribal group, and unhappy were those outside it, like the half-caste, Eric Anderson, who was openly abused for his colour, or those who had no one of their own tribe to protect them, such as Jerome Magaje, the neurotic Ninzam in the third form.

More sinister still was the way in which individual boys were able to set up small tyrannies. Peter Kure was now openly independent of authority, treating the Principal with a combination of familiarity and contempt, while, in the form below him Mark Dimka, bigger and better fed than his form-mates, had long since proved his indifference to the Principal's cane. ('I can beat him to the wall, but he still defies me.') He would emerge from the Principal's office with a sneer on his lips and a contemptuous shrug of shoulders. He now used his power against the rest of his form, who were obliged to accept him as their leader.

At the beginning of our second dry season we had a shock. The affair concerned Father O'Connell, who had been on the staff since the beginning of the year, and had become indispensable within a month of arriving. He was an organised man whose clothes were always neatly laundered, whose mail was punctually answered at the end of each month, and whose room was in apple-pie order. He was a sensible brain in the intense and overheated atmosphere of the Fathers' House who at last removed the Principal's keys from his soap dish and sorted them out for him on a set of hooks of his own design. He trained the football team to fight an unpolished but obstinate and effective game. He gave clear, methodical, and conscientiously prepared lessons and was able to take over the chemistry and much of the maths. Most important of all he had an honours degree in science, and the boys felt that as long as they did as he told them they had a guarantee of success in the most important of the subjects they were to take in the School Certificate examinations.

One September morning the messenger from the post office was hunting round the school compound for him with a telegram. Five minutes after that I was aware of the Principal agitatedly tapping on the window-pane. Breaking off my lesson, I went outside. He was obviously very excited.

'Ye must tell none of the boys. Father O'Connell has got to go home.'

'What?'

''Tis the telegram. He has to be on the plane in twenty-four hours. Don't let it out.'

'But why?'

''Tis the authorities. They do things like this. There's nothing to be done. Alexander'll speak to them in the dining-hall at breakfast.'

I returned to the classroom and tried to continue with the lesson.

We were at breakfast ourselves when we heard the increasing uproar from the dining-hall which announced the receipt of the news. A few minutes later the Principal was on the verandah, worried and flustered. 'They're holding a meeting,' he said. 'Alexander's talking to them now.' He sat down and breathed out cigarette smoke.

'There's no hope for it at all; he'll have to go.'

'But can't the Prefect do something?'

'Oh he's coming out this morning, but it'll make no difference. He can't do anything about it. 'Tis the authorities. They do things like this in Ireland.'

'Won't the Prefect explain? Father O'Connell's the linch-pin here. If he goes, the school will fall apart.'

'That may be. It makes no difference. He'll go. They won't change their mind in Ireland. The sooner he's off the compound now, the better.'

He hurried away. The noise over at the school dining-hall was increasing, so there seemed little point in going across to our classes. The Prefect arrived and went upstairs to speak to the fathers while the boys continued their own meeting on the other side of the compound. I went across to the Fathers' House to find the Principal.

'Father O'Connell has to go. The Prefect thinks they may let him come back in due course. The boys won't go into class. The Prefect is sending out Sati, the man who helps the Education Secretary. They'll listen to their own. They won't listen to Alexander. They're not going back to class till Sati comes.'

The meeting went on all morning. During the afternoon there was quiet. I met a group of boys in the middle of the compound. 'We're not going back to class. What's the use. If they send Father O'Connell away, what will become of our science examinations? If they send him away, why won't they send you away, too? We will have no staff left. What will become of us? What will happen to our examination results?'

We tried to soothe them. Perhaps Father O'Connell would be allowed back. Certainly the Principal would try to get him back. 'He won't,' said one abruptly. Just because he had gone for the time being it did not mean that anyone else would be going. 'How do we know?' interjected the same boy.

There was another meeting that evening. Mr Sati's Volkswagen was outside the dining-hall. I saw a group of the boys in my dormitory afterwards. 'We are going to tell the Prefect,' said Benedict Balarabe, 'we must have Father O'Connell back.'

'Why not let the Principal do it?'

'He won't listen to us.'

'But he is as worried as you. He doesn't want to lose Father O'Connell.'

'What do you know? You don't know the Principal. What will he say to the Prefect? He does not understand. He only loses his temper.' A long, inconclusive debate went on in the darkness. There was a pathetic tone of bewilderment about it all. The boys had been used all their lives to authority; now that it had disappeared they seemed bewildered as if they wanted someone to step in and tell them what to do. All over the compound there was the same murmur of worried voices. In the classrooms the lights were out; only in the dormitories were they on, and did torches move backwards and forwards. Only gradually did the lights go out and the voices cease.

In the morning I saw the Principal once more, more worried and flustered than ever, nervous and unshaven, tapping cigarette ash over his verandah. 'They won't go back to class. They've told Alexander.'

'Have you seen them yourself?'

'I wouldn't. I wouldn't. They won't listen to anyone except one of their own in a thing like this. I've left Alexander to do it. He's speaking to them again now.' There was again a confused roar from the dining-hall.

'I pity Alexander. Poor lad. He begged me not to keep him as head prefect. He wept.'

'What's happening this morning?'

'There's no classes. We daren't. But we must go from the verandah. We mustn't be seen talking like this. They'll suspect something.' He stamped his cigarette butt out and immediately lit another, then turned away. 'Ye'll not go near the school building, mind! There's no telling what they'll do.'

He was over to see us at breakfast. 'They're marching to Jos,' he said, 'both the two senior forms, to see the Prefect. They're leaving the youngest form. Too little, they say, to be mixed up in this.' He disappeared again.

We went over to take our classes, the only members of the staff in the classroom block. The first form was rather excited, but perfectly happy to do as it was told. We asked what was happening. 'They're walking to Jos, sir, but,' with less enthusiasm, 'we're staying.'

Half-way through the period there was a commotion outside. Benedict Balarabe came into the room, excited and dishevelled. 'I must see my brother, sir.' He went outside with a boy from the form, another Kagoro for whom he seemed to have a message, then he disappeared. The bell rang, and as my lesson was over I walked to the road. From all over the compound the senior boys were streaming to the road, dressed in their white uniforms, and talking excitedly. They took no notice whatever of the Principal, who had also come to the roadside, or of any other member of staff, but formed a long untidy column which proceeded away from us. We watched them go, their white shirts receding gradually into the distance.

'Should we try to persuade them to come back?'

'It's no good,' said the Principal, 'they'd run into the bush as soon as they saw you. Let them go.' They had disappeared. The compound was quiet.

By lunch-time they had reached Bukuru, six miles away. At this point they were met once more by Mr Sati. It was a hot day and there were ten miles to go to Jos. They agreed to turn back, while Alexander and the prefects were carried into Jos by car, where they presented their request for the return of Father O'Connell to the Prefect, who received them in a friendly manner. The rest walked miserably home through the hot afternoon. I saw Benedict briefly in the dormitory sluicing cold water over his face. He was nearly in tears. Exhausted, they went to bed early that night, and in the morning quietly took their places in class once more. Father O'Connell was not mentioned. He had to retake an examination he had failed and returned a few months later. Meanwhile the boys restored order on their own and the veil fell back into place once more.

The Ministry of Education did consider it worth holding a brief enquiry into the affair, but it was not the usual sort of trouble. A teacher was being asked to stay. More often one was being told to leave. Two European inspectors spent a few hours asking questions, but were really more interested in finding a connection with the much more serious rebellion that had taken place in the Vet., where veterinary students had marched with placards and threats of violence to demand the resignation of a large part of the senior staff of the research station. Once they had ascertained that there was no connection whatsoever they left us to deal with their own problems.

Yet an underlying bitterness had been revealed. The boys had come to school expecting great things. They were 'students' attending a 'college' administered by a 'principal' and staffed by 'tutors'. They were bitterly disappointed.

There is no-one for dis earth wey go say he happy proper. When I dey go for primary school I think say I go happy proper much when I reach secondary school, but where?

Their very displeasure had to be expressed in pidgin English, for the vernacular was forbidden by the Principal on pain of a beating, and the language spoken by their English staff was as difficult for them to understand as that of Chaucer. Other blows to their self-esteem soon followed.

When I reached Vwang I saw big and new boys. I begin say the principal no de punish the big boys. Asey all be the same for 'em. When you do something bad he go punish you as if, say, you de for children dem school.

The Principal beat them as they had been beaten at their primary schools for talking the vernacular, for being late to classes, for disobeying the prefects, for not wearing the school uniform, for being late with their work and for a host of other reasons. As he said, with some satisfaction, he got them all in the first month.

They resigned themselves to the school routine.

Them get one kind big bell wey bellman de ring often. I no like so the bell. Early in the morning at six the boy go come tanda [stand] for dormitory, begin ring 'em. The sound no go leave man sleep any more. If you no fit wake up them go book down your name. Everything na quick-quick. Go here, go there, as if say na gand-roba ['guard-robber', i.e. warder] deh for work.

This was accepted, however reluctantly, as the price for later advancement. In the early years it was the food that worried them most of all.

Sometime here we no get enough chop to wak [eat]. We go report but they say na the same kind palaver wey deh for most schools. In the morning we drink akamu [gruel] and wak bread. When you come siddown for class you feel so-so sleep then say you no want know something . . . Nna [really] man suffer for nineteen-fifty-nine. Some days na beans zalla [only] we chop.

Night own worse than morning own. The women way they cook 'em no fit. When we go for bed the beans for our stomach go just leave we sleep for some time. At about midnight the beans make one kind old noise for our stomach as if say na one kind old diesel lorry de pass, or locomotive train de pass.

Nor did the Principal's rules allow of any relief. There were harsh penalties for anyone rash enough to bring in food from outside the compound. 'If you no belly full you not fit take penny buy chop. The law done forbid 'em.'

Kevin Dagai did improve matters, and the woman whose cooking had so offended the boys was replaced by a more satisfactory man.

Now things don begin better small-small. We get oranges, eggs, bananas as light chop, though na one-one [every day] . . . We happy now for yam deh, garri deh, fish deh, rice deh, and acha, the worst of them all dey plenty. Wetting? . . . Sometime dysentery deh worry we. Our nyash [anus] de make yo-yo as if sey na old bucket de leak. Everyday na complain. 'Excuse me, sir, we wan go clinic.' It no be disease, na beans de vex for belly.

There was little that they could do. The school was the boys' only route to future prosperity in modern Nigeria. They settled down grimly to present discomforts, in anticipation of future benefits.

Make we no open eye for this world yet. This time we dey as if say no be we. Make we all pray God He help we and give we long lives. Amen.

10
The School Changes

By the end of 1963 the school was at its worst. Our own tempers withered as we approached the end of a long tour. The Principal was dwindling to a shadow of his former plump, prosperous self. One of the boys went home sick at the end of the term, Mathew Zatiyok, who had just completed his second year, reserved, hard-working, intelligent, and courteous. We were told afterwards that he had been complaining of a swelling in his stomach the night before he left. When he got down to Kagoro he was badly sick. The native doctors were called in, who treated him for two weeks. Finally his family brought him into the mission hospital at Zonkwa, where he died within forty-eight hours.

Just after Christmas the Principal was moved to the Secondary School in Jos to look after the science there. He rose from this disaster like the phoenix in triumph above its ashes. Within a month he was his old invincibly optimistic self. A new man took over in Vwang. Father Glynn had, in fact, been on the Vwang compound since October, a refugee from Ghana, where he and a number of other principals had resigned over a matter of principle. He was a quiet, grave man, rather prepossessing in appearance and with a distinct aura of authority, either the habit of many years, or the consequence of a deafness which may have been actual, but which was certainly diplomatic. 'It's a poor little school,' he said, 'a poor little school, but something can be done with it. It's got a fine site.' He talked of building, of taking in a second and third stream, of a sixth form, of new subjects, new laboratories and a proper library. 'But,' he observed fiercely one morning, 'the thing that's wrong with this school is moral sogginess—moral sogginess.' The bell had just rung for Mass and half the school was still in bed. Cobwebs trailed across the backs of the chairs in the oratory where the sacrament stood in a room with filthy walls and lumps of dried mud lying in the corners. Outside, through the greasy windows, could be seen a couple of boys with hands in their pockets, picking their way across that forlorn oval which was designated as a cricket pitch, and where pieces of torn paper lodged here and there in the straggling dry grass. 'The prefects are stupid and careless, the boys lazy, their clothes dirty. Moral sogginess, moral sogginess! In Ghana . . .'

The first problem was that of authority, and Mark Dimka was the first to present it. His form were trying out the new regime, and one evening that first week of term I found a fight going on in front of a neutral but interested form. Mark Dimka had fierce hold of Jerome Magaje, who, with teeth bared and fists flying chaotically, was making indistinct noises of anger. They separated, breathing heavily.

Jerome got his word in first. 'He tore my shirt, sir,' he shouted, his face, raised, for once, and eyes fixed and looking over my left shoulder. 'He tore it,' and he pointed to his sleeve, which had indeed been nearly detached from the rest of his rather insubstantial garment.

'He abused me,' said Mark shortly.

'He called me small boy,' shouted Jerome.

I called out Gabriel Salla, an intelligent and very ambitious Goemai who had some claim to be second to Mark in the form hierarchy. Mark seemed to be in the wrong, so he was told to pay for the repair of the shirt. He shrugged and turned with a sneer to go back to his place in the class.

Half an hour later there was a knock on the door of our living-room. An excited Jerome Magaje stood on the verandah, fairly incoherent with rage. 'Dimka tells he will slap me . . . will not pay . . . will tear shirt again . . . calls me small boy . . . says I am bushman.' He was beginning to splutter. This was beyond me, so I took Magaje, now quietly malevolent, to Father Glynn, explained the case as best I could and left him to go over to the school building and settle it there.

Mark was called into the office and there ordered to make

amends to a now quiet and self-righteous Magaje, on whose face an unexpected and disdainful smile had now appeared. It was Mark's turn to stutter with rage, with a consequence that was also unexpected, for no notice was taken of him. The new Principal did not appear to hear, and Mark left, defeated, with a face like a mask. The mighty were shaken in their places.

Poor Mark had a difficult term. A few days later he quarrelled with me, and in a moment of unforgiveable anger I struck him, the only time I ever struck a boy in that school. We raved at each other for the rest of the day before peace was restored. Then, towards the end of that long term he fell ill of typhoid.

He was taken to the Protestant missionary hospital which stood by the Birom village under the Vwang hills a few miles away, where I saw him a few days later. He was out of his coma, and sat in one of the isolation wards in the older part of that ancient and warren-like institution. It was no more than a cell, with one small window and the ancient mud walls coated black. On the metal bedstead with its grey blanket, Mark sat in a coarse nightgown. His jet complexion appeared grey and dusty, and his solidly built body seemed to have melted. His eyes, deep in their sockets, focused with difficulty, and he spoke slowly, and with such effort that it was hard to make out his words. 'Yes, I am a little better now. I was sick. I was very sick. I think I nearly died. It was very dark.' He repeated the last sentence faintly two or three times. I asked if I could bring him anything. 'No, I want nothing. I want to speak to somebody— bring Clement and Eugenus.'

There was little to be said. Clement and Eugenus came. They were his countrymen, and nobody, when they were sick, ever wanted to see anyone else except their countrymen. They brought Mark out in a wheelchair, that great sturdy fellow, wrapped up in a blanket, and brought him extra food from the village. It took him a month to recover, and though his strength returned, he never regained the power he had lost in his form.

Peter Kure was a more formidable problem. In his dormitory lights did not go out till half an hour after everywhere else was dark, work was not done, and Peter himself drew only the thinnest, most formal veil of courtesy over his disdain for school rules or school authority. His most forthright demonstration of opposition to authority occurred on Northern Independence Day. When the rest of the school paraded according to Government instructions in almost immaculate white uniforms to the uncertain rhythm of the primary school band, Peter stayed in his dormitory, and when required to make an appearance did so in a coloured scarf. The following day he spent cutting a large area of grass at the back of the classroom block. The senior forms were impressed, not altogether favourably.

When big day come then go tell we, make we go march for Veterinary ground. Na so we march for Northern self-government, independence and for Republic days. If you say you no fit march na you and langa-langa [cutlass] go become friends for the hot sun on the field. The staffs ma na wah na you [seem to be friendly but are not in fact so] and you and them go enter three [are in trouble]. If you no get white and white na you and the principal go enter the same trousers [are in more trouble]. This kind thing vex me as if no be me for tomorrow.

It was treatment altogether unbecoming to the dignity of a senior member of the school hierarchy, and the oldest form, now working for the last year of its examination course, was nostalgic for the old days.

Elsewhere in the school there was less resentment, for the petty tyranny exercised by some of the senior boys was at last alleviated. The washing that the little boys did for the older boys was rationed. The student council, which had been founded by the old Principal, now heard more complaints, and could deal with them with Father Glynn's support if necessary. The pressure on the minority tribes slackened. Eric Anderson was no longer abused.

The school began to settle down under Father Glynn, and everyone on the compound had leisure to take stock of each other. Now that relationships were so much easier we could again find out more about the boys. This was not a one-sided process. They were finding out as much as they could about us.

On display to them, like specimens swimming around in three

goldfish bowls, were three versions of the Western European way of life, all of them rather odd. The Fathers represented their own twentieth-century Irish form of monasticism. Our African teachers lived a life which combined in varying proportions the assumptions of Europe and West Africa. Our own bungalow was part Bohemia, part provincial suburbia, and at different times resembled a kindergarten, office or waste-paper depot.

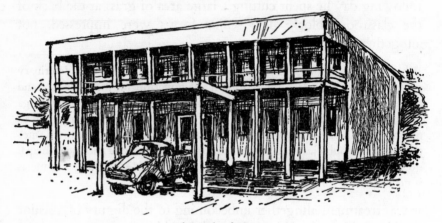

The Fathers' House

For a while the Fathers' House was regarded by the building father as a considerable architectural achievement on account of the mono-pitch roof, artfully hidden by the massive front and side walls. This enormous area of corrugated iron buckled, groaned and banged all night as it warped with the changing temperature. The ground floor was planned on a grandiose scale with accommodation for chapel, dining-room, reception room, and office. Half of it spent much of its life as a junk-room. Upstairs the community lived in the maximum publicity, revealed to the full view of the school the moment they stepped out of their room upstairs onto one of the verandahs which looked out across the school compound on either side of the building.

The Fathers' House had been the first to feel any change. In his first few weeks Father Glynn would wander desolately along the ground floor, peering into the lower windows of his new domain. Then three years' rubbish was hauled out: mattresses whose cotton filling had disintegrated into a mound of dust, broken chairs, rickety desks, empty paint tins, old tin cans, jam jars, beer bottles, cardboard cartons, rusty cutlasses, old shirts, an aluminium vaulting pole, various tin trunks and one or two bags of cement. The kitchen was cleaned out, and the cockroaches at least temporarily dislodged. The cook was sacked, another servant taken on to do the washing, one of the boys who helped around the house was placed in the first form, and the other one sent to Kafanchan to train as a teacher.

The builders were brought in, or rather a couple of labourers closely watched by Father Glynn with a plumb-line in his hand. The front door was knocked down, and light admitted to the hall by two new windows on each side, each perfectly vertical and in line with each other, which showed dramatically that nothing else in the building was. The huge table was moved from the downstairs sitting-room. A nun selected and sewed immense and rather expensive curtains that shrouded the place in genteel gloom, and the lurid daubings of Mediterranean ports which had hung on the walls under the old regime were replaced by a lithograph of a schooner in desperate straits at sea, and King Charles I in the days before he had heard of Cromwell.

Father O'Connell returned, to everyone's relief, to control with equal firmness and efficiency the laboratory and the football team. About the school he was a magisterial figure, unbendingly just, and hard on evildoers. The boys apparently called him 'Julius Caesar'. Poor Father Kelly developed shingles and later pneumonia. He had to be invalided home. Another young priest, Father Sheehan, was brought up from the Teacher Training College at Kafanchan, rather glumly, because he had been happy there. He became infirmarian, doling out the aspirin and the epsom salts, and awakened once a week to cope with soaring temperatures and delirium. He also looked after the table-tennis. Then he organised a band, in red pill-box hats and tunics, and long white trousers, which played 'Scotland the Brave' on tin whistles with impressive verve. Then Father Murphy arrived, who had known and worked for Father Glynn in Ghana. He was older than most of the priests, and when the Prefect finally broke the school up it was on his charity and affection we depended in the months before we left the country.

I doubt if it was possible for us to know most of the priests particularly well. We were ourselves so preoccupied with our work and our children; in addition we did not share their celibacy, their communal life, their loyalty to their order, or their nationality. Now, however, we saw more of them. It was Father Kelly, who, before he left, gave Nicholas his first cigarette when he was two years old.

The Fathers' House was a much happier, friendlier place than it had ever been, but it was a still a bachelor household, and a religious community at that, where personal rights and privacy were at a minimum. From the time he got up, before Mass, on his way to the bathroom in the early morning, to the time he walked back to his room late at night, each man and all his doings were on full display to the whole compound. A visitor to one was bound to wake all the others with his knocking, and a particularly persistent and unmannerly resident on the compound once reduced Father O'Connell and Father Sheehan to lying on the floor of one of their rooms, with curtains drawn and the lights out, so as to have peace and quiet for a couple of hours while they listened to the All-Ireland hurling final, broadcast from Wembley.

Few of them had wanted to be teachers. They had most of them been attracted to a missionary vocation when they were still children, a vocation seen in terms of the missionary magazines of ten years before where dedicated priests and nuns gave their lives to God in romantic circumstances, far in the African bush. They had gone through the junior seminary from the age of about thirteen, then to the senior seminary, after which they might once have expected to be sent out to the missions. The changes in West Africa had taken them unawares. It was as teachers that the missionaries were now most in demand, and whether they liked it or not, off the society sent them to university to get their qualifications. For the rest of their life, it seemed, they were to be schoolmasters. Few of the younger priests would have stayed in any school, given the choice. As soon as the term ended they were off to the bush, the more remote the station the better, and if a flood cut them off during the first few days of the next term, they were the last to complain.

Our Nigerian staff had been unlucky. By the time Father Glynn arrived their chance of getting the scholarship for which all of them studied, which would take them on to university, wealth, and privilege, had almost gone. Our first three teachers had all gone on to higher things: Edmund Jibiri, Alexander's brother, to study education in England; Patrick Ohadike to Ibadan, and then to Australia to study demography, and Moses Onwegbuna to Sierra Leone to take a degree at Fourah Bay. Their successors, Clement Ibi and Stan Onokor, were no less able or hard-working, but the scholarships were going to secondary-school students now, and their hard-won qualifications in English, religious knowledge, and British constitutional history availed them nothing.

All of them were married men, but we met none of their wives, who all stayed down in the East, for they were Ibo or Ibibio, and worked for their living as teachers among their own people. They occupied those cramped airless little bungalows in which the fathers had once lived, made suitable for African habitation, in one case, by the building father, who tore out the bath that had been briefly installed and left it outside the house in the rain for the next two years. Each had a young relation living with him, who washed his clothes and kept the house clean, in return for the cost of his education at the primary school. We seldom met the Nigerian teachers, for the staff-room hardly ever functioned, and Moses Onwegbuna had been the only one we had known at all well. He was a most likeable and conscientious man, very earnest and very hard-working. Like the other Nigerian teachers from the East, he lamented, at intervals, the laziness and grubbiness of the boys he taught. Things were different in the East, we gathered. None the less Moses was earnest in his endeavours to make the school a good one, assisted on the football field, and was ready with advice to the senior boys. He seldom smiled, and was very concerned for his health. On one occasion he refused to eat any of the ice-cream that Constance had prepared for a meal, saying that his doctor had warned him against such things for fear of pneumonia. He disliked the North, hated the cold winds of the Plateau, and refused to leave his house for days on end when the harmattan was at its worst. He received with delight the news of his scholarship, and the last we saw of him was with hands clasped in triumph above his head, as he sat on the lorry, speeding down the main road toward Jos. He was smiling. A few years later we received a letter from him. There was a photograph. He was on the eve of graduation, dour, but very happy, in gown and mortar-board. He had succeeded.

Mr Nwobina was the exception. His family lived with him. He was a round, cheerful little man, and we never found out how many children he had. His wife, a slightly built girl, much younger than he, had more while we knew them. Apart from his own children, there were the inevitable relations who worked for him and went to school at his expense in return. It was difficult to tell which were which. Altogether nearly a dozen people, babies, small children, and adults, lived in one tiny, three-roomed bungalow. The province was not extravagant in its treatment of its Nigerian staff. Mr Nwobina owed a great deal to General de Gaulle, whose endeavours to assert the place of French as a world language had made a number of scholarships available in Nigeria. Mr Nwobina left for Dakar, in the Senegal. His wife went south to look after that enormous family during the two or three years that were to elapse before Mr Nwobina returned.

When Father Glynn became Principal our own family had just been added to. Elizabeth had arrived, in a much more civilised manner than Nicholas, at the near-by Protestant hospital, which had just started to accept wealthier patients than the poverty-stricken Birom whom it had served for the previous forty years. The Zawan sisters came to see her. I think that they were a little puzzled by the familiarity with which we treated Protestants, having been Protestant ourselves for such a long time. The amusing aspect of the situation was that the women in both missions, devout, courageous, and slightly eccentric, had more in common than either group would ever suspect.

With Elizabeth back at Vwang a routine now confirmed itself. We now, at length, settled into the whole bungalow, putting the children into a bedroom each, and confining the accumulated paperwork of two years to a store at the end of the back verandah.

We put up more curtains, had a couple of cots and little cup-board painted white, and stuck transfers of pink fish on to the last. It was about this time that we first had bars fitted into our win-dows, the normal precaution against burglars in this country. Perhaps we at last considered that we had something to steal. Any doubts we may have had about the efficacy of these bars were soon confirmed when the dog took to forcing his way in and out of windows between them, and reinforced when Nicholas pulled one out with one hand.

We took on another servant, a girl to help us look after the children, Teresa, a sister of Anthony C., of whom more later. She was to work for us for a year before she went on to a teacher training college. The first day she visited us she left behind a little parcel. We opened the screw of paper, not realising, at first, what it was. Inside were two large grasshoppers and a sparrow. The Birom did not eat too well at that time of the year, just before the harvest. When she came to us a few weeks later we arranged for her to go and eat with relations in the village. By the end of the year she was about twice the size she had been when she started, and all the dresses Constance had altered for her were on the point of explosion. She was a bright, shrewd little girl, and well used to looking after herself. She got on well with Elizabeth, who also turned out to be a bright, shrewd little girl, well capable of looking after herself. As soon as she could walk, off they would all go, Teresa, Nicholas, and Elizabeth, into the fields opposite the school, to a Birom farmer a quarter of a mile in bush. There they would buy a penny stick of sugar cane, and all of them would sit and chew. Our children were well on the way to becoming naturalised Nigerians.

Other little Nigerians came across the road from the junior staff quarters, attracted by Nicholas's strange toys: bricks, a wooden engine and trucks, a small tricycle, and a plastic donkey on wheels. It was normal during the afternoon and evening to have half a dozen of them playing with our two in the rather gritty sand of which the drive was composed. There was usually a worried little boy of nine or so, whom the others all called Johnson, who appeared to be in control, or trying to keep control. The most frequent visitor was called Chidi. He was about Nicholas's age, a very corpulent three-year-old, normally naked from the waist down. He knew Nicholas's name and Nicholas knew his, and together they would pile up the bricks, or scrape in the sand. Occasionally Nicholas would stand on the verandah and shout for Chidi, and sometimes, in the evening, after Nicholas had been put to bed, Chidi would appear, wordless, round-eyed and solemn, looking for Nicholas. From time to time Chidi would overstay his meals, and a relation would arrive to haul him off, shrieking and protesting. On other occasions he sneaked away to our garden, to be followed half an hour later by a worrying sister. He spoke no English. Nicholas spoke little enough himself. Both got on very well.

But we were colonialists after all. Our servants, Bonaventure and Teresa, regarded these visitors with suspicion and tried very often to warn them off. There was a little boy of about five, Martin, rather small, with a cast in one eye. He seemed to poke Nicholas from time to time, and occasionally a toy would disappear. Bonaventure was very insistent about him, saying that he had a bad and neglectful father, that the child stole, and was not to be trusted with Nicholas. I sent the child home. He came back the following day. We let Bonaventure send him home. He did not come back. Once, in a spirit of enquiry, we asked Teresa's brother Anthony, what would happen if we sent Nicholas, when he was old enough, to one of the local primary schools. 'Oh, madam,' said Anthony firmly, 'the other children would beat him.'

For all that the life seemed to suit the children well enough for the time being, out of doors all day long, all but naked, playing brown and barefoot in the sunshine, watched by Teresa, and usually by one of us back from the school during a free period. It was as well that they played outside, for the living-room inside, at the height of busy school day, looked rather like a badly organised parcels office. Exercise books lay in heaps along one wall; paper in all its forms, note-paper, duplicating paper, exam paper, drawing paper, cartridge paper, clean, scribbled on, torn, screwed up or drawn on, was scattered everywhere; reference books stood in heaps on the dining-room table, old newspapers were shoved on top of the bookcase, unfinished paperbacks were left open under the armchairs, stationery and children's toys jostled higgledy piggledy on the desk top, the bookshelves and the cubby-holes. At break-time Bonaventure would find room on one of the stools by the armchairs for some coffee-cups. At lunch-time he would push aside some of the marking to make room for the dinner-plates.

All in all, amid the muddle, we and our children were happy now, even if our pleasures were rudimentary enough. We have never, for example, enjoyed the Sunday papers so much as when we used to read them on Tuesday evenings. Without a radio, till Father Glynn eventually lent us one, we had to wait a whole week before we knew what was going on in the world around us. This sometimes had its advantages. The Russian merchant ships had been turned back from Cuba before we learnt that they had set out on their momentous voyage. Penguin books, too, which came in a batch to Jos once a quarter, were bought by the armful when they arrived, and we would gorge ourselves on their contents, like people faced with a whole meal after months on bread and water.

The delights of the flesh came sparse enough, but again no one has really appreciated fresh apples or grapes unless they have bought them unexpectedly from a cold store in tropical Africa, or enjoyed fresh bread (freckled with sesame seed from a Syrian baker) with fresh butter and cheddar cheese unless they have tasted it only once a week after thirty miles' dusty driving to the only supermarkets within two hundred miles. Once a week, too, we went to the swimming pool. Some went almost daily, and swam. We just sat. It was as much as we could do to take the children to the little paddling pool at one end. There were magazines in the library, too, but not many decent books, and on a really good Sunday Constance might even find two new copies of *The Tatler*, a journal whose delights I had never really considered before we went to Nigeria. Just occasionally I even saw a familiar face among those glassy smiles and boiled shirtfronts. We sat, read, ate bacon and egg sandwiches, watched the children spread a tube full of Smarties over themselves, and wondered if we had enough money to afford another glass of beer. Then we would drive home, a little sleepily, twenty miles across the open sun-filled stretches of the Plateau. In the evening we did our marking for the next day.

It was life lived in a glass house, however, and the closest observers of the exhibition were Constance's pupils in the first and second forms. Some, of course, were almost as old as she, and surveyed her tolerantly and paternally from the back row of their forms, but the little ten- and eleven-year-olds who came increasingly into these forms were openly fascinated by our household. As their elders had once done, they probed as tactfully as they could, were keen to find errands that brought them to our bungalow, came in groups to deliver exercise books, lingered long in the living-room doorway, and went sideways past our house on the way to the post office.

Nicholas attracted their attention. He had always done so from the time when I had occasionally carried him over to Mass on my shoulder in the early mornings, or a little later when Constance had wheeled him across to the school in his little carry cot, which her pupils called 'the box'. He conferred prestige as a male child, far more than poor little Elizabeth when she came along, who could never, for all her efforts, persuade the boys to give her more than a passing glance.

Of all those who made friends with Nicholas, the most constant in his attention was Anthony C. Anthony was not really one of those cherub-like, earnest little boys, who sat eager and clean in the front row of those younger classes. He was small enough. He appeared to be about ten when he came to the school. He was, in fact, fourteen. Thin and wiry, he occupied one of the front seats, with long legs and arms, bony joints, prominent Birom cheek-bones, projecting front teeth, and a high-pitched giggle. He never, if he could help it, stopped talking, but though his spoken English was fluent, his written work was usually abominably written and spelt, short, untidy, and handed in late.

It was in order to hand in one of his books which should have been delivered days before that he arrived outside the living-room door. Having got rid of the book he took a step into the room where Nicholas sat on the floor, put his hands under his armpits, and lifted our son high into the air, giggling and chirruping at him as he did so. 'That's Anthony,' we said. 'Anthony,' he repeated, as he backed on to the verandah, 'Anthony, Anthony, remember—Anthony.'

The following morning he appeared in the doorway with his form's exercise books. Having deposited them on the breakfast table, he made a chirruping noise at Nicholas, who was sitting in the middle of the living-room. 'There's Anthony,' we said.

'Come, Nicholas, come,' and without a word, Nicholas, who was now about a year old, got up and rushed to the door. Once more Anthony seized him under the armpits, and hoisted him up, both of them giggling at each other, and for the next three years he and the other Birom boys in that form were common features of the household scene. Nicholas was slow to talk, but one of his first words was 'Anty', followed by 'Willyum', the name of Anthony's acute and wary friend, William. With Nicholas, and sometimes without him, Anthony sat on the verandah for hours piling up the wooden bricks or pushing along the wooden engine with the trucks. The fragile struts of the little German tricycle we bought for Nicholas at Christmas soon buckled under the weight of Anthony and his friends, and rather too many of Nicholas's books had been embellished by them.

Again and again it seemed to be Nicholas's toys that attracted the boys. They had not known toys as such. The miniature weapons and tools they had once been taught to handle, bows and arrows, hoes and spears, were not given to them for their play value. Even the labour of the smallest child could not be neglected in a subsistence economy. The child's world was not separate from the adult one. Only in the towns did you occasionally see little boys pushing before them through the dust wire impressions of mammy wagons, running on wire wheels, real toys. I commented on this to my house-prefect, Hyacinth Rowang. He observed: 'Ah, sir! They do not play like your children—but they do not have such fine things to play with.' So Anthony and his friends played among the bricks and the wooden trucks, on the threshold of a European education.

11
Teaching in a Strange Country

We were ourselves on the threshold of an African secondary education. Now that the school was settling down we could begin to learn how to teach in Africa. An inspector was later to tell us that there was no advice he could give to us about how to teach our particular subject, history. He was wrong, of course. As English teachers teaching African history to Africans, we were only learning how to begin.

We eventually discovered that there was a revolution taking place in the teaching of our subject in West Africa, but that was in the universities, and in 1960 that meant Ibadan 700 miles away. Even that revolution was rudimentary enough, summed up in an indignant question from a senior lecturer in 1957: 'Why in an African country, about to achieve the status of political independence, is African history not taught as a basic subject in the secondary course?' By the time we left the country a G.C.E. paper, after much soul searching and debate, in African history was about to be presented to African schools. The universities had yet to propose how the subject could actually be taught.

Long before this, on the assumption that we ought to try to teach some African history, we started to look for some to teach. In 1960 it was hard enough to find even that. The Historical Society of Nigeria had recently produced its first volume. *The Journal of African History* was just beginning to appear. There were two or three sketchy primers on Hausa and Yoruba history. The only existing history of Nigeria at that time devoted but forty of its 280 pages to the history of Nigeria before the coming of the Europeans. The researches of earlier explorers and administrators filled about three dozen volumes, almost all out of print or inaccessible, and there were a number of pamphlets and magazine articles. It seemed then that the last place to find out about African history and how to teach it was in Africa.

It was impossible for us, as it was for most expatriate teachers, to ask anyone how to start. The nearest history teacher, five miles off, expressed surprise and some disbelief that such a thing as African history existed. There were no other history teachers within a hundred and fifty miles. Professionally speaking, we were on our own.

Nor has any teacher in a small African school much time for his speciality. We both had to teach more English than history. In a school like ours was, when the teacher is not preparing or marking an English lesson, he is taken up with a variety of responsibilities: a house to supervise, a library to stock, a magazine to edit, a debating society to run, a play to produce, an athletics or football team to train. In a school like this, and perhaps most African schools are like this, it is almost impossible to carry out all these things successfully, and prepare one's lessons adequately into the bargain.

Nor are there usually many resources. In a school of less than two hundred a history room was out of the question. Our posters and friezes and photos had to compete with everything any other subject had to post on the classroom strawboard. Our storage system, too, often degenerated into a heap on the floor of the one store-room the school possessed. A set of shelves or trays for maps and photos was something we never contrived. We developed instead a system of suspending pictures from loops or strips of metal hung inside a cabinet. An article we read insisted that this had worked in Rhodesia. We suspended our maps from lengths of steel reinforcement rods. The system weighed a couple of hundredweight and looked like a builder's yard. Our visual aids had to be posters, maps or drawings. There was not, for years, a single electric socket in the whole of the classroom block, nor a single blind or curtain to darken any of the classes. Films or projectors were out of the question. Eventually a cheap battery-operated tape-recorder became our most useful audio-visual aid.

These were relatively minor inconveniences. The most formidable problems were intellectual and psychological. There was, to begin with, the exam system. It was absolutely necessary for the boys to gain their School Certificate. A failure in those terrifying examinations meant the difference between further education and a high standard of living on the one hand or a return to tribal life or unemployment on the other. Teachers and taught were pre-occupied with the examinations. Again and again a little boy in the first and second year would raise his hand to ask nervously if he was likely to be asked questions on the current topics in 'the examination'. The history teacher in northern Ghana who was writing in 1957 and who stated his aim bluntly as 'scholars must have the best possible chance of passing the final examinations' spoke for almost every teacher in Africa. His methods, moreover, were much the same as those of any teacher in Africa. He began the School Certificate course at the beginning of the third year and for three years dictated notes.

Of course, it was easy enough to say that this was all wrong. What to do to put it right was quite another matter. Too often, in an African school, it seemed enough for a well-meaning European or American teacher to attempt to teach African children to be good European or American citizens. Phrases like 'the idea of personal responsibility and service that make a reality of citizenship'—occurring in this case in an article on visual aids in *The West African Journal of Education*—flow turgidly off the pen of almost all those who write about teaching Africans anything. It was far more difficult, in our subject for example, to work out what the children actually understood when we taught them history, what the term meant to them anyway, what could be taught to them successfully, and what they ought to be able to understand.

To begin with, of course, the children possessed their own historical traditions, though—as they were uninitiated into full membership of their tribes—they were excluded from a full acquaintance with their tribe's knowledge. These traditions shared nothing of the objectivity and time sense that are supposed to distinguish the study of history in the West. They were often little more than a justification of tribal claims to territory and tribal pride, or to the pre-eminent place of one clan or group within the tribe. They were ruthless of earlier tradition if it clashed with the interests they were upholding. Historical knowledge, in the boys' experience, was therefore on two levels, either of epic or anecdote, stories treasured and retold by the old men of an evening over the fire, or of case-history, an enormous collection of precedent preserved by the older men, to be referred to when disputes broke out, and occasionally deliberately adapted, as medieval monks adapted their legal documents, as circumstances required. Historical knowledge had also been used as a source of moral education for the boys, and to build up their pride, and their self-respect in belonging to their particular community.

Nevertheless, whatever the limitations of their viewpoint the the boys were interested in things historical. In this discipline, probably with most disciplines that have been brought by the European into the African classroom, there existed a road into the boys' own experience. There is no denying the passionate interest of all Nigerians, of all Africans probably, in their own past. The nationalist revival in Nigeria began with the writing of history, a deliberate attempt, perhaps, by Nigerians to preserve their identity against the menace of European culture. One of the earliest of these histories, Samuel Johnson's *History of the Yorubas*—a great book by any standards—was completed in 1897, four years after the British had declared a protectorate over the Yoruba states.

The interest was there. It was up to us, then, to make use of it. In the first two years of the school course the problem as we saw it was to train some objective sense of time, perhaps also some appreciation of common background transcending both European and African traditions, and, finally, to entertain.

The development of a sense of time in a child is not, of course, purely an African problem. It is not properly developed in a European or American child before the fourteenth or fifteenth year. It is a more complex problem in Africa, where traditions are seldom accurate for more than three or four hundred years back, and often not as far, and where a stone ruin which may be a thousand or more years old may either be ignored entirely by more recent tribal traditions or have attached to it some totally anachronistic legend. When the sense of time had not been developed the consequences were often agonising. I remember unhappily a lesson on the South African Australopithecenes of two million years ago, delivered to a fourth year, who regarded me darkly, and asked if that was really what I thought Africans looked like before the Europeans came. This sort of chronological muddle has caused African university students to credit Renaissance Europe with the invention of the steam engine. Constance had all this to deal with. Time charts were built up all round the classrooms, were measured off in all her exercise books. I think that at least this part of the children's intellectual training worked.

In the first year, also, it was relatively easy to offer that common cultural background to Europe and Africa which we thought the children needed. The physical development of man is, after all, largely an African affair. The rise of the ancient civilisations went on more in northern Africa and the Middle East than it did in Europe. Even the Greeks and the Romans are far more than the personal property of Europe. The subject-matter for the first year, in fact, was very similar to that of an English school, with as much African knowledge roped in as we could find: African cavemen, African iron-smelters, African builders of stone fortresses in Rhodesia, African merchants crossing the Sahara, African kings in Ghana, Benin, and Oyo.

All this had to entertain, and it had to be understood. The sad fact was that for most children all but the easiest of textbooks was incomprehensible before the end of the second year. Even the rather humane book by Elliott and Russell, which we used, called *We Are Their Heirs*, was a little too difficult for them. Fortunately an increasing number of simply written booklets on this period was being produced by English publishers from the late fifties onwards, pioneered by Ginn's 'Museum Bookshelves' and Longman's 'Then and There' series. These also had lots of pictures. The more pictures the better. We bought postcards, cut up magazines, ordered posters, even drew our own. If the boys found difficulty in reading at least they could look. If they could not write fluently, they usually liked drawing, often in a pleasantly stylised manner, sometimes with painstaking pride and attention to detail—such boys could then produce posters for the rest of the class.

There had to be a story. The cavemen were good for a story, so were the Myceneans, the Cretans, the Greeks and the Romans. The Ancient Egyptians were a more prosaic, less anecdotal civilisation, so they tended to lose out as our syllabus developed. The boys had to tell the stories back and illustrate them. Sometimes they composed magazines, sometimes newspaper stories. The latter had advertisements in them, for soap, wireless sets and ointment, and pictures cut out of the *Daily Times*. One, on the first arrival of the Europeans in Benin, featured the Portuguese ambassador. The accompanying dialogue seemed rather familiar:

Nigerian: What for you come here? To make you kill we?
Portuguese: No! No! No! Of course not.
Nigerian: What for you come, then?
Portuguese: We come to make trade.

I had a horrid suspicion that this was a line from one of my lessons. The Portuguese was represented by a newspaper cutting of a vague balding European, rather overweight, with a hearing aid plugged into one ear.

Oh wad some Power the giftie gie us . . .

The end of the second year and the whole third year were given up, perhaps too much so, to Europe. We still brought in Africa where we could, but the problem was that so little was really known of such a large area and such a large period of African history, that it was not possible to fill more than a fraction of the total syllabus with African material, particularly since much of that material was appearing in learned journals and was very difficult both to grasp and to present.

Our other justification for the use of so much European material was that European culture and influence bulked so large in recent African experience that it had to be studied, and that, carefully chosen, the European past could very often illuminate the African present. Much of our second year's work was still on the lines of the first year, lots of simple books, as many pictures as possible, and a good story wherever we could find it—the fall of Rome, the Irish and Latin missionaries in Europe, Vikings and Normans, castles, weapons and armour, crusaders and Marco Polo, explorers, Henry VIII chopping off heads, the Armada sinking off the British coasts. Already, though, we were beginning to explore momentous issues for Africa as well as Europe. Gunpowder and printing: they printed with potatoes and made little cardboard cannon. The Reformation: they listed those multitudes of churches that subsist in every African township, Catholic and Protestant and semi-pagan, Jehovah's Witnesses, Seventh Day Adventists, Church of the Brethren, Quakers, Methodists and Baptists, Cherubim and Seraphim, over fifty sects listed from the boys' experience alone. The rise of nationalism: the rebel Dutch hanged by the Spaniards outside Haarlem, the floods creeping across the fields towards Leyden. By the middle of the third year the boys were being invited to discuss the ideas that were making modern Nigeria much as they had once made modern Europe. It came as a shock to discover how deeply Luther appealed to those supposedly devout communicating Catholics.

At the end of the third year the boys spent a term looking at the origins of modern Europe and America, examining, in fact, the possibilities that faced modern Nigeria. There were the great despots, Peter the Great and Frederick the Great, representing the brutal power of military force, of personal ambition, of government by the powerful and ruthless despot. There was the developing power of Britain, economic power, the initiative of the individual citizen, undirected and hardly controlled by national government, the power gained and conferred by thousands of enterprising farmers, inventive and ambitious industrialists, avaricious and audacious financiers and businessmen. There was, on the other hand, Washington, and, if I had time, Lincoln, representing alternative ideas about modern government, the proposition that individual freedom could also be fought for successfully and prosper. We ended with the French Revolution and Napoleon. We debated them all. What were the virtues of all these? Which of these men would they have liked to have seen as Nigerians? Individual boys sometimes showed considerable sophistication, and could explain the benefits of a democratic government, but for most it was the despot who appealed. 'Ah,' they said, 'but Peter the Great would have had no difficulty with Nigerians. He would not have had to kill so many.' All would have been proud to own Napoleon as their own. National glory was seen, at that stage in their education, in military terms, in terms of bombs, aircraft, and guns.

It was in the fourth form that we really began to examine African history. Here were the most useful opportunities to experiment. All our teaching up to that point had been carried on within the formal classroom arrangement. The boys sat obediently in the rows of desks and listened, then talked, drew, made models, or wrote. Increasingly we realised how artificial that teaching situation was. In Europe and America we have accepted the classroom and all its limitations as an immutable part of education, forgetting that it is only within the last hundred years that the majority of our children have ever had to enter one. The boys themselves made the point whenever we discussed education in that recurrent debating topic: 'It is better to be a schoolmaster than a farmer/policeman/lorry-driver, etc.' 'Everyone,' they said, 'is a teacher. Did not our parents teach us . . .?' The process of education that they were used to had been carried out in the fields and in the villages by parents, siblings, and elder tribesmen—how to farm, how to herd, how to build huts, how to remember tribal tradition—all by example, by imitation and activity, by observing and asking questions. The passive situation in the classroom was part of an alien tradition.

In any case, with our alien wares, our knowledge, our methods of thought and research, it was quite possible for the boys to listen, write, repeat, and regurgitate, and yet admit and retain nothing. Increasingly we felt that the boys would not be able to learn a thing unless they were obliged to learn it themselves, make their own observations, ask their own questions, and draw their own conclusions. It would avail them nothing to listen to us in the classroom, even about the history of their own country, even of their own tribes. The secret of teaching, not just history but any subject, lay in getting the boys to do the learning.

It happened that we had an enormous advantage. Jos was the home of a real museum, the property of the Federal Antiquities Department, and both Mr Bernard Fagg, the Director of the department, and later Mr Robert Soper and Mr Ekpo Eyo were prepared to let me use some of their resources. I proposed, therefore, to let the boys study some of the stages in African development, making use, as far as we could, of what the Museum could lend us, what pictures we could get reproduced, and what we could find in the country round about.

We could go back to the very dawn of African history, for out of the tin-mines came an abundance of stone tools that went back to the earliest Palaeolithic. We started by borrowing these: two cleavers, two or three hand-axes, a couple of pebble tools, a couple of spherical lumps of stone whose use was totally conjectural. Grinders? Missiles? Weights for a bolas? After talking about the early forms of man, and discussing a few pictures of a skull of a form of Australopithecus, the objects were handed out.

This I did in the dining-hall, where the tables were flat. Otherwise the spherical stones had a nasty habit of bouncing off a desk lid on to the concrete floor, to be followed by a rueful silence and the exclamation, 'Oh God!' There was room there for groups of boys to sit round each object and try to work out what it could have been used for, and how it could have been made, drawing and writing, and then looking at another object, while I circulated between the groups to discuss and explain.

There is a reality about a hand axe that no amount of talking can convey. Its very weight comes a shock. A fistful of rock. What power there must have been in the wrists and muscles that wielded it. Its significance as a technical achievement is realised as the fingers explore the concavities left by each blow that shaped the tool. No modern artificer can achieve that pear shape with its point and its scalloped edges. Its very beauty is an astonishment. The later specimens are finely finished, the grain of the rock beautifully exposed, the cutting edge pared finely, the tool slender, almost, as a leaf, its edge, when held end on, curving in a slight but evident and elegant S-shape. I have heard the boys exclaim in awe as they realised—I did not have to tell them—that what they held in their hands came from the hands of men half a million years before them. This was a real teaching situation for them, as it was for me. A few weeks after one of these lessons one of the boys even came back with a tool of his own, and together we explored the bed of the stream which ran down to the lake away opposite the school, to come back with three of those spherical balls.

We did the same sort of lesson with the microliths—two dozen slivers of quartz in a couple of polythene bags, unrecognisable at first as any sort of artifact. This disc, the size of a sixpence, a scraper, held between finger and thumb to shave away the fat and the hair from an antelope's skin; this little crescent an arrow-head; this tiny dart a barb; this curved and pointed, less than an inch long, perhaps an awl for piercing leather, to make clothes and satchels. What intricate workmanship they all required. There were places in the Kagoro hills where the stone-workers had sat on the hillside in the sun, and the ground was still strewn, centuries later, with scraps and fragments of shining quartz, thousands and thousands of pieces of shivered stone, the waste left behind by the tool-makers.

Then there were the stone axe-heads. These were so frequently discovered that I hardly needed to borrow them from the museum. They lay under the surface of the ground everywhere; they were wedged between the boulders on the hills. As the boys said, they were bound to be common, they were thunderbolts. I distributed them in all shapes and sizes—long heavy ones almost cylindrical in cross-section weighing two or three pounds; smaller ones, flatter, equilateral triangles in stone, perhaps nine inches long at each edge; little ones, one or two not much larger than a thumb-nail, almost rectangular in shape, with a bevelled cutting edge. The groups discussed them. I walked round once more. This one perhaps an adze, this perhaps a hoe, this heavy one for clearing trees, this little one for cutting rope, shaping wood, cutting up meat, trimming skins. Each one bound, probably, to a haft, or socketed in the same way, perhaps, as the little school hoes with their triangular blades. 'Ho-ho,' said an Angas boy, 'and we have these big ones, these very big ones, or bigger still. We put them outside the bridegroom's door at night. When he marries. That gives him power.' They chuckled.

'Yes,' they all said at the end of the lesson, 'they come when the lightning falls.'

'But they don't,' I protested. 'You said yourself how they could be used. Men made them, lots of them, and left them everywhere. They will never be destroyed, because they are of stone. That is why you can always find them wherever lightning falls.'

'Oh, yes, yes!' Though some looked a little doubtful, others still insisted: 'yes, but it is still the lightning leaves them there.' I desisted. I could not convince them if they did not wish to be convinced.

We collected our own iron tools: little triangular hoe blades; one of the massive square-shaped hoes of the type with which the Birom turned the soil at the beginning of the rains, back-breaking things with two handles and a great shovel-shaped blade; wicked little arrow-heads beaten in this case out of six-inch nails; a couple of spears; a Birom sword, a savage broad-bladed stabbing instrument, eighteen inches long like those of the Roman legionaries; a shield, made of palm leaves, wickerwork style. These were purposeful, malevolent instruments and we talked about these and their advantages over the brittle, easily blunted stones. They told me how they made them, of the hills covered with iron slag, so much of it that long ago it replaced the red laterite as a source of iron. One of the boys brought in the black gritty stuff and showed me how they pounded it with clay in Pankshin division, and heated and hammered it to the consistency of metal.

This brought us to the Nok culture, for the boys, though they did not realise it, had an ancient culture all their own, represented by heads shaped in terracotta, excavated from the mine-workings and the laterite pits on the roadside all round the southern edge of the Plateau. Two thousand and more years old, in their ornament they showed a direct tradition connecting them with certain ornaments and hair styles worn by various Plateau tribes in the twentieth century. In these strange stylised shapes, the ovals and the elongated conical cylinders on which the heads were based, and in the simplification of eye, ear and nostril, they betrayed an elegance and sophistication that represented a long period of artistic tradition. There was, moreover, a nobility and individuality to some of these clay masks that gave them the quality of great art. As it happened, the culture that made them was one of the first iron-smelting cultures in the whole of tropical Africa, and thus seminal, not merely in the history of Nigeria, but in that of the whole continent. And this ancient tradition was the boys' own.

We reproduced photos of these magnificent pieces from the Antiquities Department collection, blown up to full plate size, as large as we could get them. They looked marvellous.

'Your ancestors!' I said proudly.

There was a short silence. Then the boys rose in indignation. 'They cannot be.' 'These ugly bush things.' 'We do not look like this.'

I spent the rest of the period talking myself out of that one. Aesthetically the boys regarded the heads as an insult. They were prepared to accept a connection between them and themselves, but more or less on sufferance. One or two volunteered a few scraps of evidence for such a historical link. They were not enthusiastic about the proposition. It had been a mistake to interpose my own interpretations and enthusiasm between them and the subject of the lesson.

These artifacts enabled us to discuss how, at different stages, Africans had reacted to their environment. Another means of access to the boys' history was to find out about their own oral traditions. This was far more difficult than I had anticipated. Essentially the boys were ignorant of all but the bare outline of their tribal past, and some of the stories narrated about the more famous hero figures. Reference had to be made, when they could be obtained, to the provincial gazetteers, and to whatever historical information had been gleaned incidentally by anthropologists or European travellers in the area, sources normally rather suspect. Otherwise the various traditions of the past had to be sought for in whatever written records might lie in divisional files, or from the lips of the old people themselves. In the end the last was the only possible process, an immensely laborious business if done properly, and for all the tribes in all the enormous area from which the boys came, a total impossibility. Nor was this a task which could be left to the boys. These traditions were not for children. It took three journeys of over a hundred miles each way to obtain one authoritative oral tradition. Two things were clear, both that a collection of authentic oral tradition was an essential tool of the history teacher and that the acquisition of such a collection was a task that required much time and preparation.

With or without such traditions the business of teaching had to go ahead. By the second term's work on African history I had developed the visual aid of which I was most proud. It consisted of every map of the Plateau area which the Nigerian ordnance survey produced, each sheet pinned to the next till the map covered the whole area of the wall across the back of the classroom on a scale rather larger than an inch to the mile. Only one sheet, that of the mines-field itself, was depicted in full colour, with the contours in brown, and all the symbols that are so familiar on English maps for woodland and settlement, for major and minor roads, for post office, railway station, and church. Off that sheet were half a dozen more with rivers and lakes picked out in blue, and the spot height, at reasonably close intervals. Beyond that, for sheet after sheet, for mile after mile, all that was recorded were the details that had been gleaned from an aerial survey of ten years before—an intricate network of streams and rivers, the main roads, the railway, a couple of dozen minute named settlements, and a few widely dispersed spot heights. To all intents and purposes that enormous stretch of country was unexplored.

Over this expanse of paper were pinned sheets of transparent polythene, and on this I could draw with wax crayons, or stick on little plastic letters or symbols, visible, I hoped, from the back of the class. Village names, trade routes, commodities, tribal boundaries, or whatever else was needed, could thus be indicated on the polythene. There were drawbacks. The pins fell out, the plastic stickers fell off, the dust settled, the wind came in. The polythene fell in festoons, and the paper flapped in the breeze. The whole affair needed constant servicing. The answer was probably to glue the whole lot to a sheet of hardboard and varnish it, a task I never started.

In front of this rather uncertain monument we proceeded to the influences that had come into the area from outside, in particular the part played by trade—in tin from the Plateau, antimony from Wase, salt from pans on the Benue, palm kernels from the south, and perhaps blue cloth, and silver passing across the Plateau on the way to the north, horses, and perhaps copper going southwards. We plotted as far as we could, the routes along which these goods were carried, and the whereabouts of one of the historical mysteries of the Plateau, the bridges piled up from stones and boulders of all sizes, of unknown origin, that could be found down towards Pankshin and Shendam division. Oddly enough these may not have been built for commercial reasons at all, but for some religious or political purpose. A Kwa boy suggested that in his area they had once focused on the centre of the local cult, at that time located in the chief's compound.

We considered the forms of pagan, animistic religion that flourished throughout Africa, particularly those which centred on a divine corn-king, on whom the government and the whole existence of the tribe depended. The boys knew enough about the rulers of their own tribes to recognise these. Their people had come under the control of one of the most mysterious of all, the Jukun who had once controlled most of the area of modern Nigeria from their forgotten capital north of the Benue. They still retained in their cults, particularly among the Goemai, Jukun rites and Jukun religious terms. It was easy for them to understand the references to the pagan king of Ghana a thousand years before, or of Benin but fifty years past.

Then there was Islam. We had photographs of the great Sankore mosque at Timbuktu, and the ancient fourteenth-century tower at Katsina, the oldest structure still in use in Nigeria. We had reproduced the etchings from Clapperton and Denham's account of their travels in Northern Nigeria early in the nineteenth century, of Muslim lancers in padded cotton armour, of the strange court of the Mai of Bornu, whose government was in the hands of a devout Muslim theologian, but who survived without power, and received his visitors according to ancient pagan custom, concealed from human eyes by a screen. The boys knew much more. They were able to describe how Islam gained its converts, by what gradual stages the pagan assumed first the charms, and then the ritual prayers and ablutions, then the clothes and the manners of the Muslim, and finally the Koran itself and its language, so that little by little a man ceased to be a pagan of his own pagan people, and became instead a Muslim with his first loyalty to the Islamic religion and state. The boys knew all that there was to know of the power of the Islamic empires which have waxed and waned for the last thousand years over the greater part of West Africa.

We looked at the Christian missions, and tried to consider why it was that people became Christians at all. The boys' usual answer was that it was 'destiny', but if you looked close enough you found that the same reasons which accounted for the spread of Islam also accounted for Christian conversions. The appeal of trade and wealth, the existence of superior political and material power in the hands of the alien religion, the attraction of the written word, and of a cohesive structure of belief and behaviour in a period of fluctuating values, had all served to extend Christianity into the boys' lives.

So for two terms we talked our way through the various themes that had influenced African history from the physical problems of survival in a tropical country and the ways in which these had been overcome, and then the influence brought to bear from inside and outside Africa, religious, political and social, and finally the brutal material force of the European with his firearms and his technical competence.

Finally we reached the examination syllabus. Events justified my belief that the exam could be passed on the basis of four terms' work on the actual syllabus, and that even on the anarchic paper with which we were faced, with its questions on Islam, British government and European exploration, three-quarters of the work could be done on the West African past.

The foundation for success had already been laid. There existed some sort of historical sense, an appropriate framework of ideas about the main developments in African history, and considerable practice in the discussion and handling of historical fact. The material we had to cover in the last four terms was fresh to the boys, retained their interest, and was thus easier for them to understand and remember. The emphasis over four years on discussion had prepared them to organise the facts they required to answer an examination question, and guided them away from the repetition of long-prepared, and possibly irrelevant, notes. To make quite certain that the boys did not relapse into the routine of copying and rote-learning I insisted that they turn my skeletal notes on the blackboard into their own words, so that I could check that they thoroughly understood what they had written. To make absolutely certain that they had revised and understood they had to write a weekly essay under examination conditions.

Moreover, I was able to keep the most difficult, and perhaps the most interesting part of the course to last. The work on contemporary Africa, and the attainment of national independence, was done in the very last term, so that six weeks before the exam they were interrogating me on the complex and slightly shady details of pre-independence politics. There were off-days, but generally the work remained useful and fruitful to the end. The examination results, still the crucial test of success, were a justification. Of my last group of forty-two candidates, of every standard of intellect, I lost only two. Over two-thirds gained the credit level which indicated the equivalent of an Ordinary Level pass in an English School Certificate.

There was so much else that remained to be done. Much more African history remained to be incorporated earlier in the school curriculum. More active and sophisticated methods of bringing the subject into the classroom, or the boys out of the classroom into the countryside, needed to be worked out. Above all, they and we needed to know far more about their past. We had been lucky enough to get a great deal of printed material about the area into the school library, the provincial gazetteers, the accounts of the earlier travellers and administrators, the annual reports of Lugard and his successors from 1900 to 1911. Now we needed to collect every available tradition, taped, and then recorded verbatim, with both vernacular and translated versions, with the name and the authority of the source noted, from every tribe on the Plateau, all to be kept for reference in the school library. We needed to build up our collection of artifacts, weapons, tools, anything—it was all passing. For the boys' sake we ought to preserve it. Above all, of course, we needed a properly qualified Nigerian to teach all this. We would always be little more than interlopers. But we left the school, and there was no one to take over the tasks that remained behind us.

I am sure that we made innumerable errors of omission and commission, and probably in the end any effort by an expatriate teacher to intervene in the affairs of another culture will be vitiated by his own isolation. Essentially, though, it seemed that we were right in our approach. In any subject, in any African school, before any African school-children the task of the expatriate is only incidentally to teach what he knows, and what his values are. It is rather to use his special insights and intellectual training to enable his pupils to recognise, respect, and come to terms with their own culture, and their rapidly changing environment. In this strange teaching situation it is for the children to find out, and for the teachers to learn. It is for us to attempt to make up for centuries of arrogance by the humility with which we approach the ancient values of the children we teach.

12
English in an African School

We were also English teachers. Almost every expatriate teacher in Africa ends up teaching English. Skill in the use of the English language was central to the curriculum. Until 1965 the boys could not get a School Certificate without it. English is the medium of government and commerce, of education above the junior primary school, of most journalism and politics, of scholarship and literature; even, in some Western-educated families in Southern Nigeria, of personal relationships. The primacy of the colonial language was endured as a very real humiliation by the majority of our older boys, but reluctantly accepted as a necessity. No vernacular could win universal acceptance in a federation where over three hundred different languages were spoken. Not one gave access to world affairs and education as English did. Not even Hausa, Yoruba or Ibo appeared completely effective in meeting the demands and terminology of the twentieth century.

As with history, the teaching of English in Africa was also undergoing a revolution. When we arrived the English language was being taught as it had been in the English grammar schools, as if it were as dead to common use as Greek. The textbooks we used guided us through a post-mortem on its corpse in the archaic terminology of clause analysis and parts of speech. The artificiality of the old grammar was only too plain in the African situation. Three-quarters of the boys' linguistic errors could not be identified grammatically at all. Their usage was at fault. Their patterns of speech—this was the new phrase—were based on vernacular patterns. The aim of the new English teaching was to train the children to use recognisably English sentence patterns. The new theory was that the children should learn the English language as they had learned their own language at their mother's knee, by imitation and repetition. Volume after volume of simple sentence forms were being printed for use in schools like ours, to familiarise the children with sentences conforming to various simple patterns: noun + verb, noun + verb + noun, and so on at increasing levels of complexity. The children read, recited and constructed scores, hundreds, of simple different examples till they could, in theory, express themselves in orthodox phraseology without any thought at all. The teaching process could be refined by introducing little question and answer dialogues and little plays to illustrate the pattern being taught at any time.

It was an excellent system, though even its exponents agreed that only the younger children were prepared to accept the sheer monotony of the work. It could also lead to its own aridity. Like the old grammar it could become an end in itself—the pursuit of pure English without any consideration of what it could be used for or what it meant. When this happened its failure was complete, for it served no use outside the English lesson, and its sentence patterns naturally gave place to the patterns of market English, or Hausa, or the vernacular, whose use was evident, and in which practice was incessant.

Ideally, of course, the vernacular and market English should have been incorporated into the school course. The patterns of the English language, which have adapted themselves to different periods and different countries, are infinitely flexible, and are adapting themselves today to West African conditions, as the teacher of English in Africa should be aware. The vernacular should be taught to the children, and the English teacher should himself be able to speak it. A large number of linguistic and conceptual problems might then be clarified. The occasional work using the local dialect ought to be set. This and the vernacular only too often provide a more accurate and flexible vehicle for personal and emotional expression than the more 'correct' versions of English we are bound to teach in our classrooms. Moreover, it may then become possible to transfer some of the qualities of both forms of language into the children's use of the standard English they need for most of the formal conduct of everyday life.

If we had any theory about the teaching of English, it was that the language the children used should mean something, when it was read, and when it was written. As far as possible the principle that we applied in the history lessons should be followed in the English lessons. Wherever possible they should read books about their own environment. A number of simple books with an African background, by African writers, was already being produced by English and African publishers. Cyprian Ekwensi alone had written three such readers. Further up the school Camara Laye's *Dark Child* and Chinua Achebe's *Things Fall Apart* were achieving general recognition. The African novels that were not suitable for class use could all be put in the library, where a number achieved a degree of salacious popularity. European writers were more difficult to choose. By the end of the fourth year the boys' intellectual maturity had outgrown their linguistic skill, and we were not able to make any very satisfactory choice of books to deal with this problem. Orwell's *Animal Farm*, Swift's *Gulliver*, and Hardy's *Mayor of Casterbridge*, which was too difficult, were my main choices to go alongside Laye and Achebe. I should have liked to have tried out Cary's *Mister Johnson*, which the boys liked when I read to them, and Karen Blixen's *Out of Africa*. In the drama periods I made use of abbreviated versions of Shakespeare, put out by Ginn, from the end of the second year, noisily produced by groups of children in the dining-hall, before we started an un-abridged *Macbeth* in the fourth year.

The boys' writing, and their poetry, followed again the same principles as those of the history lesson. They were used to explore their background. The trigger for their weekly writing might be a passage for comprehension which related to their experience—a description of a person, a journey, a story, an experience of some sort. In the first couple of years after our arrival it might have been an account of some personal experience, though one had to take care that this experience was sufficiently personal, entertaining, and comprehensible to them. Then we could launch into the discussion that preceded such writing.

The English lesson was a process of exploration, as the history lesson had been, for teacher and taught. About a month after I arrived I had asked Form II if they knew any good stories. I had to do no more that lesson. They stood and told story after story, largely about animals. The climax of the lesson was one told about a tortoise by an Ibo whose English I could hardly understand. The details were a little unexpected. The point of the story lay in the animal's ability to break wind in the face of his enemies.

Once a term thereafter the boys would write, and we would read the best. One will do as an example, told by a little boy from Gindiri, which lay in the strip of flat infertile territory between the edge of the Jos Plateau and the Pankshin hills, the route followed by the slave raiders on their way down to the Benue. Here are the heroes of half West African folklore, the tortoise and the hare, the latter, of course, reincarnated in another continent as Brer Rabbit:

One day a hare went to a tortoise's house so that they might go to the bush and hunt. When they reached the bush they started hunting. After a while the tortoise saw a dead rat and said, 'Here is my dead rat.'

Then the hare said to the tortoise, 'I saw it first before I invited you to go hunting,' and he took the rat from the tortoise.

A little later the tortoise saw a dead partridge and said, 'This is my dead partridge.'

At once the hare rushed forward and offered to fight the tortoise. 'I saw it first,' he said, 'before I invited you to go hunting,' and he took the partridge from the tortoise.

A little while later, while they were still arguing with each other, a lion heard them, so it lay on the ground with its mouth open, with the flies buzzing inside it just as if it were dead. When the tortoise saw it, he did not know it was alive. 'This is my dead lion,' he said.

'Are you mad?' said the greedy hare, rushing forward. 'Before we started hunting I told you that I had seen all these before I invited you.' So he took the lion and gave the two small animals to the tortoise.

On their way home, the hare, who was carrying the lion, heard it breathing. Then he pretended to be tired. 'I am very tired,' said he to the tortoise. 'Won't you help me, and let me carry your load?' The tortoise agreed, and so they exchanged the loads. Then the hare said he wanted to lie down. When he saw that the tortoise was very, very far away he shouted: 'Throw him away! He's alive.'

Said the tortoise: 'Shall I throw him among your goats?'

'Your grandmother!' exclaimed the angry hare. 'Throw him away. He's alive.' So the tortoise looked around for a way of escape. Seeing a crab's hole, he threw the lion away and scrambled in.

Then the hare changed himself into an old woman, with a basket, went up to the lion and greeted him. 'Why are you digging?' he asked.

'I am digging for a tortoise,' growled the lion.

'You will need more strength,' said the hare. 'Go to the stream, not this one, but the one far away, fill this, and have a drink.' And the hare gave the lion the basket. The foolish lion took the basket, all full of holes, and went to have a drink. When the lion was out of sight the hare called the tortoise out, gave him a rope, told him to tie it round the lion's neck and pull hard.

When the lion came back the hare told him to dig. After the lion had dug for a little while the hare told him to put his head in the hole and see if the tortoise was there. No sooner had the lion put his head in than the tortoise put the rope round his neck, and pulled with all his might. The hare took up a big stick and hit the lion again and again and again till it was dead. Then the tortoise and the hare divided the meat up and went home.

This was straightforward enough, though I have often wondered what sexual and anal fantasies may be connected with the tortoise in much of the folklore I was not told. Gradually, I realised that I was entering into strange territory through these tales. Images of terror and of beauty moved through them in strange symbolism, masks, demons, wizards, and the ghosts of the vengeful dead. Emotions and relationships foreign to Western traditions were hinted at. Folk memories reached back, half understood, over a thousand years. Here is Alexander Kebang's story from the Lowland Angas of Kabwir:

When I was still young my blind grandfather often told us stories. This story is one of the most famous among my people.

Once a hunter and his son broke in, unintentionally, upon a witch, who sat in her hut feeding her many mouths, which were about ninety-eight in number.

When the witch saw that the hunter and his son had discovered her secret, she was extremely angry, and decided to revenge herself. She transfigured herself into a very beautiful maiden, and went to the hunter's house.

On her arrival the lads of the village gathered round her, each hoping to speak to her about marriage, but she was only interested in the hunter and his son. Therefore she put her vessel on a stone. She told all those who were interested in her to throw a stone to see if they could knock the vessel over. She promised to marry whoever did so.

The hunter warned the boy not to participate in the contest. The others tried very hard to knock down the vessel, but none of them was successful. At length the hunter's boy took a handful of gravel and threw it jokingly at the stone. To his amazement the vessel fell before the stones could reach it. The girl sprang up, gratefully kissed the boy, and so married him.

After some years they decided to pay a visit to the girl's parents. On the night before they set out, the girl asked him many questions. She asked him to tell her the name of their previous king who was reputed to be very strong and brave. He did not tell her, because it was illegal to pronounce the king's name. He therefore told her indirectly in this famous verse:

> The brave, for sure, sleep deep tonight,
> When the moon is bright, and the wind in the trees,
> But cowards have much ado to sleep,
> Though the young lie often unconcerned.
>
> When the day is bright, all things sing,
> All with hoe and shield on shoulder dressed,
> But our brave king, unknown, goes always empty-handed.
> The greatest is this king who ever lived among us.

The woman seemed still unsatisfied, and asked more questions. She asked him again to list the names of all the things into which he could change in order to save his life when attacked by a wild beast.

He told her that he was able to change into a whirlwind, into a lion, and into many other things besides but when he began to name a butterfly his father stopped him when he scarcely had had time to begin the first syllable.

On the following day they set out on the journey cheerfully together. They arrived at the woman's former hut as the shadows were lengthening. The woman deceived her husband into thinking that her parents' house was still very far away, and that they would have to sleep in that hut till the following day. The man agreed and she prepared a sleeping place for him on the ground. He was so tired that he fell asleep as soon as he lay down. Meanwhile his treacherous witch-wife left him and went out to plot against him.

As he was sleeping a snake fell from the roof and warned him about the evil woman. He was very confused and frightened by this, but he mounted his horse and rode away. He had not gone far when the woman saw him and called after him to wait and collect his clothes, but he paid no attention to her. Within a moment she was near him, and had cut off three of the horse's legs. But the horse did not stop. She cut off the last leg, and the horse fell.

The man changed himself into all the things he had told the woman, and she also changed into them. At last he changed into a butterfly, and was saved, for the woman did not know what he was, since his father had not allowed him to complete the name.

The witch was there in many stories, waiting in the depths of the forest, with her rapacious mouths. The animals, too, appeared again and again, and in story after story the pursued man, in a series of nightmare transfigurations, changing and changing to avoid the avenger, reached always that last configuration whose title had not been revealed to the pursuer. The potent symbolism of the serpent also recurs. It has been the centre of West African cults for at least two thousand years. The Higi king, said Kevin Dagai, had a hut full of serpents. In his sleep they crept over him and licked his body, which might not be touched with water while the crops grew. At the other end of West Africa, Camara Laye, in *The Dark Child*, described the black snake that came into his father's house to tell him secrets and predict the future.

How important, too, is the power which lies in a man's name. It is knowledge of the hunter's title which gives the witch power over his several incarnations. When she does not know the name she is powerless. At the centre of the tale is the riddle of the king's name, which may not be spoken, or referred to except in riddles. Here, too, is a puzzle, for this great king 'unknown, goes always empty-handed'. Five years later I became certain that this is a Christian or Judaic conception, 'a man forsaken and rejected of men', one of many such memories of a religious heritage which predates the missionaries by over a thousand years, preserved not only by the Angas, but by tribes of all sorts down the eastern side of Nigeria, from Lake Chad to the coast round Calabar.

Soon our weekly essays became an explanation of the boys' experience and environment. Often this was concrete enough. They explained how they built huts, made pots, wove mats and cooked meals:

Usin is made from starch, palm oil, water, palm kernels, onions, pepper, tomatoes, natron and the meat of snails and crabs. The palm kernels are boiled, pounded and crushed. The oil is then put into a pot and ground pepper, tomatoes and onions are added. While it is boiling you add the flesh from snails and crabs. The natron is then broken into the pot, stirred, and taken out. Salt is added to taste and then the soup is taken off the fire. The starch is mixed with water and palm oil, put into hot water, and boiled. You stir all the time till the starch thickens like fu-fu. It is then taken off the fire, rolled into a ball and eaten with soup.

Sometimes they described how they hunted, sometimes how they farmed:

Acha is of great importance to the Birom. The scarcity of firewood has made it necessary as the main food. It can be eaten raw, and requires only a little cooking before it can be taken as food.

The unit measurement of acha is a 'buema'. It contains about five full headpans. A farmer may produce about a hundred 'buemas' or more yearly.

Acha is a grain obtained from a certain type of grass. It needs much rain, but little heat. The acha is scattered on the ground. After the acha has ripened, it is cut and gathered. The grain is obtained by beating the grass. After that it is collected and stored in granaries. The grass is used in making mattresses and native potash.

We explored all the physical circumstances of the boys' lives, the villages they lived in, the towns they had visited, the schools they had attended, the countryside in which they played, farmed, herded the animals, and hunted, the roads they travelled along, the people they had met, the accidents and adventures they had undergone. In our most interesting lessons, as the boys grew older, we would talk about the customs and beliefs of the tribes from which they came. They knew that they had to come to terms with two cultures. They said so on several occasions. They were conscious of belonging to neither the old tribal culture nor the new European one, and yet were tied to both. They were attempting, as objectively as they could, to choose from the two heritages, in order to build up, painfully, an adequate intellectual and moral equipment with which to face the tensions of their life in twentieth-century urban Nigeria.

It was a vivid impression that I received of their lives outside the school. They described an environment that was at once beautiful and frightening, to which they looked back with both awe and nostalgia. At the same time they were conscious of inevitable and violent change. The very animals that they described were disappearing from their old haunts as the bush receded. The ancient skills on which their people had relied in their childhood, blacksmithing, and weaving and mat-making, were already becoming obsolescent and would soon be forgotten. Their affection for the past, for their own childhood, was often expressed in terms of their appreciation of natural beauty. Even the clumsy English of the earliest years could not conceal Andrew Gwaza's affectionate memories of the wind that blew refreshingly off the Rock at Kagoro, or Michael Kwardem's recollection of the peaceful hill-sides near Nbamu where he had lived with his mother, or the sinister beauty of the sacred pool, the centre of the Kagoma cult of which Peter Kure might have become the head.

At the same time there was the terrible awareness of violence and death. All of them had seen it on the roads, the deserted lorry, silent, on its side, with the shattered windscreen and the pool of blood in front of it, the man, white-faced and vomiting blood over the tailboard of a wrecked mammy wagon. All this was a common experience. They were used to death in many forms. Peter Kure had watched a hut burning to death its owner, and described the explosion of the wretched man's stomach, and the appalling stench. Benedict Balarabe knew a prosperous farmer whose family had also died in a fire, and who had gone out of his mind and hanged himself. Kevin Dagai's village had been invaded by elephants, smashing huts and crushing men to death. Ignatius Longjahn, travelling to a near-by village, had passed a corpse abandoned by the roadside and toyed with by vultures.

As well as the essays the boys wrote poetry, almost all of it traditional in origin. There was never any difficulty in any poetry lesson. They taught me far more than I taught them. Rhythm, the essence of poetry-making, was developed in them to a degree that was not possible in a European environment. From the time they learnt to speak they learnt not merely rhymes but working songs to accompany almost every daily activity. They chanted in the fields, hoeing the land, threshing the corn, cutting the grass. One called; the rest responded:

> What killed Nwakatinkporo,
> O Nwakatinkporo!
> A bunch of breadfruit killed Nwakatinkporo,
> O Nwakatinkporo!

What made the breadfruit fall?
O Nwakatinkporo!
A fly made the breadfruit fall,
O Nwakatinkporo!
Who ate the breadfruit up?
O Nwakatinkporo! [etc., etc.]

In the dancing, daily, nightly, since they first walked they had learnt to respond elaborately to the complex rhythms of the drums. Toddlers of two or three shuffled and swayed to the high-life records in the Vwang compounds. In their social evenings, each Saturday in the school dining-hall, the boys danced together, a totally sexless process, pure rhythm play, often executed with a grace and suppleness none but a trained European ballet dancer could exceed.

The words that accompanied the dances they had learnt in the villages were an exercise in verse-making, extemporised as they often were, the lines repeated by the congregation of dancers in response to a caller:

Nabaam was a wizard.
Yes he was a wizard.
And his family they were wizards.
Yes they were wizards.
Rice and ground-nuts were his wives.
Yes they were his wives. [etc., etc.]

As the children grew older they had received the traditions of the tribe in verse:

The Goemai land is under Muduut,
O the land is under Muduut.
The land of our fathers is under Muduut,
O, hey-ho, the land is under Muduut.
Carry the bones of our ancestors up,
And let us go back to Muduut.
The Dorok land is under Muduut,
The land is under Muduut.
O, hey-ho, the land is under Muduut.
The ghosts of our fathers have gone to Muduut,
The land is under Muduut.

146

They learnt the chants which accompanied their religious ceremonies. This one laments a dead Goemai chief:

> There was a wall,
> Thick and strong,
> Held by steel.
> The steel is broken;
> The wall has fallen;
> Therefore we cry.

On a similar occasion the Kwalla had a war chant:

> Tim, Tim, Tim,
> The strongest on the battlefield
> Has brought the captives' heads.
> Let us rejoice.
> Let us play with the heads.
> Let them be angry who fled.
>
> Now the battle is ended.
> Now we are cool as rain.
> Let the war break out again.
> Let our men conquer again.
> But what has gone shall never be again.

Most of these incantations were simple enough, though they
incorporated imagery and illustrated customs that were often
difficult to comprehend. Some of the boys' poetry went further
than this and explored human relationships. A mother speaks to her
daughter in this Kagoro poem:

> Remember what I did for you.
> Come nearer, come nearer, come closer.
> Come nearer, come nearer, if you can.
>
> Go. You may go now.
> Remember, remember what lies you told me.
> Remember, remember the words you told me.
> Remember, remember. No longer, no longer.
> See what you have done to me.

As I read more of the essays, and as I looked through much of the
poetry it was striking how frequently the process of eating, digesting,

and evacuating was referred to. In the stories there was the suggestion of cannibalism, 'a witch who sat in her hut feeding her many mouths'. In the descriptions of the rituals there was the eating of the sacred food. There were the references to evacuation in much of the folklore I had to reject for the magazine, the reason, I think, why one of the priests described the stories which the Angas told as 'obscene'. When I sent a group of boys to prepare an article on Bukuru market, they brought back a detailed account of the laxative products for sale, the leader being extremely explicit about the satisfactory effect of one type of local pepper on his own bowels. Occasionally I overheard conversations in which the physical act of eating seemed to receive unusual emphasis, 'with my thick lips' was a phrase which recurred, while a Kwalla poem speaks of rolling a locust bean on the tongue. Jocular references in pidgin to the anus were common . . . 'our nyash de make yo-yo as if sey na old bucket de leak'. There are parallels enough to this sort of thing in English, but here the effect was sometimes akin to the strange grossness of phrases in *The Pardoner's Tale* in which the speaker is so vividly aware of the digestive process that the organs concerned gain an individual, almost dehumanised existence:

> O wombe! O bely! O stinking cod,
> Fulfild of donge and of corrupcion!
> At either end of thee foul is the som.

Such a consciousness, if it in fact exists, seems alien, even grotesque to our traditions, but it could achieve great force and dignity. In Anacletus Tunkuda's translation of an Angas poem, made shortly after the death of his own father, the image of devouring, associated strangely with act of giving birth, is given extraordinary power. The resurrection theme with which it ends almost certainly long pre-dates the missionaries, one of those relics of a far-off Judaistic past.

> O Death, direful Death, dear,
> O most cruel ghostly master,
> Where be thy supernatural eyes
> That watch the dwellers of the earth?

O Death, direful Death, dear,
Thou who killest, why bearest not thou?
Why bearest not, though thou hast eaten?
Lo thou eateth, but produceth not.

O Death, direful Death, dear,
Where livest thou, mine enemy?
My Maker shall his creatures call.
Then shalt thou also give thy soul.

O Death, direful Death, dear,
Since thou diest as well as we,
Why dost man fear thee?
Nay, rather fear thou man.

O Death, direful Death, dear,
Woe most painful will thy downfall be.
When man riseth, thou wilt sink deeper,
Lo, thou hast lost eternal bliss.

From this sort of material I began to develop the school magazine which had begun in my first year as a dozen sheets stapled in the middle. The second edition at the end of 1961 was intended to involve every boy in the school. In every class groups of boys dealt with particular topics—games, childhood lessons, meals, tribal traditions, culture, history, sport, education—'as if,' I suggested, 'to explain to another African boy what sort of a country Nigeria is, and what sort of people Nigerians are'. The result was a ragbag, a highly unreliable collection of largely unrelated tradition shaken together to form a number of disconnected essays, but at least everybody wrote something.

The most spectacular effort was a poem produced by Gabriel Zi, at that time labouring under a considerable inferiority complex, and soon to quarrel finally with the Principal.

Hate me not because I am black,
My colour is the will of God;
He made me rational and strong;
He made my colour beautiful;
Hate me not because I am black.

149

Hate me not because I am poor.
My Maker knows the reason why,
Gave me my body and my soul,
Gave me also many gifts,
And crowned them all with poverty.
Hate me not because I am poor.

Shortly after the Principal met him riding a bicycle, a fairly common breach of school rules, and suspended him. He left, to attend the agricultural college at Zaria, thus stealing a march of three years over many of his form mates who were to follow him there, and went to Italy on a scholarship, where he met the Pope and considered himself a considerable success with the girls. He returned, a man of mark, to settle down as an agricultural officer on the Plateau and marry a girl from Zawan.

The next edition, a year later, did not please the boys so much. It was to be an anthology of material from each of the tribes in the school. This, in itself, was a popular venture. There was a flood of material, stories, songs and traditions of every type, much of it unprintable, since it dealt freely and exuberantly with defecation and sex; and much of it untranslatable without a very thorough grounding in anthropology.

The main disappointment was that there were no pictures. The provincial secondary schools had their magazines printed at considerable expense, and neatly bound in high-quality card, with the school device emblazoned on the front. More important still were the photographs of the school team and of those who were leaving, undeniable proof of secondary education for those who possessed a copy of the magazine. We did not run to such things. The whole affair was duplicated, using thirty-seven stencils, and strenuously turned off on the school Gestetner before being stapled together between sheets of yellow tinted paper.

Another disastrous shortcoming was peculiar to the country, and was a direct result of the Goemai preponderance at the school. There were three Goemai contributions, an unexceptional song used by bird-scarers in the fields, and two anthems.

One of these was long and had a rather strong rhythm:

This land, this land is under Muduut,
The land is under Muduut

was the chorus, Muduut being the term for the town of Shendam, and for the Goemai kingdom. Much of it, however, was open to objection:

The ghosts of our fathers have gone to Muduut
The land is under Muduut.
The bones of our fathers lie in Muduut,
The land is under Muduut.
The tribes in the hills come down to Muduut,
O-oh, hey-ho! The land is under Muduut.
Kwande is under Muduut,
Oh the land is under Muduut.

Since a large part of the school belonged to 'the tribes in the hills', and several came from Kwande, and none was prepared to accept that his land came 'under Muduut', a few age-old sores were touched, the scars of forgotten wars. The resentment was not assuaged by my innocent choice of another Goemai song to introduce the magazine. The theme was that of unity, which seemed an appropriate choice for such a magazine in modern Nigeria. It was in the nature of a chant, two sides calling and responding with rather a catchy tune.

You young Goemais, do you hear what I say?
We young Goemais, we like what you say.
Ah, d'you like what I say?
Ah, we like what you say.
Ah, if you like what I say, let us be one, so we may progress.

[Together] Let us be one, one, one! Let us be one, one, one!
Let us be one, let us be one, and we may progress.
Let us be one, one, one! Let us be one, one, one!
Let us be one, let us be one, and we may progress.

The song was full of implications for those whose people had once come under Goemai domination or been threatened by it. Unity proposed to them by a Goemai had sinister associations. The magazine was not a great success with those who were not Goemai.

The cohesion of any Nigerian community, from the school to the State itself, was a precarious affair.

The 1963 edition was the most ambitious of all. The theory was that the boys should go out and ask questions, and thus be required to use their English in the most exacting circumstances possible. A committee was set up, and by popular request we had a page of riddles, to which we omitted to put the answers, which caused some annoyance, and an article in Latin, entitled 'Lepus et Testudo'.

Apart from this one group of boys went out into the hills to look for ruins, a prospect of which one or two were rather nervous, so that they went equipped with torches and cutlasses to probe their way into the caves and clefts among the rocks. The grass was still high, so they found little. They claimed to have discovered human bones, and reported on ruined cattle enclosures, hut foundations, the positions of old graves, and the variety of useful plants that had been preserved on the tops of some of the rocky outcrops. Finally they talked to an old man who could remember the fighting which had gone on in the area at the beginning of the century before the European occupation.

Jerome Magaje looked after the group which was sent to investigate the fields opposite the school, assisted by Ignatius Longjahn and a number of juniors. Twice a week they drifted noisily out into the countryside, usually ending up gossiping around a culvert by the side of the main road, Joseph dour and silent on the edge of the group. Finally they were obliged to write something, and Jerome showed his usual disdain for the locality and its people. 'Without mining this area would have been a desert.' He insisted on his homeland as being one of the places from which the Plateau bought their food. Inevitably there was argument. The Biroms denied that they were employed by the Hausa to grow sugar cane down by the stream. They were quite capable of doing it themselves, and did so. Nor was it true, they said indignantly, that acha was grown because it needed no cooking and saved fuel. Jerome sulked and left the rest to make their own contribution. The Biroms therefore described the cultivation of the nine different types of acha which grew in the area, while others dealt with the millet, beni-seed, yams, coco-yams, sweet potatoes, and sugar-cane that were grown in smaller quantities as cash crops. 'I noticed,' said one writer, 'that some of the farmers seem to finish the sugar-cane bundles themselves. They find it very sweet and keep only a little for sale.'

The efforts of the group which went to the market-place aroused some suspicion, only partly allayed by Athanasius Chukwu, who assured the stallholders that he was representing the Principal, for whom he would shortly be placing large contracts. We published little of this work apart from a description of the methods used by the butcher.

More successful were the boys who were sent to interview Nigerians from the local villages. There was a lorry-driver who said he travelled mostly at night to avoid the traffic police, who normally loaded up to eight tons on a vehicle built to carry five, and considered burst tyres and broken springs as a normal part of a long journey. A labourer in the tin mines walked eight miles each way to his job, carrying arms if he was out after dark. He received twenty-six shillings a week.

Every week I pay seven shillings to the 'uwar-tuwo' who is a woman who cooks meals for me twice daily. I pay ten shillings for a sort of collection or deposit (you see five of us pay out ten shillings weekly and one man collects that money. Next week five of us pay out ten shillings and another man collects that money). I spend about five shillings a week for clothes and the remaining three shillings for some food and wine. When it is my turn and I collect £2. 10s., I spend some of it on women. But I buy some useful things for the house.

Poor Clement I sent again and again to ask more questions of his farmer—how he lived, what he wore, what he farmed, how much he earned, what his religion was and why. Jatau, whose son worked as a steward in the school kitchen, farmed in the fields opposite the school and earned a cash income of about £150 in a good year. He had a family of twenty-eight people of all ages, including four wives and a number of children, living in a compound of eight huts and six granaries. He was a prosperous man.

Most of the farmers dress very poorly, but Mr Jatau is one of the lucky ones, and throughout the period I have been visiting him I have always met him wearing a pair of trousers and an old coat (though it may be an 'auction' coat i.e. second-hand, from the many tons of cast-off clothing exported from Europe each year and sold in Nigerian market-places). Because of the coldness of the Plateau during August and January, Mr Jatau buys old coats for his children. Those that are at school possess, in addition, their school uniform. His wives are always seen wearing their 'gwados' (calico wrappers).

In his attitude to religion Jatau, a man of about forty, was typical of most Nigerians of his age and generation.

Mr Jatau with all his family are Christians. As for himself and his four wives, they hope to be baptised at the hour of their death. He said that he has been a convert for ten years, and when asked why he should have become a Christian, he said that it had been predestined by God before his creation. Being a Christian Mr Jatau has rejected all forms of pagan practices but he still keeps in contact with Hausa mallamai as a way of getting the most effective preventive medicines against human poisons.

Most of the enquirers tended to adhere to the suggestions they had been given about questions to ask and topics to find out about. Only one broke entirely loose from the formulae he had been provided with. Aloysius Shilong, sturdy and rebellious, went to interview an old Fulani who had settled in Vom after a lifetime of wandering with his cattle. Almost verbatim he took down the old man's biography, confused and rambling, but full of life, and went on to add to it details of Fulani dress and custom which he had found out for himself. Such curiosity and initiative were unusual. They were not qualities which were encouraged by the boys' environments. Aloysius brought back a strange story of movement and marriage, birth and death and misadventure, and all the different place-names where the herdsmen had camped.

We passed to Wase. I was at my twentieth birthday. My wife Hadiza delivered a child here and the child died after three months. We then came to Yelwa and passed to Bakin Chawa. Our cows became ill here. My second wife Hanna delivered a child. We went to Goeyil Merniang and the Dokas. We were well received here and made the biggest hut we ever made at Dunglong. As the part we stayed on was very fertile we planted vegetables and millet. The natives bought our millet and butter. My son Hamma was three or four years old. Sickness came upon our cows. I had fifty or sixty cows while my father had three hundred.

The committee were relieved to hear that the results of all this were to be printed. The job was to be carried out at the Rainbow Press in Jos, an enterprise run by a couple of Ibos in one of a row of cement-walled sheds not far from the mission. It stood between a bar and a bookshop, and within three small rooms exhibited a sort of history of printing. At the back, in an ill-lit cubby-hole half a dozen inky and undernourished young compositors sat in front of the ancient trays of type. With their tweezers they selected the little leaden sticks that made up each letter, and laboriously and myopically assembled each paragraph, and then added it to the forme on the bench before them. Then the result was leaded out, clamped, inked, and a proof was rolled off. The type was worn and the faces confused. There was a shortage of commas and full-stops, while 'n's had to be reversed and used as 'u's. Despite every stratagem there was never enough type to assemble more than one page at a time, and after each one had been printed the pieces had to be cleaned, laboriously dismantled, and returned to their trays before the next page could be commenced. A page printed a day was the fastest rate we could hope for.

In the front workshop, which was only about twenty-feet long, a brand-new printing machine had been bolted to the middle of the floor. It glistened in shiny black enamel and had been imported from Heidelberg. It hissed and whirred with a mechanical vigour that threatened to shake the whole dilapidated building down about it. It chattered its way through 250 pages of our magazine in less than ten minutes, and then returned to its more usual diet of pools forms for the 'Tin City Football Pools', religious tracts, laundry bills, invoices, membership cards, and rule books for the dozens of unions and tribal societies that flourished in the town.

In direct contrast was the ancient hand-operated press that stood beyond it, with its crude wooden type, from which were run off posters for sports meetings, entertainments, political parties, and religious functions. At the opposite end of the shop sat the manager, reading proofs, checking numbers and orders, gluing, sticking, or trimming on the huge guillotine. Opposite this I found a table where I could wedge myself with my proofs and cope with the numberless errors that result when illiterate compositors try to assemble a page of writing in a language they hardly understand, from an inadequate collection of type.

The last page was printed with twenty-four hours to spare and the committee was brought in a body to the Rainbow Press to put it together. The manager eased himself heavily into his seat after lunch, and we squeezed ourselves round the table where I had done my proof-reading to sort out the bundles of pages into their correct order. Then for the rest of the afternoon we sorted and stapled, while the manager, complaining that it was 'A bloody job! A bloody, bloody job!' folded the covers and gummed them on. At last the magazines were put into the press and trimmed, and we loaded them into the car for the journey home. We showed them to Father Glynn in their green marbled paper covers with the title of the school across the top. 'Crooked!' he said. They were. The name of the school was just out of alignment with the top of the cover. Perfection is far to seek.

The boys were well enough pleased. They were issued with them free, for no one dared to charge them anything. Most of them had their names printed somewhere inside, and there were three photographs, of the school-leavers and staff, of the athletics team, and of the football team. They were blurred enough, but if they were studied carefully the faces of the boys could be made out reasonably accurately, all presented to the camera in profile or three-quarters to achieve the most flattering effect. The usual complimentary copies were sent out to every Northern Nigerian school.

It was our last magazine. The next year I proposed an issue devoted to the federal elections which took place near the end of 1964. It would have been a marvellous topic if it had not been so dangerous. Not surprisingly the Provincial Commissioner refused to let us go ahead. We were offered a talk by a Government official instead. Then the preparation for the G.C.E. examinations started, and no other preoccupation could be allowed to intervene. After we left in the following year there were no more magazines.

13

An Extra Curricular Experience

We worked hard at our lessons and at the magazine, and yet there were many times when I felt that it was the athletics team that lay closest to my heart. It was something shared with the boys. The days of its triumph were some of the proudest and happiest of my life.

The athletics team had also been the first indication for Father Glynn that there was any hope for his new school at all. We had to be hosts for a meeting with Kafanchan a few weeks after his appointment. For the first time we beat them, and the Ibo Secondary School from Jos, and the Junior Seminary from Barrakin Ladi. Our 440 relay team, beaten on so many occasions, now sped away from its rivals. In the fierce, clear Plateau sunlight Kevin Dagai raced straight, minute, determined and alone, with his supporters going berserk with triumph around the track. At the end of the day the school had won more points than all the other teams put together and the scoreboard became a memento, left under the notice-board for the next week, before being locked reverently away in the storeroom. 'It's a poor little school,' repeated our new Principal, 'but there's no denying it—they're fine little runners, great little runners.'

Once again we embarked on the ritual of early-morning exercises, followed by the privilege of that substantial bed-time snack of bread, margarine, and Marmite. Then we had the luck to find a V.S.O. with a lot of spare time on his hands in Jos, and a great deal of athletic experience gained in his time at Ampleforth. Several evenings a week he came out and put Clement through his interval running, adding an unexpected white face to the group of dark ones constantly circulating the track. We hoped that at last it would be Clement's year. Nothing could be less certain. Two years before he had been disqualified for cutting too quickly into the lead. The previous year he had lamed himself playing at the pole vault. There was no knowing what he would do this time. However, he won the provincial contest easily, while Lucas Dangaana

A View of the School

Scores of tons of concrete were built into the classroom block—and still failed to keep out the rain. The storms drove horizontally at sixty miles or more an hour straight at this end of the classroom, with the result that the interior walls at this end of the block had a curiously mottled appearance throughout the wet season.

with equally little difficulty won the high jump. A gaunt Angas boy, Alexander Kebang, won the 440. We failed to gain the cup for the meeting, as Gindiri possessed a sixth form and there was little we could do against that.

That year it was my turn to manage the province's team at Kaduna. It was rather a disgruntled group. The best sprinter had been gated by his school. Their accommodation was uncomfortable, and the food, they said, was inedible. The meeting itself went its rather vague way. Nobody seemed to trust the starter despite his spectacular starting weapons, which looked rather like a pair of sawn-off shot-guns. The team did not do particularly well. The most formidable opposition came from Keffi, with its sixth form and its full-time P.E. specialist, and from an American Protestant missionary school at Waka whose boys appeared to be natural athletes, and well trained into the bargain. Event after event fell to them. It was these two schools who were to provide Lucas and Clement with their most dangerous opposition.

Later that afternoon, as nothing seemed to demand my attention as team manager, I sat down by the high-jump pit to watch Lucas take part in his event. I plucked a piece of grass and chewed it. The first competitors had gone out the previous day at five feet six inches. It was clear that only one contestant was expected to go very high, a strongly built Tiv from Keffi Government College, who had watched the other jumpers with a patronising smile, not participating himself at the lower heights. His coach was also in attendance, a jovial, well-fed young man, probably also a Tiv, who looked at the other jumpers with considerable condescension. No straw-chewing for him. 'Hoh, hoh!' he boomed. 'There's no need for him to start yet. He does five foot eleven easily.' Lucas's face was expressionless, but his mouth tightened a little, and his eyes seemed to focus somewhere in the middle distance. He bounced lightly on his toes, and shook his left foot backward.

Once the bar began to rise above the jumper's head the least hesitation would ruin everything, a few inches out in the run up, the jumping foot misplaced by ever so little, a falter in the leading leg, a tenseness of the hips, a slight clumsiness of the hands, and off would come the bar. Even the valiant Alexander would try to fling himself over, lengthening his run, hurling himself with ever greater violence from further and further back, only to bring the bar with a painful thump into the sand beneath him. For Lucas, the higher the bar, the more serious the opposition, the more deadly calm he became. He had trained all his life. At his primary school the competition had been to throw yourself off moving trains, the faster the train, the greater your prestige. 'I would not advise anyone to take up this game,' he wrote. 'Boys sometimes lose their arms and their legs. Even they can get killed.' He waited his turn, flexing his legs lightly, the suggestion only of a smile on his set lips.

At that point I had to dash across the field to prevent the starter blasting off the hurdlers while the Plateau boy was still in the hop step and jump, an action for which I was later reproved by the Permanent Secretary himself. When I returned the bar stood at five feet nine inches, only three contestants remained in, and the Keffi boy had condescended to jump. At five feet ten inches he loped up vigorously and came over. Lucas danced his seven paces to the take-off point and came down neatly on the other side. There was perhaps a shade less of the casual manner about his rival. The third boy succeeded on his third attempt. At five feet eleven the Keffi boy jumped vigorously once more, and came over clear as he expected, but not too far clear. Lucas once more tensed himself and was over neatly and economically. The third boy went out.

At six feet the Keffi boy frowned. The smile had left the face of his jovial coach. This was to be a great effort. The run started a little further back, the extra energy apparent in the run up and leap. His take-off was slightly too far from the bar. He jumped high enough, but he came down on top of it. It bent and bounced off its supports. Lucas was expressionless. I chewed another piece of grass. He had never jumped so high before. There was a brief silence. He breathed in, took his run up, struck the ground smartly with his left foot, was up in the air and over. The bar quivered. We waited. It stayed. The Keffi lad scowled. Now his effort was great indeed; each step forward swayed his whole body, and with a grunt he left the ground. This time he was over. The smile reappeared. His coach gave every appearance of having won the competition. I chewed grass. Six feet one inch was asking too much. Perhaps it was all over. Lucas remained expressionless. His rival looked confident now. He seemed twice Lucas's size. He jumped strenuously up and down, measured his run up, came back, and pounded toward the bar. He had miscalculated. Once again he came down on top of the bar, and once again it fell. Lucas, too, checked his run up, placed his hands on his knees, breathed in, then skipped on his starting-point two or three times. Automatically I counted off the paces, one, two, three, four, five, six, seven and up, level with the bar, over, in the sand. The bar stirred slightly, I leapt to my feet and shouted. Lucas said nothing and walked impassively back to his place. The Keffi boy tried again. He failed. He tried a third time, with every effort he could muster. The bar fell behind him. Lucas walked away. He had set a new record for the North. His rival and the coach stood. Their faces were blank, as if they had just suffered a violent and unexpected robbery. There was no time to dwell on it. The mile was about to start.

Clement's instructions were fairly definite. We proposed the times at which he should run each lap: sixty-five seconds for the first lap, seventy for the next two, and as fast as he could for the final lap, reserving his main effort for the beginning of the back straight, when he would have all the time he needed to bear down on an obstinate opponent. We waited for the starter. Clement was tall now, but still deceptively slight, with long slim arms and legs. His face, long and fair-complexioned, was not the heavily boned structure normally associated with muscular strength. His broad shoulders and heavy chest were concealed by sloping shoulder muscles. The slenderness of his legs belied their sinewy strength, but he was no longer the stripling he had been at Kafanchan years before. He won easily. His only competition was a boy from Waka who rushed ahead in the first lap, to be overhauled in the last. Clement won by twenty yards, and set a Northern Nigerian record.

Ten days later, with Michael, I drove down to Enugu to see them. Reports from the team had been gloomy. The food was no better; the nights remained uncomfortable; and the training, for which an American from Michigan was responsible, lacked purpose. The 350-mile journey along a road that was two years later to be a refugee route and then the battlefield for a pitiless civil war, took us two days. There was no match at the Enugu sports stadium. It had rained hard all morning, and the track was under water. In the enormous sports club building at one end of the stadium we ran to earth my friend, the coach from Keffi. He was very pleased to see us, so touched that we had come all that way that he nearly wept. There was a strong smell of beer in the air. He bought us a drink and then disappeared to a committee meeting. When he returned we discovered where the team was supposed to be and drove off to find Clement, Lucas, and Alexander, who was a member of the relay team. We found them, as directed, sitting in the dormitories of the largest Catholic secondary school in the town, perspiring in their bright red track suits, which appeared to have been stitched out of blankets. They were waiting for the bus to take them to the field. My friend from Keffi had forgotten to tell them that the match had been postponed. Morale was not improved. That night we packed the Plateau boys into the Volkswagen, eleven of us inside altogether, and drove cautiously to see Harold Lloyd clinging to the wall of a skyscraper in a film from the thirties. They laughed uproariously while I sweated to the tips of my fingers. I hated heights. Michael observed that it had all been shot at different times of the day, as was perfectly obvious if you looked at the shadows on the film. It was his ambition to be the *Cherwell* film critic.

The match at last took place. It was not a good day for the North. The team had trotted, dispirited, in their heavy red track suits, round the stadium, and were now content to come last in race after race. The Gindiri boy took a fifth place in the hurdles. The Kuru boy came third in the javelin. To all intents and purposes the match was between the Eastern Ibo and the Yorubas from the Western Region.

I spent most of the meeting searching restlessly for a vantage-point. Eventually I found it, at the top of an observation tower built for the use of the Nigerian Broadcasting Corporation, and which provided note merely a view of the whole track but a bird's-eye view of all Enugu, the railway yards behind me, and in front the corrugated-iron roofs, and two miles beyond the steep forested hills down which we had driven the day before.

We had given Clement his instructions. Nobody had given him any advice. A first lap in sixty-five seconds, two in seventy, and the last as fast as possible, with the final effort to begin in the back straight. This time there was a Nigerian record at stake.

There were ten runners, far too many for a fast race. They pressed shoulder to shoulder along the starting-line, Clement on the outside. He would lose yards on the first bend, but at least it minimised the chances of falling in the press. There was the usual appalling silence while they came under starters' orders. The runners waited. I felt sick with apprehension. On such occasions I always longed to be anywhere, absolutely anywhere else at all. In an access of devotion I muttered a prayer for calmness. Success was now Clement's affair.

The pistol fired and the line of runners sprang forward. It was a fast pace. Clement was to the rear, on the outside, forced to run yards wide on the bend, adding measurably to the distance he had to run. In the front a singlet caught my eye. The Waka boy had gone into the lead. Well ahead of the field once more, he was running just as he had run at Kaduna. The ground was quiet. The runners paced steadily through the first lap. Clement disappeared from my view on the near straight, behind some urchins who clung to the railings at the top of the tower. He was still to the rear of the field, but running exactly to time. The field remained static during the second lap, the positions of the runners unchanged. As they passed under the observation tower Clement was still on time despite having run wide on all the bends. Now the pattern was changing. The Waka boy, tiring more quickly this time, was falling back appreciably. A steady realignment was taking place. A figure in white was moving through the crowd of runners toward the front. Clement, more gradually, was changing places with the two runners inside him. Seen from the tower the changing formation of the runners as they came into the third lap was like that of a slow, obscure dance, working itself out to the steady rhythm of the athletes' feet. Clement disappeared from my sight in the near straight, once more, still running exactly to time. The bell clanged, and the runners were suddenly charged with a new intensity. Silently the figure in white, a Lagos boy, began to move forward at a faster pace. Behind them there was a quickening, as runners shifted their places in the pattern. Clement still moved steadily, now about fourth, still fairly wide on the bend, maintaining his distance from the flying pace of the leader. He came into the back straight. Now his figure also took on a new intensity. The level of excitement was rising as Clement bore down on the two runners immediately in front. He was second to the bend. The crowd, once quiet, now shouted encouragement and warning. The leader, clearly aware of a challenge, dared not look round to gauge it. Both were strong runners and though both were now running at the limit of their endurance, neither showed any break in their pace nor their power. Clement, a couple of yards behind, was running wide on the bend. He came into the straight, pulling up to the Lagos boy's shoulder, their legs flashing beside each other, disorientated in their rhythm. Then they disappeared from my view. Howling encouragement, a useless performance at that distance, I pushed my way across the tower. The two figures reappeared before the tape, shoulder to shoulder, legs and arms flailing. The tape broke. There was no doubt. Clement had won. Instinctively I clicked the stop watch. There was no doubt, either, that four minutes thirty point one seconds set a new Nigerian schoolboy record. Clement freewheeled off the track. I clambered down from the tower. My ears were singing; my arms and hands trembled.

Lucas had yet to take part in the high jump. The meeting was running late. It was the fag end of the match, and the Northern team was already thinking of its train home. When the jumpers at last assembled there was a storm threatening and a stiff breeze was blowing in smuts from the neighbouring goods yard. The air was growing heavy, for night and the storm clouds were approaching together. Lucas, small and wiry, only five feet seven inches high, was dwarfed by his tall, slenderly built Southern competitors, many of them over six feet, all equipped with jumping shoes. As the light worsened the judges made haste to put up the bar two inches at a time, not the best way of carrying out a jumping competition. The bar rapidly reached six feet. Once more Lucas was equal to it. To my surprise I realised that he had not so far touched the bar. Even the Ibo crowd applauded his slight, unequipped figure. Six foot two was too much. One after another in the gathering dusk the athletes jumped and fell. On the third attempt four got over. Lucas was one of them. The bar went to six foot three inches. The sky was now threatening and overcast. The breeze stiffened and an increasing shower of smuts blew into the field. Only one boy succeeded at that height. There followed the elaborate process of working out who came next from the dead heat. Lucas had fewest falls. He was second. The thunder rumbled in the distance. The North had been thrashed. That hardly mattered. Our school of 180 boys had provided that region of twenty-eight million with its only first and second places. We got back to the car as the storm burst. It was Sunday. I still had to go to Mass. Having totted up how long it was since I had swigged a bottle of orangeade, I went to Communion. Somebody deserved to be thanked. Outside all Enugu dissolved in the tempest. Rain scattered through the open brickwork of the cathedral. Lightning flashed horrendously over the city, and in the dark the surface of the land outside the cathedral was a flood of black water fitfully illuminated by the storm.

GLIMPSES OF AN AFRICAN CHILDHOOD

PART THREE

GLIMPSES OF AN AFRICAN
CHILDHOOD

14
Kagoro and Balang

Through their writing and through the preparation of the school magazine we were beginning to gain some insight into the boys' lives. Our family life had brought us into closer contact with a few of the boys. Some we knew in our home, the others in the classroom and in the school compound. Yet we were far from appreciating what their experience and upbringing really was. We could only compare it with our own childhood, and with that of our children, now two in number, and growing from babyhood into fat self-confident toddlers, friendly, secure, and a little spoilt.

In terms of that experience what our pupils had known was incomprehensible. We saw what our boys must have been whenever we went to Kuru. This was the nearest Birom village, about two miles off, in the shadow of the hills, one of them sacred, across which the storms came in the rainy season. We went there once or twice a week to buy eggs. An enterprising member of the chiefly family ran a chicken farm next to the chief's compound, with hens of European stock which laid eggs of European size and flavour. Each week we saw the children of the village in the dusty clearing in front of the chief's house. Our own children would peer curiously through the car windows. They, in the dust outside, would stare back. Sometimes a little boy would be encouraged by one of his friends to touch Nicholas's white skin.

Once I looked a little harder. There was a girl of seven, perhaps, with a baby brother tied to her back with a cloth, three four-year-old boys, and two of six or seven in torn khaki shorts. The rest were naked. They were, all of these children, more or less sick or distorted. Their eyes were sore and bloodshot and around them the flies settled. Their bellies were all swollen, their legs thin as sticks.

Two of the boys had a protuberant blob of flesh where their navel should have been, umbilical hernia, the result of crude midwifery. There were sores on the girl's legs, a filthy bandage on the baby's fingers. The oldest boy was half blind, his face disfigured by small-pox scars.

For once, my normal indifference pierced, I was appalled. What, I suddenly thought, if these had been our children, filthy, naked, and diseased, standing in the dust. The idea was insupportable. How could children, who might have been my children, stand so neglected. Yet this was how most of the boys I taught had once been. Until I could understand more about their experience and upbringing, and the marks, physical and mental, this had left, I could never expect to understand their behaviour and attitudes in the school.

It was as a history master that I first gained any direct contact with the environment from which the boys came. I had always wished to explore the Kagoro Massif, a huge platform lifted up from the continental bedrock of Africa, whose edge marches for twenty miles along the road to Kafanchan. It rises precipitously over the high forest until in Jemaa emirate the forest opens out into the plains which were the prey of Fulani slave raiders sixty years ago, and here, above Kagoro village, the edge of the Massif rises to a peak from which the rock falls, sheer, polished granite, a thousand feet, vertically to the plain.

The Kagoro people revere the Massif. To them it is simply 'the rock'. Their ancestors had lived there, and on it they had preserved their freedom. They still hunt there. Benedict in one of his essays, spoke of an enchanted tree somewhere among its boulders, whose fruit, foliage and branches were luminous in the dusk and whose fragrance filled the air around. I remembered the first line of Darley's poem

Oh blest, unfabled, Incense tree

According to him it had already exacted one involuntary sacrifice. In the compound at Kafanchan were two graves, one of which was of a young Englishman who had gone with his wife, without any local guide, on to the rock, according to Benedict, to seek this tree. The man fell and the girl had been left all night with her husband's corpse till she was rescued in the morning, all but out of her mind.

The rock was a fortress where traces of the past might well be preserved long after they had been erased from the plains below. I arranged with Benedict, Hyacinth, and Andrew Gwaza, another Kagoro, to take me to the top along with an Irish friend who was teaching at Kafanchan. Two Kagoro farmers went with us as guides, accompanied by their dogs and carrying bows and arrows. They were gaunt figures, lean and gristly. They and their equipment seemed much weathered, their shorts grey and tattered, their cloaks, greasy with age and use, made out of a blanket and thrown over one shoulder; their bows were unpretentious and much handled strips of brown wood, their slender arrows, with their black, delicately barbed steel heads, were annointed with a trace of venom. Their animals were vicious half-fed mongrels of the type which lurk about the huts of any pagan village, but they took on a new appearance on the mountainside where they appeared spare efficient creatures, threading their way purposefully through the long grass, loping easily ahead over the rocks, ranging to the side of the hunters, quiet and alert.

There is an easy way up the rock. I followed it the next time. It is a well-trodden pathway, west of the peak, which winds up the hillside. Half-way to the top you can even rest in the shade where a stream splashes under some rocks into a pool of clear, fresh water overhung by bushes. On the sand and shining pebbles vivid scarlet-winged dragonflies settle, then dart to and fro over the pool. Instead we went eastward over a plank bridge across a torrent rushing from the hills, past the little plots behind the village, beneath the brown-barked iroqo trees, to the foot of the rock which rose straight up before us, blocking out the early morning sky.

'Come,' said Andrew, 'you can see where the people used to go and hide when the Fulani came.'

Although the foot of the rock was green and grass-covered, huge outcrops of granite thrust out of the ground and to one of these in which there was an insignificant fissure Andrew led us.

We squeezed into a crevice so narrow that we could touch both walls with outstretched hands. It was cool and damp and the ripple marks in the sand on which we stood showed where the rain water had washed down the previous day. The narrow floor sloped steeply upwards. The roof was invisible above our heads.

A clatter of rocks further up showed where our guides were already moving ahead. A match struck and glowed in the darkness. They had gathered a bundle of long-dried plants, rather like rushes, and one of these was being lit. It was held downwards and a smoky yellow flame threw shadows on the walls. We scrambled upwards after it.

'There is a wall here. We must climb it.'

The yellow flame was guttering above our heads. We heaved ourselves up till beyond the wall the crevice widened into a cavern. The yellow light fell only indistinctly on distant walls. There was a slight echo and a feeling of emptiness in the dark around us.

'You see that the whole village could get in here. The women and children would sometimes stay in here for a whole week.' It was damp and cold, the floor a litter of hidden rock clammy to the touch. The flame guttered out, and as another taper was lit, I tried to envisage what it had been like to wait with the children in the pitch dark, while outside the raiders were searching to take the women into captivity and to murder the babies.

'It will be a bit difficult now, sir,' said Andrew, 'but do not mind, for I will help you.'

We moved upwards out of the cavern till we reached a sort of funnel which rose above our heads. A circle of light, fringed with grass, was thirty feet up and from it the sunlight flowed down on to jumbled grey rocks, while the darker recesses of the cave still continued ominously upwards. The guides and Benedict climbed up to a ledge just short of the exit, then swung their way out and upward into the daylight. With much less ease I also reached the ledge, then, as I nervously placed my hands and feet in position, I was seized by the arms and hauled out to land breathless in the dazzling sunshine on the grassy hillside which sloped away beneath us.

By midday we were over the brow of the rock and into a

shallow valley on the top where forestry workers were preparing to plant trees. Almost the first object I saw in this inaccessible part of West Africa was an umbrella, jammed point foremost into the ground. The top of the massif was level, slightly undulating, composed of nuggety red laterite scantily concealed by thin grass on which some Fulani cattle grazed in the distance. At the skyline the grassland ended abruptly, and where it dipped another far-distant horizon was revealed at the edge of the plain below. Kagoro village had once stood up there. Now all you could identify were the hearthstones where the huts had once stood.

We were taken to another hole in the ground. 'This,' said Andrew, 'is where my people still come to get the white clay which they paint on their faces in the festivals. They have done it for many years. You can see that the hole goes far into the ground.'

We went back, straggling in a long line, toward the edge of the massif till we reached the granite again. To the left, about half a mile away, a terrible smooth shoulder of rock fell an infinite distance to the forests below. We were close enough to see the turf which edged its summit, and the occasional tuft of grass lodging imperfections in its otherwise flawless descent.

We stood among the tumbled slabs at the back of the peak itself. The top appeared to be a pyramid of rock rising from the neighbouring outcrops, and surmounted by a boulder the size of a large house. Our guides walked nonchalantly over the rock face of the pyramid, disregarding a forty-five degree slope which dropped sharply to a hundred-foot fall. With Hyacinth's gentle encouragement I averted my eyes and took the brief jump across a narrow chasm on to the slope which led to the top, then hunched my way across the crystalline granite to the narrow ledge which ran around the boulder crowning the summit. Once there I straightened up and walked round to join the rest of the party seated in a row at the top of the peak. Before our feet the rock fell sharply away, and the hillside beneath was invisible. A murmur of conversation spread along the ledge.

'See down there, the mission compound. You can see right down inside it, inside the walls.'

'There—see the college.'

'The road goes straight to Kafanchan.' We looked down on the plain. 'That is where I live, sir,' said Hyacinth. 'That is the Kaje country, where the hills rise.' The land rose slightly beyond Kagoro.

We sat there quietly for about a quarter of an hour before the guides and Benedict found what they claimed was an easier way down, across another little chasm, and then down a rocky valley toward the village. Half-way down one of the dogs saw something. He made no sound, simply checked suddenly, then moved forward eagerly to the edge of a rock and froze there with one paw raised and his narrow muzzle pointing. The guides also froze, then edged forward across the rocks to the side of the valley, stringing their bows and fingering their arrows into place as the dogs sidled alertly ahead of them.

'There are leopard here,' said Hyacinth. 'When my father was a young man he met one here by himself, and he killed it with his spear.'

'If you meet a leopard and you have no weapon, you know,' said Andrew, 'you must hold it by the tail. It has so many ribs it cannot twist its backbone round to bite you.'

'What happens then?'

'Oh, you shout. If you shout long enough there will always be someone who will come.'

'Then he must stab it in the stomach. That is the best way to kill a leopard, as my father did.'

'Does he still have the skin?'

'Yes, but the head had to be given to the chief.'

Whatever it was that the dog had noticed had now escaped and we continued down the hill.

'Our soldiers would come here in the old days,' said Benedict. 'They would hide here and shoot arrows at the Fulani.' The only way along the valley here went through a passage between two high outcrops of rock whose vertical walls were only six feet apart. The guides were talking to Benedict.

'We will go up here,' said Benedict. 'Would you like to see a place where our soldiers hid in the old days?' On one side of the valley the rocks reared, one above the other. The lowest, obscured by the thick tentacles of some creeping plant, sloped upward like a ramp. We thrashed our way up through the vegetation to the top of the ramp, thirty feet above the valley floor, which was over-shadowed by a huge projecting outcrop. Underneath it was another cave. Out of the floor rose a rounded shelf of rock on which, in the darkness, could be made out the remains of two huts that looked as if they had once been granaries. The place was dry and capacious. The end nearest to us seemed once to have been open, but was now filled up with clay. It seemed as if the cave had extended further into the hillside, for to the side of the great over-hanging outcrop there was a small hole sheltered by some trees. Through it the light shone on to a floor twenty or thirty feet below us. There were times when the whole hill appeared to be hollow. Benedict had said that the whole tribe could disappear underground when the occasion required.

It would have been a nasty place to fight in. Near the eastern frontier of Nigeria the British had once had to do so in a similar place. A group of pagan Chibbuk, accused of raiding the trade paths, had withdrawn to such an outcrop riddled with caves and subterranean passages. A company of Nigerian infantry had had to follow them in and for a week a battle had gone on in the dark. Had the British commander not found the source of the tribesmen's water, there is no reason why it should ever have ended. It cost ten dead soldiers. Forty Chibbuk corpses were pulled out of the gloomy passageways. Others must have remained uncounted inside the hill's recesses.

Eventually I had enough material to give a few lessons to the third and fourth year on their local history. For these lessons, too, we had to search the countryside. We tried to use objects such as the prehistoric stone implements from Jos Museum or Birom weapons and tools from Vwang.

We made lessons on the use of fire, using two primitive methods of firelighting common on the Plateau. The most usual was to strike flint or quartz on steel or, if you had the skill and the steel, to strike two pieces of quartz together. The spark would then ignite an oily cotton substance gained from the interior of the orange fruit of a small palm which grew in the Birom villages. Caught under the thumb which holds the striking block, this would catch the spark, smoulder, and could then be used to light dry grass.

More elaborate and ritually far more significant was the firestick, which is the method Boy Scouts are supposed to know about. A bamboo stick is revolved against a notch cut in a piece of soft, fibrous wood, and the resulting friction lights the fire. A bow is sometimes used in the Lowland Division to act as a drill, but I did not see this equipment. The process is a gruelling one which takes an expert five minutes' hard work. A team of six sturdy youths taking it in turn would need twenty minutes, and still bore a hole right through the wood without success. The worker is bound to be soaked in perspiration before the acrid smell of burning strikes the nostrils, and smoke, first in a wisp, and then in a steady stream, curls up from the spinning stick.

The Birom use a firestick for all ritual occasions, lighting the first fire for a new compound, starting the fires for a hunt (the white stone where this had once taken place could be seen north of the crag opposite the college, with a deep groove worn in it by the stick over many years) or for the reconciliation of friends, who manipulate the stick together. Its use has a curious story of origin. The Birom boy who first learnt to use it did so from the little muturu cows that were once kept in stone kraals on the hills round Vom. These creatures are believed to be the first species of cattle introduced to tropical Africa and have existed so long further to the south that they have acquired immunity to the tsetse fly. The muturu cows on the Plateau do not possess this immunity, perhaps because they have been brought up from the south so long ago that they have lost it again. These dwarf cows taught the herd boy the trick and told him to keep it a secret. Unfortunately for him his family returned home one evening to discover him using the firestick. They forced him to teach them. The dwarf cows smelt the smoke, and in their anger tore the boy to pieces and flung them into the bush, where they changed into dwarf buffalo. I assume the legend refers to some form of culture contact in the past, and that one of the cultures involved was associated with both the dwarf cow and the use of the firestick. I have seen it stated that the firestick is a method of firelighting peculiar to the forests, and if this is so the technique presumably is connected with some ancient migration from the south to mingle with earlier settlers on the Plateau.

Another of our more active performances was the work on the hunter-gatherers, those people who lived a life midway between that of a hunter and a farmer, supplementing their hunting by gathering whatever they could of the other resources of the countryside. This way of life is still followed, of course, by a few remote pygmy and bushman tribes in parts of Central and Southern Africa, while Jerome Magaje claimed that a group of his people, the Ninzam, had been found living in exactly the same way a few years before in forests south of the Plateau.

In the evening, after the lesson, I would send the whole class out to gather anything that might remotely have been of use to hunters on the move who needed to use every available resource in order to survive. A group went down to the stream, more went up into the hills, others out into the plain. They would come back an hour later with leaves, branches, fruit, and seeds. This was for building roofs, that making thorn fences, this for a purge, that for a poultice; these seeds could be boiled down for a poison; those pods provided oil for cooking, and so it went on. The greatest discovery had a little escort round it. The smallest boy in one form, Alphonsus Lucas, with a face like Flopsy Bunny and an excessive willingness to please, held, stretched out before him on the end of a long stick, a branch with a number of objects which might have been seed pods. Each was rather larger than a horse chestnut, and each appeared to be covered in tawny mottled fur. They looked like tiny pouches of leopard skin. 'Do not touch, sir. It is too poisonous.'

With each form we used to chart the names of each object in each of the languages on a map, on the assumption that there ought to be a pattern. A rather vague picture seemed to materialise, by which the Birom seemed to be associated with Pankshin and the hilly areas of Lowland by their terms for some of the trees and poisons. On the other hand, a different terminology, that for the chiefly title 'Gwom' used by the Birom, seemed to associate with a priestly term, 'Aegwan', used by the Katab round Kagoro.

It became my ambition to find out more about these fragmented and mysterious peoples of the Plateau, among whose traditions might lie the clues to much Nigerian history. The Prefect bundled us, protesting bitterly, out of Nigeria before I came near to realising this ambition. I have but one minute contribution to make.

It concerns the people of Balang, the centre of a small group of villages in the Pankshin hills. The only son of this village to receive a secondary education was Gregory Golu, who wrote an essay in which he said that they made stone tools at the beginning of each harvest. There are a few people in some of the remote places of the world who still do this, and very few have ever seen it done. I reported the matter to a friend in Jos Museum, who went down by Landrover the 120 miles to Pankshin, taking with him Gregory and Clement Sati, and came back at the end of the day with two sheets of notes, and the news that no one was prepared to go any further and make any knives for him until after the harvest a month later. Then he went to East Africa and I took over. The first time I went down to negotiate, or rather to let Gregory, Clement, and Eugenus Tokzaka, another local Angas, do the negotiating, while I went back to Pankshin and ate sandwiches. I collected the boys after lunch, the arrangements having been made.

I came back at the end of term with a photographer from Jos Museum and a tape-recorder, and accompanied by Clement and Eugenus. Gregory had already gone home and would be waiting to welcome us. Just before it reaches Pankshin the road turns off towards Lowland. It dives sharply over the edge of an escarpment, winding down towards Kabwir and the country of the Lowland Angas. Half-way down we parked the car. The hills rose on either side of the road, rocky and scantily covered with small trees. There was no sign of path, settlement or human life.

Eugenus led the way, and pushed through knee-length grass for about a hundred yards till we reached something like a rabbit track which wandered around the stones and rocks that made up most of the subsoil.

> pausing to throw backward a last view
> O'er the safe road, 'twas gone; . . .

The road had disappeared from sight almost as soon as we left it, and with it went a European's most common view of Nigeria. The roads often discipline what he sees and give him a misleading sense of having subdued a territory, when, instead, it has more often confined him from movement beyond its gutters, and the compounds and installations it serves.

We followed the path over a rocky spur and then into a small, steep-sided valley down which fell a little stream.

> a sudden little river . . .

The path chose a place where the water fell less sharply. It flowed into a pool, and it was possible with a little exertion to pick your way across dryshod.

Eugenus trotted up beside me as we made our way along the side of the valley. 'You see that stream there, sir,' he said eagerly, 'if there comes a thunderstorm up in the hills there above, the water comes down so heavily, and so quick. It is too dangerous. Even me, sir, it almost drowned last June. It was during that time of the census, and I was coming late, and because it was dark I came to cross, when the water catched me. It came right up to here.' He touched his neck. 'I lost my feet. If not for this bag I think I must have died.' He patted the large green plastic satchel with the federal badge on the flap with which the census-takers had been equipped. 'It seemed to float, and I caught it, and I just came to the side. It is lucky, I think, that I was not dead.'

> . . . so petty yet so spiteful.

We climbed up the side of the valley. We could hear the stream gushing through the rocks about fifty feet below.

'There,' said Eugenus, 'is the bridge. Can you see, sir?'

It was quite difficult to see, since it consisted of no more than a strip of concrete about six feet wide, with no balustrade or central support, spanning the little gorge, which was about twenty yards wide at that point. It was surprisingly high above the water, which was just visible as it flashed among the rocks beneath. I wondered how high the stream must reach in spate, when the flood roared down the hillsides after a storm.

'The people were asking for that for many years, sir. More than ten. Every rains people were getting drowned, and when it was raining properly no one could even cross for weeks. No one whatever could get to Pankshin. Each year people would drown. It was six who drowned three years ago, sometimes four in a year, sometimes more.'

Two women trotted across with baskets on their heads. This was what independence really meant, I supposed, to these little villages, a thin strip of reinforced concrete costing, perhaps, £300 for which the D.O. up at Pankshin had not been able to allocate the money for reasons of economy stretching far back through Kaduna to colonial policy in London. Another woman trotted across the bridge, followed by a small naked child, about seven years old, with a basket on its head.

The bridge disappeared to the right as we followed an increasing stream of people up the little path. A murmur of voices could be heard in the distance.

A Nigerian Road

The lorry bounces and grumbles in a cloud of red dust over the corrugated road, across the crude wooden culverts. Its gears grind as it sways over the pass to Kagoro. A foot from the off-side mudguard the ground drops away to the forest, which stretches to the horizon. Above your head climbs the rocky hillside. A flight of dark green hornbills swoops across the road behind you, rising and falling in undulated flight. A monkey flits out of the bush. The battered lorries with their wooden superstructures, the second-hand cars and dented mini-buses could carry you almost anywhere in Plateau Province for ten shillings. For a couple of pounds you could reach the frontiers of Nigeria.

'Soon we shall come to the market,' explained Eugenus. 'Every Saturday it is held here. There will be one further up tomorrow. Each village has a market on the same day each week. On Fridays is the one in Pankshin. They sell a lot of potatoes there.' The murmur grew louder and quite soon, where the hillside levelled out, there was a dusty space among the trees which covered the hills. It was full of people, some squatting round the edge, with little piles of peppers, or yams, or baskets of grain, or rows of small pots, or oddments from Pankshin. Others moved about with baskets on their heads. Others stood or squatted, examining, bargaining, arguing, questioning, gossiping. There was a sharp suggestion of haggling in the air. People were constantly coming and going to and from the group.

As we left the market-place behind us, we were now passed by men and women, particularly women, with baskets on their heads, and sometimes with a child or two trotting over the stones behind them. Fists were raised in greeting, and the Angas formulae of welcome passed backwards and forwards. Curious heads were turned as we passed.

'They do not often see a European up here, do they?' I asked.

'Father O'Connell came here. I don't think anyone else has,' said Eugenus, 'maybe the parish priest, but a long time ago. Perhaps the D.O. once.'

We followed the path along the terraced hillside. Above us, through the trees, there rose to a wall of brown rock the crags at the top of the hills, the haunt of leopard and baboon. Below it every inch of ground was guarded by the terrace walls which followed the contours, stepping below us to the bottom of the valley, visible through the trees, rising on the other side. Here, where the slope was steep, each terrace was about two feet high, holding back a strip of hard yellow earth, apparently without humus content.

'There are men who know how to repair these walls. Every two or three years they will come and put back the stones which have fallen. If not, the walls must come down. Nobody knows how old they are, not the oldest man even. They have always been here.'

Some of the terraces had been left fallow that year. It seemed impossible that any living organism should subsist on that harsh ground, but in patches of apparently sterile soil strange flowers would explode in extravagant colours, bright orange, vivid scarlet, purple, maroon. In one of the fields below us, among the acha, a pole stood in the ground. Tied to it was a strange polished piece of wood like a deer's antler.

'What is that?'

'The farmer's crops are ripe. Soon he will harvest them. That is his ju-ju. He puts it there so that people will know, and will not touch his crops. There are other ju-jus that look after some of the trees.'

'Are many of them guarded like this?'

'Oh yes. You will see some with a broad leaf, which we use for making roofs. We must not touch it till a particular time of the year. The ju-ju forbids it. All the trees that are of use are guarded.'

It was cool and peaceful as we walked among the trees, between whose light foliage the sun filtered, much as it does through olive trees in the Mediterranean. It was a gentle contrast with the harsh uncompromising sunlight of the high Plateau. The hills, in an area regarded as one of the most primitive in Nigeria, seemed quiet and harmonious. The ju-ju in the field and the minute control that was exercised over every stone and every tree suggested a quite religious harmony between human society, nature, and the super-natural forces underlying both.

We were approaching the edge of the hills, and ahead, between the trees, and beyond the terraces, glimpses of Lowland opened out. Far away a shower was hovering over the green plain, trailing shafts of grey across the fields.

We reached Balang. There was Gregory. He was the nephew of the headman, and Gregory had dressed in his very best to welcome his visitors and to impress his seniors. He wore tight jeans, held about the waist by a chrome buckle with the legend 'Wild West'. He wore a check shirt, an open velvet waistcoat, and a little embroidered smoking cap on the back of his head. His shoes were black and highly polished, 'winkle-pickers' in England, 'pin-toes' in Nigeria. They were rather high-heeled.

He shook hands with all of us, Clement, Eugenus, the photographer, and myself, and we sat down in his uncle's compound. It was a complex of small mud-walled thatched round huts, granaries, and storehouses, which stood to one side of an open compound looking toward the Lowlands. Some baulks of timber lay about, mortars and chopping blocks, and some large stones were distributed about the edge of the compound and in a circle at one corner. A pleasant breeze blew through the place. The smooth walls of the huts were well maintained, and the mud floor of the courtyard swept free of rubbish.

The cleanliness and order, not just of the compound but of all that I had seen, surprised me. The Birom settlements near Jos were usually untidy, squalid places. Their inhabitants were normally dismissed as 'filthy'. One of the authorities on their habits related that a compound was normally built with enough sleeping huts for the inhabitants to abandon them as they became verminous. I had no reason to expect anything different in Pankshin. Clement himself, on one occasion, had said that he was hopeful of eradicating the last of the fleas from his pants. That had been at school a year back. I anticipated both body vermin and a degree of filth as inseparable from farming life on the Plateau, just as it had once been in rural England. But Pankshin Division seemed to be clean, fresh, and well ordered. I was reminded that Nigerians are more in the habit of regarding Englishmen as filthy. 'We,' Gabriel Nongo had observed to me, 'wash our hands before all our meals. We bathe every day, and do it in the stream. We oil ourselves. Unlike Europeans, we are clean.' I had recollected then how too infrequent were our baths at that time in the little concrete enclosure open to the winds that served as our bathroom. I had been suitably chastened.

We had lunch first of all. I handed round sandwiches and a couple of bottles of beer. Half a dozen small children appeared shyly behind us. They were quite naked, though one of the little girls wore a thin yellow bracelet. Clement, to whom I handed over a packet of biscuits, gave one to each of them, with an air of great liberality. They nibbled these unaccustomed objects curiously.

Gregory and his father tried out the tape-recorder. The photographer set up his tripod.

Then the old men assembled, the heads of the households which belonged to Balang. There were about fifteen. Two or three appeared not to have come, regarding it as a waste of valuable harvest-time. Their age was impossible to tell, for all were lean, and all their faces were bony, scarred, and grizzled. Their dress was almost identical: shorts, a blanket draped over one shoulder, a satchel hanging beneath it, a small knife at the waist, a floppy cap on their head, their feet bare and dusty. All of them bore the priestly title 'Ndekum' and had the responsibility for manufacturing the stone tools.

Gregory's uncle stood in the centre of the compound. His beginning was rather ceremonious, a statement of credentials, in which he pointed out that he was about to describe the village traditions, with the presence of the senior men of the community as proof of their validity. Then the account began. At the end I played it back piece by piece, and Gregory translated. Later he was to transcribe both the original Angas and its translation.

The account began as follows:

In the whole of the village of Balang of which I am the head, we have commandments handed down to us by our ancestors. The greatest of all of those which concern food production, and therefore our lives, is the commandment to use stone knives. It is believed by all farmers in this village that as a rule anyone who uses a metal knife instead of a stone one for reaping his dawa or his acha is violating a great rule. Nowadays the punishment for any man or woman who disobeys this rule is to bring three goats and a big basket of dawa or acha to be offered to Furlong, the god of harvest, who introduced the knowledge of the stone knife. But in the old days when the slave trade was in progress they were enslaved. Furlong was the oldest of all our ancestors, and for his bravery during the wars, and his intelligence, we worshipped him as our god. All these rules or commandments respecting prosperity and health depend upon him. He is believed to send his messengers, Kower, Wong, Moriok, Malu and Kumpel, whom no woman or uncircumcised boy is allowed to see. These stones are prepared by these Ndekums whom you see have come to demonstrate how they are made to you, three weeks before the harvest starts. These Ndekums and myself are the only people allowed to speak to Furlong and his messengers whose names we have mentioned before.

We asked him why Furlong had forbidden the use of metal knives.

'Furlong said that we should not use them, because if we did so our produce and our lives would be in danger. Furlong is, as we know, our greatest teacher, and cannot make a mistake.'

'Where did Furlong come from?'

'Furlong, as we know well, was from a place called Jim, and from Jim he settled at Gi, and lastly at Balang, our village, of which he is the founder.'

'Were there people at Balang when he came?'

'No, there were no people when he came. He brought with him his family and some slaves.'

'Why did he leave Jim to come here?'

'Well, being an ambitious and strong teacher, with intelligence, he wanted to found a kingdom.'

'Which of you, the Ndekums, saw Furlong in his youth?'

'None of us here knew him. Even our grandfathers never caught sight of him. We all in Balang, with the exception of Christians, pray and beg our daily bread from Furlong.'

'Which of the two knives existed first?'

'The stone knive was the first to be introduced. The metal knife was introduced later, but not by Furlong the god. The knowledge of the metal knife was introduced by some slaves captured during the wars. These slaves taught us the knowledge of iron smelting. The iron was dug from the ground in combination with a certain soil we call Kurci, and then the iron is extracted from the soil, and is then made into shape. From this iron smelting we were able to make knifes, hoes, and spears. Perhaps the reason for not respecting the metal knife as much as the stone one is due to the simple fact that it was introduced by a slave, and not by one of our own people. But the definite reason is not known to us.'

'Do you still smelt iron in this village?'

'Yes, it is practised.'

'Where else beside Balang is the stone knife used, and where else are the commandments of Furlong obeyed?'

'Well, is not my business to know what others do about their own affairs, for I am only concerned with my own village.'

I now had a perfectly valid historical document, authenticated by the witness of the fifteen old men whose families it concerned. What significance it had was quite impossible to tell. Hundreds of similar documents needed to be collected and checked before anything could be deduced. The reference seems to be to a cult based on the use of stone, which may well have antedated all later iron-using cultures on the Plateau. I also suspect that this cult may be related to the use of rock gongs, pieces of rock which give out a musical note when struck, and which appear to have been connected with fertility cults not only on the Plateau but also in other parts of Africa and in Europe. The name 'Balang' is perhaps an example of a village name taken from the sound given out by a rock gong. I was informed that Furlong's shrine was under a rock, at which rituals took place. I wondered afterwards whether this might not be a rock gong. Had I asked I doubt if I would have been told.

We saw the Ndekums make the tools. The process was crudity itself. A piece of white quartz was produced and flung on the ground, where it shattered. A few triangular fragments were selected and put on one side. One of the large pieces was knocked a couple more times, and a few more suitable fragments were selected. Stone Age man had to go to surprisingly little trouble to make his tools, and the results were hardly distinguishable from any other chance fragments.

Bob Soper from Jos Museum had already understood that these tools were manufactured a couple of weeks before the harvest was due to begin, and issued by the basketful to the heads of each compound. They also appeared to have an important part to play in sacrifice to the god Kumpell, who is credited with a far larger place in the Angas pantheon than this tradition suggests. Small quartz knives are also used to mark the scarifications that decorate the faces of most Angas. The knives were used only for about three weeks. Then the chief Ndekum would announce that iron knives might be used from his own compound high up on the hillside, and the news would be spread from compound to compound by men shouting from the top of the cediya trees which grew in each of them.

There were still many questions I would have liked to ask. It was not clear who became a Ndekum, except that most of the older compound heads had this position. Nor had I seen the shrine. Nor did I know anything like enough about Furlong, and his origins, or about his successors. But I appeared to have obtained all the information Gregory's uncle seemed to think I ought to receive. We prepared to go.

I gave the Ndekums fifteen shillings for their work. As far as I had been able to gather from Eugenus this was roughly what they needed to compensate them for their time. 'Was it enough?' I asked Clement later.

'Yes,' he said. 'I think it was more than they expected. They were pleased.'

We left, crunching over the stones. Eugenus carried by the legs the fowl which was the present given to most visitors to these little compounds. There were no more women passing to market now; just the occasional young man, usually dressed in shorts and a shirt, carrying a blanket and a bag. 'They are coming back from work in the mines,' Gregory explained.

There was one more event. As we came near the market a distant horn sounded through the trees. Somebody was singing. Half a mile away a group of young men were dancing toward us. They were fine muscular fellows, dancing and laughing. On their ankles they wore iron bracelets which clattered as they stamped their feet. Around their waists were skins, delicately patterned. Over their shoulders were slung satchels, woven and embroidered. Around their bodies were furs and skins. In their hair were feathers and ostrich plumes. They carried small drums under their arms, and one had a twisted buffalo horn through which he blew, from time to time, a long-drawn-out bellowing sound. They gyrated, stamped and sang.

'What are they?' I asked Clement.

'They come from a village on the edge of the plain. They are celebrating.'

'What are they celebrating?'

'Their harvest is in and they are happy. They have come to this village to celebrate.'

The dancers caught up with us; they danced around us, the horn braying in our ears. One of them saw Clement. There was a whoop of recognition, and the two of them put their arms around each other and danced.

'Do you know him, Clement?'

'Yes, he is my brother,' Clement said, a little breathlessly. 'They come from my village.'

We all tramped along the path together, Clement and his brother talking and shouting, the rest dancing round them. There was a heavy scent of perspiration and beer. We were approaching the market-place.

'Would they mind if I gave them a shilling to get some beer with?' I asked cautiously.

'No,' said Clement, 'I believe they would be happy about it.'

I gave him the shilling, and he dashed ahead to give it to the leader with the horn. There was renewed noise. They danced round us once more, and then gyrated ahead of us up the path, the music gradually getting fainter.

When we reached the market the business of the day was over. The place was still full of people, but now the air was thick and drowsy with beer fumes. Voices were louder than in the morning, but now the keenness of bargaining and argument had evaporated. The atmosphere of the clearing among the trees was that of a bar-room half an hour before closing time, noisy, friendly, incoherent. The celebraters from Clement's village were in one corner. Around them a group of young men were already joining them in their dance. We left them. The noise gradually grew less as we wound our way down the valley by the stream, towards the car, and the road back to Vwang.

15
Notes on an African Upbringing

On the way to Balang I had, for a few hours, been admitted to the world from which the boys had come. The image of the sick children at Kuru was obscured. What I had seen at Kagoro and Balang, and glimpsed elsewhere, was an environment which, for all its dangers, was rich and deeply satisfying in its relationships and traditions. No wonder that the boys looked back to their childhood with such nostalgia. I returned to their essays with renewed interest and understanding.

On Friday evening during Sallah the Beri-beri beat the kalungu, a four-sided drum a yard long. When the boys hear it they come yelling and screaming to the chief's palace. The boys and girls stand side by side after shaking themselves in salutation. The kalungu is beaten by a stick with a bent head like a question mark. Round and round they dance, facing the drummer, then they all turn away at once like birds flying in the sky, the boys yelling and screaming at the top of their voices, and the girls shouting Onyayere songs and dancing all over the place.

 The Goemai play at tumbling. First a boy must learn to walk forty yards on his hands. Then he must run in front of the men, swing his legs in the sky over his head, and stand again on the ground.

> Come, come, let us swim,
> Let us have a little pleasure.
> When we've dived under water
> We'll see fish, fish, fish.
> Everyone will catch, catch, catch,
> Until he dies.
>
> Come, come, let us sing,
> Let us sing and have our pleasure.

It was, in so many ways, an idyllic childhood, lived out of doors, full of physical activity. As their people's most valued possessions, the boys had been cherished as very small children, the most important people in the tribe. They had been nursed at their mothers' breasts for the first two years of their lives, seldom rebuked, toddling unchecked, dusty, pot-bellied, and unclothed about their family compound, and then into the village outside.

I was never, however, allowed to reject completely my memory of those children standing in the dust at Kuru. The boys had grown up in the shadow of their environment.

'During the rainy season, when the farmers' supplies begin to finish, and because of the hard work during this period, most of them usually look hungry and thin. This appearance of weakness and thinness can best be observed in their children.'

Like the children at Kuru many of the boys had been marked at birth with umbilical hernia. The soggy cereal mash on which they had been weaned had stuffed out their bellies. The germs had festered in the excrement at the backs of their villages, and they had suffered sporadically from dysentery and diarrhoea. The flies had buzzed about their inflamed eyes. The food they touched had been infected with the spore of parasites they still carried with them: hook-worm, tape-worm, and ringworm. The streams that flowed by their villages had carried bilharzia and fularia. The mosquitoes had whined about their stuffy huts at night, and they had fallen feverish and anaemic with malaria. In the damp of the rains tuberculosis and pneumonia had bred, and in the dry season in their unventilated huts meningitis struck. Three out of every four children were said to die in the remote Plateau villages. The boys, like all Nigerians, were used to seeing children dying.

'The fact is, sir,' said Thomas Kaagnan with a broad grin, 'that if you lived at all, you lived till ninety. You see it is so from our old men. Not at all like today.'

Cherished as they were, their upbringing had been as unpredictably violent as their environment. A photograph in one of Meek's books about the pagan tribes of Northern Nigeria shows a Birom mother feeding her child. The baby is held almost upside down on her knees. With the fingers of her cupped hand she is stopping its nose, while into its gasping mouth she pours the distasteful acha gruel. The process is dying out, but small children still had to submit in many parts of Pankshin to the ordeal of scarification, performed with a sliver of quartz passed through flame. After a couple of years' undivided attention the boys' mothers had probably become pregnant once more. Her breasts were no longer available, and the children would have been abruptly weaned, and often violently rebuffed by their preoccupied mothers. For the rest of their lives the boys had had to move in a masculine society, and to form an integral part of it, learning the masculine skills of farming, hunting, and hut-building. Almost as soon as they had been able to walk they had been given hoes, for even at that age they had to work, and life was not too gentle for the learner.

When we went to farm my father brought a little hoe. First he held the hoe with two hands and farmed a ridge with it. Then he gave it to me and told me to hoe as he had done. I started to farm the ridge I had been given. I had done one foot and then I felt tired and looked up. My father left his portion and came to me. He told me that if I left my hoe again and stood up he would flog me. I tried again and then I was tired and looked up. Unluckily my father saw me and came towards me. I thought he was going to beat me and ran all the way home.

After the hoeing the boys had been taught other skills.

After the land had been dug I was nearly beaten by my father for scattering the seed all over the field. I was told that I had not scattered the seed in the right way. I should have taken the grain, and, after making a small hole in the ground, I should have put in the seeds.

As the grain ripens the children had to shout and sing in the fields to drive off the birds.

> Birds have eaten father's corn, ha oyi ye!
> Birds have eaten father's corn, ha oyi ye!
> Some are birds which have red beaks, ha oyi ye!
> Some are birds which have black beaks, ha oyi ye!
> Ndeng please go away.

> If you don't go away I'll shoot you with a pointed stick.
> If you don't go away I'll shoot you with a pointed metal rod.

A pointed metal rod, whom has that ever killed?
A pointed stick, whom has that ever killed?
Ha wo-we kwaklak!

Most families had possessed a few skinny sheep and goats.

When I was young I stayed with my uncle. Every day my work was to drive a flock of sheep to the forest so that they could eat grass. After a while my uncle bought a horse. It was white. It had large ears and a bushy tail. My uncle taught me how to cut grass for the horse before going with the sheep to the forest. After a short time my uncle taught me how to ride the horse.

Out in the fields with the other boys, watching the sheep or guarding the corn, the children had passed their time wrestling, swimming, or in snaring birds or hunting rats, which were welcomed as a useful addition to the family's diet. Around Akwanga they had constructed the little wigwams of grass and sticks that stand in the fields. They were insect traps, for some of the creatures that were caught inside could be eaten.

In the dry season the boys had gone with the older men in order to hunt bigger game. Sometimes they had gone on the great annual hunts when whole areas were surrounded with huntsmen, light was set to the dry grass, and the animals were driven by a wall of flame on to the spears of their attackers. These were dangerous affairs. One of our boys had seen a man clawed to death by a leopard. Another had been present when two young men were encircled by the flames and burnt to death within sight of their friends. Even the smallest children were expected to show considerable physical courage when out in the bush with their spear or their arrows.

When I was four, while I was creeping through the grass, I suddenly saw a baby leopard. I shot it in the eye, and when it did not fall I shot it in the stomach and it fell down and died. When the other animals in the forest heard the noise they ran away and hid themselves. When my brother heard the noise he was afraid and ran towards me. I showed him the leopard and he was amazed that a small boy like me should have killed him.

Though their life looking after the goats and sheep in the bush had been spent with the other boys, nevertheless the boys had grown up as part of an adult world, and their contribution to it, in their farming and their hunting, though small, had still been useful. For all that theirs had been a lowly position in the community. It had been dangerous to develop too close an attachment, even to the closest relation, for the boys had often been the possession not just of one couple, but of all the aunts, uncles, and grandparents on both sides.

When I was five years old I was taught how to aim with my bow and arrow. Because of my practice my father was pleased with me and carried me with him wherever he went. One day my uncle told him not to do so any more because people were jealous and wanted to poison me. My father was sad, but sent me to my uncle to preserve my life. I stayed with my uncle for two years. He was very wicked. He did not want me to play. He would beat me. Although my father was sorry for me he could not do anything for he did not want to quarrel with his brother. I worked so hard I forgot about my hunting.

The lowly position of the children had been impressed on them. Young children were sometimes obliged to accept the authority even of other children who happened to be a bit older than themselves.

In my village, Nassawara, when the maize is ready for harvesting, boys usually gather together and choose two or three of their number whom we usually call 'Ngyoh'. This is done because the boys sometimes steal the maize without their father's knowledge, at night, after supper. The 'Ngyoh' will cover their bodies with leaves so that no one can see or recognise them. After supper the boys will go to the bush and cover themselves with leaves. They disguise their voices and creeping behind the houses they will shout in unearthly voices that any boy who has stolen or given trouble should be given to them. If the father of a boy gives him to the 'Ngyoh', they will whip him till he says he will never steal again.

Sometimes authority had taken on the guise of the supernatural. Every inexplicable happening was ascribed to the work of spirits. At certain times and in certain places the gods and their representatives were known to be abroad, and the boys who had not yet been initiated into their secrets were warned to keep well away.

> The roots of the trees are not for play.
> The wizards, the wizards are gone to the bush.
>   Fear, fear, fear, then!

The roots of the trees are not for play.
  Daniel Dashe came away.
The roots of the trees are not for play.
The wizards, the wizards are gone to the bush.

Some performances were far beyond the threat of a bogey man.
This is the account of a Goemai boy from Demshin:

Of all . . . gods the fiercest . . . is the goddess Matgoelaa. This goddess is
supposed to be the head of the gods and to possess great powers. She is
supposed to have a husband 'Goewan' and to have a child called Dashittian.
She can destroy or give fortune to men, so there is always a great fear among
the people when her season for worship approaches. This season is usually in
the month of December when the harvest has been done, and the farms have
been put in order. I do not know for certain who or what announces the
news, but I usually hear a voice which does not seem like a man's though I
understand what is said. The news is announced thus in a hoarse kind of tune:

'The season approaches,
  The maker of our great one approaches
  To show her great wisdom and power.
  Prepare you, then, your shrines to receive her.'

This message is announced twice in the last two weeks of November.
People, and especially women and young boys and girls are usually frightened
by the news, for boys who are nearly mature are taken to the secret place to
be shown to the goddess, since she is responsible for their existence.

When December comes, not many people leave the town to go to the farms
or to go hunting. Life is quiet and full of fear. The goddess is often heard
about seven in the evening. I do not really know what happens, but I have
heard what she is supposed to say, and I have noticed that she travels faster
than an aeroplane. You hear her voice for a moment here, and then you will
hear it three thousand yards away. When I once dared to say that there were
two, one standing here and another standing there, I was abused and warned
not to speak such things again. She often speaks in a very loud and clear tone,
but different from that of any normal man or woman, naming the witches
and thieves in the town. Any mischief done by anybody is revealed by this
great and invisible goddess. She often repeats these sentences:

'Goewan, my son,
  Where have you been,
  The son whom I love so much?
  Come here to me and make me happy.'

Then her husband will answer:

> 'Matgoelaa, the creator of all,
> Reveal to them their terrible deeds.'

This story may seem fictitious, but it is what really happens, and I have seen it happen for many years. It may be concerted by men, but that is what I have experienced.

Even as he wrote these words it was possible to sense the narrator trying to free himself from the impression left by a childhood over-shadowed by this strange ordeal. Laurence Buenyen, who wrote this, concluded his story:

The most enjoyable part of this great worship is the dance devoted to the goddess. The dance takes place after the serious ceremonies have ended, everything has been set in order, and the goddess wants to depart to her castle under the earth. On the last day of December the men and boys go to the secret place called 'Nmei' where they paint themselves with lime. The drawings on the bodies of the men are sometimes in the form of jackets and shirts. From the loins to the feet a wrapper is tied, while the painting covers the upper part of the body. The dance usually begins at six in the evening since the goddess does not like the light.

She appears among the dancers, but few see her except the men closely connected with her. The song is sung by a man who holds a calabash called 'Shia'. In the calabash holes have been bored, and small stones are tied to short strings which are threaded through the holes in the calabash. When they are shaken these stones strike the calabashes, and a very loud sound is heard.

The singer sings and at the same time shakes this instrument and the crowd answers as he sings. There are many other instruments used only for this dance. The melody is very enjoyable. The song is repeated over and over again.

The singer sings: 'Men, our noble goddess shall go.' The dancer answers: 'Yes, our beloved mistress shall go.' The singer again sings: 'Dance you then to mark her end.'

The dance is performed in sections, each group with its own style which differs from the others. It is usually very competitive, since it is thought that the goddess will reward the best group. Moreover, from this dance, wives sometimes choose their husbands.

At periods such as this a considerable emotional tension must have been built up, but throughout the year the stress, for various reasons, must have been incessant. The communities were small. A cluster of small compounds making up a village might contain less than 500 people, all related to each other, who were born and would die each other's close neighbours, whose interests were inextricably involved in each other. Together they lived always on the edge of survival. Disease, drought, famine, and bereavement were threats which could never be forgotten.

Death at times seemed to be the invisible, familiar inhabitant of the Plateau compounds, addressed almost with affection:

Oh Death, direful Death, dear,

Nor were the dead ever absent. Sometimes they might return malevolently. Always their spirits were waiting and watching, to be remembered and placated. When, in the dusk, the warmth of the day still lingers, dark, almost caressing, amongst the euphorbia hedges or between the narrow walls of the mud compounds, the Birom believe that the spirits of the dead are clustering together there for comfort.

Thus the fears, the personal antagonisms and suppressed desires of these small communities were visited on the dead, who were credited with ill-will and mischief-making. Such passions sometimes found their outlet through rituals where memories of human sacrifice and sexual aberration still lingered. The violence and cruelty of their tribal traditions were not forgotten by the boys. One recounted a Chamba legend which tells of a pregnant woman sheltering in her compound, while outside the spirits of the dead who had not been buried but hung from trees, rock the hut as they try to get in. Under her bed her husband hides, defecating in terror. Outside, voices, referring to the woman and her unborn child, thunder, 'I smell double meat.'

In other ways an outlet was found for pent-up passions: through the rough and tumble of violent games, through drinking, and above all through dances. Through the nights of the full moon the drums beat, and the dancers follow the beat of the drum sometimes till they fall into a coma. At certain times of the year among the

Angas and some of the Lowland tribes the dancers are permitted to howl all manner of personal abuse and insult as they move in their trance. No retribution may be exercised. Thus they released antagonisms and tensions that might otherwise have broken loose to harm these confined communities.

The boys came into school used to repressing their resentment of their fellows, to accepting authority, and even to restraining their judgement, for they had been obliged to accept the disguised voices, the masks, and the secrecy of their tribal cults. They were commonly reserved and non-committal in their personal relationships with those outside their tribe. They acquiesced peaceably in poor administration and bad teaching. When authority failed them completely they appeared bewildered and indecisive. In other schools, in other areas, they broke loose, rioting, burning cars, sacking classrooms, and attacking teachers.

Despite all these restraints and fears, almost all the boys looked back to their childhood among their people with nostalgia and affection. But the communities among which they had been reared were already breaking down. The young men had been leaving Pankshin and Lowland to go to the mines for years. If they returned, they brought with them new wealth and a new scepticism of the tribe's standards and authority. The products of Western industrial society that were sold in the markets were replacing the traditional tools and making obsolete traditional skills. New religions and ideologies, Christian, Muslim, and materialistic, were making inroads on ancient faiths and systems of government. The outside world of Jos and the Nigerian cities, and the opportunities offered by the new Nigerian State became more and more tempting. To seek these the boys came to the schools, abandoning, as they did so, the right to become full members of their communities.

At puberty they would have been initiated as adult members of their tribes. They would have been taken to one of those schools in the bush that almost every pagan African society establishes for a few weeks or a few months during the dry season. There they would have been taught the ritual and theology of the tribal cult, would probably have been circumcised, and perhaps received a few additional scarifications. They would have left their sorrowing families as children, and returned from their ordeal, greeted as if they had come back from the dead, as men. They would then have been able to marry, at any age between twelve and fourteen, would have received land from their father, would have had an important part to play in the family's rituals, and would have aspired, quite early in some cases, to a responsible place in the life of their village. Hardly any of our boys had been through the initiation ceremonies. They had chosen instead to leave their villages and undertake another initiation, at another type of school. They were to be initiated into a modern state, by passing through something resembling an English secondary school.

Occasionally the boys had been sent by their families. 'Go, my son,' one of them was told, 'and be my eyes in the world of the white men.' A few came to school because their father was a chief or a village head liable to pressure from the administration, who wanted them to set an example to their people. Others had relations who had already benefited from some education and who had become clerks, policemen, tin-miners, soldiers, or pharmacists. These wished their children or their relatives' children to benefit still further. Some boys came to school because they wanted to, sometimes in the face of family opposition or indifference. Clement Sati had been beaten when he first abandoned his father's goats to attend the junior primary school and was only allowed to attend when his elder brother agreed to leave school and take over Clement's duties instead. For others the decision was less traumatic:

It was one evening when I began to think about school. When I saw an aeroplane passing in the air with a great noise, I asked my father what it was. He told me that it was a kind of lorry, and that in it there were many people. Then I began to wonder about it. I asked him whether it was made by God or a human being. His answer to that question was that it was made by men who attended schools and learned important things.

Then I left him and went and asked my mother what my father meant by the word school. She told me that it was a place where boys and girls were taught something about citizenship and the invention of cars and lorries.

That night I thought about these great things as I lay on my bed and wished to go to school and make a car for myself. The next morning I forgot all about it, but remembered it again when I saw one of my father's friends reading. I first heard him speaking to himself. I thought that he was mad, but I saw him sitting still. Then I drew near and listened to him reading some marks on the paper. I thought it was magic.

When he discovered my curiosity he asked me whether I would like to know how to read. I answered him earnestly that I should like it. He persuaded me to go and ask my father so that he would send me to school. I was very happy with this advice but I was afraid of my father, and I did not go straight to him but to my mother. She asked me why I was willing to go to school. I told her that I would like to able to read and to make aeroplanes and cars. She laughed at me and told me that she would allow me to go. I was pleased by this and thanked her.

After this I began to attend school, hoping that one day I would satisfy my ambitions. But at last I discovered that it is a very hard task to make cars, aeroplanes and lorries.

Relatively few children ever started their primary education, less than a quarter of those of school age in the Plateau Province in 1960, and there were far more schools in that area than further to the north. Of those who started only a proportion finished the three years at the junior primary school in stuffy, ill-lit buildings, writing on a slate, without paper and with hardly any textbooks, taught by teachers who could hardly claim to be literate themselves and kept order, often enough, only by the most ruthless use of the cane.

The next stage was the senior primary school. In Shendam by 1960 only a third of those who started their primary education attempted the four years which would complete it. Very often there was no school available, and then only the most stubborn would undertake the thirty-mile journey every week-end to the school in Pankshin or Shendam, or would undergo the hospitality of relations who would keep them at school only so long as they agreed to work as undernourished and abused drudges. Here the teachers would have probably received a little more training, and there would be a few more textbooks, a few more subjects, and a great deal more English. None the less classes would be crowded, noisy and ill-equipped, with the teacher more often showing a greater interest in preparing for his own examinations than in teaching the children. Punishments showed a little more variety than in the junior primary school. The boys were made to run round football pitches, hold bricks in the outstretched hand for hours, carry water, or stand in 'the bean-planting position', on one leg, with one finger touching the ground, and one leg extended behind.

A third of these children would achieve some sort of post-primary education; the majority training to be teachers and sent back to the primary schools after another three years' education, a few more going, reluctantly, to craft schools or technical schools; and only about one in ten of all primary-school children actually reaching a secondary school.

16
Notes on an African School

The boys came into the school at Vwang seeing the world in terms of their own homes, with their farms, and their clans, their little compounds and their isolation:

How is it that your people do not starve if they do not all farm?

Where does their food come from? Are they not all poor?

Are all your houses so big with two storeys, and so many rooms?

Are there so few people in your family? I think there are more than sixty in our family.

Their view of European life was summed up by Gabriel Nongo. England, he proposed, was a poor country where a great many people lived, but where there was very little farmland. Most Englishmen had no work to do. Their only hope of prosperity was to emigrate, preferably to Africa, where they would earn high salaries, and possess cars, servants, and large houses. English women were particularly ambitious in this direction. The luckiest were those who after much plotting, obtained an African husband. If this failed, some were fortunate enough to marry English men who were going to work in Africa. Those who remained in England were obliged by law to limit their families, and did so by undergoing an operation after their second child. An exception was made, as Gabriel observed, for the Queen. His close acquaintance with the private life of Father Smith made him an authority on the habits of Europeans, and no one presumed to contradict his views.

The world view presented by the School Certificate history syllabus was almost as preposterous. For the examiners, England was the centre of the universe. Thus a quarter of the paper was devoted to a survey of all the constitutional bric-à-brac of British government: the kangaroo, the guillotine, and the closure, Black Rod, the Mace and the Sergeant-at-Arms, county councils, urban district councils, rural district councils and parish councils, county boroughs and municipal boroughs. A close acquaintance with the dehydrated work of Messrs Hussey and White, bound in bilious orange by the Cambridge University Press, gave many a West African secondary-school student the belief that he held the clue to the efficient working of a parliamentary democracy.

More popular still, because the questions were so easy to answer, was the section dealing with European exploration and discovery. This also had the advantage that the stories were good, if not very elevating. It started with Prince Henry, rounded the African coast, reached India, did Columbus, studied the North-east and North-west Passages, knew all about the North American settlements of both France and England, and the major constitutional points about the government of the Spanish Empire in South and Central America. It drew complacent attention to European vigour, courage, and enterprise, while accepting apparently with approval, European cupidity and violence. The main textbook used in Muslim schools quoted with approbation Albuquerque's barbarous threats to capture and desecrate Mohammed's bones.

The part of the paper which dealt with Muslim history was normally avoided like the plague. The section devoted to tropical Africa, from the Sahara to Rhodesia, expected candidates to show a keen interest in the slave trade, the European forts on the coast of Ghana, and the details of their subjection in the late nineteenth century. 'It is no wonder,' observed Ambrose weightily, 'that the Europeans despise us if we were always their slaves. Do we not despise those whose fathers have been slaves?'

An even more spectacular distortion of history emerged after it had been processed by West African teaching methods, for there exists a corpus of notes for the study of world history in a Nigerian school. The first volume fills a whole exercise book after a year's work, three periods a week, copying from the blackboard, page after page. It starts at the beginning of the world, skirts round the theory of evolution on the first page, and goes on two pages later to a heading entitled 'The True Theory of Race' which distinguishes Aryans and Mongolians, dismisses the Negroes in one sentence, and is scathing about the Jews, whom, it states, are 'not much good'. The Middle East occupies little space, and the bulk of the first year's work is classical. Pericles, the Peloponnesian War, Pyrrhus, the Punic Wars, the Gracchi, Marius and Cinna, Caesar and Augustus are described in exhaustive, polysyllabic and misspelt detail.

A version of these notes has won itself a place in the literate culture of modern Nigeria. Somebody called Pitti, who owns a printing press in Lagos, has printed them in all their lovely detail. He has even persuaded a friend, acknowledged in his introduction, to lend him his old exercise book, and from it he has reproduced the drawings and maps so lovingly executed in his schooldays. The *chef-d'oeuvre* is Mr Pitti's friend's interpretation of a Roman soldier, in pen and ink, absolutely enormous, with rather short legs, and apparently wearing chain mail. Mr Pitti offers this memento of his schooldays at three shillings and sixpence, with considerable reductions if bought by the gross. Complimentary copies have been issued to most Nigerian secondary schools.

Outside their textbooks and outside the school the world was affecting their lives and changing them. The boys knew quite well, for example, that the French were exploding atomic bombs in the Sahara. Every Roman Catholic in Northern Nigeria had been to confession in 1959, believing that the French planned to exterminate the people of West Africa. They knew, also, the term 'apartheid', though it was little more than a word to them, since South Africa was further away than England. Communism aroused a stronger reaction with the older boys—a favourable one. They were too conscious of the poverty of their own people and of the wealth of others in the same country to feel anything else. It was noticeable, also, that those who were most sympathetic to Communism were also those most critical and sceptical of authority whether in their own societies or in the school.

These were remote problems. Others, more cruel, which faced the whole of Nigeria, menaced the school also. The Plateau had always been a frontier. For a hundred and fifty years it had held back the Muslims from its foothills. It was still one of the frontiers of the Muslim world. But for fifty years it had also been on the frontier of the Western world of Europe and America, of the towns, of the Christian missions, of trade and the mines, of the material culture of the radio and the gramophone, the new fashions in clothes, food, and language. We, the teachers, were bearers of this culture, but more important by far were the immigrants from the south, and above all, the Ibo from Eastern Nigeria, who had come up to the North by the hundred thousand from their overpopulated forests, and who formed probably half the population of Jos, Bukuru, and Kafanchan.

These people had provided Northern Nigeria with its gravest social and political problem. They came equipped with their literacy, their ambition and their acumen, loyal to each other and to their families in the south, and alien to the societies of peasants, traders, and feudal magnates among whom they settled. The colonial administration had depended on them for clerks, crafts-men, nurses, shop assistants, cashiers, and policemen. The new economy which had developed under colonial rule was staffed with Ibos, for they ran the railways, the post office, the mines, and the new factories. The ability and energy of the newcomers had brought into their hands businesses of all kinds: shops, bakeries, workshops, printing presses, road-haulage concerns, hotels and bars. Everywhere they settled they had flourished, hardworking, thrifty, competitive and avaricious, and everywhere they were hated. 'We in the North look upon them as invaders' (Alhaji Sir Abubakar Tafewa Balewa addressing the Nigerian Legislative Council, March 1948).

In the towns of the province the bulk of the Catholic population was Ibo, and so the school took in a proportion of Ibo students, up to 15 per cent of the whole according to Government regulations. An important section of the school community they were, more hard-working and ambitious than most of their Northern classmates, providing us with valuable footballers and athletes as well as sound scholars. Their background had much in common with that of English schoolchildren. They came from a people who were wage-earners and lived in the towns. Their families were literate, Christian, and monogamous, and usually more secure and affectionate than those of most Northerners. The best of them, like Athanasius Chukwu, would have fitted without difficulty into an English classroom, which could not usually be said of the Plateau boys, who had been far more toughened by their environment.

We first knew Athanasius as a very little boy, very intelligent, and very shy. He was one of the first children my wife met, an odd little figure, composed entirely of a white night-shirt, from the extremities of which appeared his slender hands and feet, and at the top his face, which split astonishingly, when I introduced him, into acres of smiling teeth. He giggled, managed to get out 'Good morning, madam,' and fled. We watched him grow into a very big boy. So many of the Plateau boys hardly seemed to change their shape. They grew a little longer, a little wirier, and their faces a little more bristly, but Athanasius seemed to swell before our very eyes, and from a shy little boy with a nervous smile he expanded into a muscular adolescent. Yet his face stayed the same on top of it all, still liable to crease into a disarmingly nervous smile. He was related to a baker in Bukuru who was a taller, slimmer, older version of Athanasius, good-looking, fine-featured, and a little shy, and a good way to becoming a very rich man with a string of bakeries across the Northern Region. Athanasius was always willing to please, and his charm could take the edge off even the sourest of his form-mates. Even at the end of his time at the school, when the hatred of the Ibos was eating into Northern society like a canker, Athanasius was still popular.

Other Ibos bore a grudge, for they knew that the Northern Nigerian Government provided no funds for the further education of Southerners, and that they would have no chance of getting into a sixth form or of reaching a university. Some made up for this, therefore, by bullying the smaller boys or being rude to their seniors. One, in the first year of the school's history, called a

Northern Nigerian teacher 'Northern trash' and tried to found a students' union on the same principles as the many tribal societies in the towns.

Another way of gaining acceptance was by running the school's social life. Those who did this were the 'guys'—the popular name for those who led the fashionable life, as distinct from the 'jews', who took no part in it and kept to their studies. They took 'guy names', titles they gave themselves, based on the names of film stars, pop idols, or characters in fiction. The habit spread. Alexander's brother was transformed into 'Sir Sylvester Jibirison de Kwande'. These boys wore the tightest trousers, the shoes with the sharpest points, the brightest-coloured shirts, the most flamboyant scarves, wore dark glasses, and carried the most fashionable hair-styles. They were the source of the magazines from whose pages came the photographs of the Beatles and the Rolling Stones which began to decorate the dormitories of the older boys. They adopted the more fashionable of the urban vices, smoked, wrote risqué letters to their girl-friends which were sometimes opened by the nuns, occasionally used marijuana. On social occasions it was normally they who organised the timetable, chose the dances, collected the records, and elected a master of ceremonies.

They, too, faced the school with peculiar problems, of which poor Nathaniel was the most tragic example. He was generally admitted to be one of the most stupid boys in the school; he was also under great strain. His father was a prosperous official in Jos with some political influence, without which it is possible that the Prefect would not have visited Nathaniel on us at all. For Nathaniel the sky was the limit, and on the persuasion of his mother he would go as far as his father's purse and his influence could get him. Even when his failure at the School Certificate had been predicted, his way had been bought into a famous southern college.

As a result Nathaniel's preoccupation with his failures was perpetually finding a way out. In an essay he proposed mutilation as a punishment for one who kept back his school fees for his own use. The class gasped. Somebody suggested that this was what he had been doing himself. Two years later he suggested public hangings once a month as an incentive for lazy schoolchildren. 'Even infants,' he wrote, 'fear death.' He found some compensation in his social activities until the nuns intercepted one of his letters to a near-by girls' school. When a despairing staff proposed that Nathaniel should take only five subjects in his School Certificate, Nathaniel spent the afternoon roaring on the verandah of the Fathers' House that he would commit suicide that very night. As the performance looked like being repeated, Nathaniel was allowed to take his examinations.

He failed, of course, and his end was unspeakable. His new school could make no headway with him, and his father proposed instead to send him to England to study. Nathaniel had always wanted to study in the United Kingdom, preferably at Newcastle, where he had reliable information that the landladies were particularly 'social'. The strain was too great. While the debate was going on about his future Nathaniel had been reading the newspapers. It was 1966, and various Vietnamese monks had been burning themselves in public places. Nathaniel retired to a piece of waste land with a can of petrol, there doused himself, and lit a match. I doubt if he even expected it to hurt. He burned to death.

From the North came the more ancient challenge of Islam. Under British protection the Muslim religion had spread more quickly in this part of West Africa than at any time in its history. Further north it had consolidated its hold over the Hausa peasantry, and even in the market-places of Shendam and Pankshin Muslim traders, officials, and clerics had begun to attract converts. On the high Plateau the very Birom were prepared to buy charms off Hausa mallamai to ward off evil or to cure disease.

The approach of independence had hastened this process. The political party which dominated the Northern Region, the Northern Peoples' Congress, was originally the instrument of the emirs, the inheritors of Usman dan Fodio's power. Its leader, Sir Ahmadu Bello, was a lineal descendant of the Shehu, a member of the royal family of Sokoto, a convinced and proselytising Muslim who still seemed to equate belief in Islam with membership of the State, as his great ancestor had done. Regularly and publicly he received large congregations of converts into his faith.

The Plateau boys regarded Sir Ahmadu Bello and his party with suspicion. Many of them came from homes where there was an ancient tradition of resistance to Islam, the religion of slave-raiders and tyrants. Even in Shendam, where Islam was making inroads into the compound of the Long Koemai, those who accepted it were accepting the faith of the Hausa, and with it Hausa language, customs, and dress. In the eyes of many of the boys they had ceased to be Goemai, and had become Hausa. The boys knew that they would have to contend with the reigning political party and its religion when they left school, and feared that without member-ship of the Northern Peoples' Congress and acceptance of its religion, advancement, and even employment, might be limited.

The Government was well aware of such resentment. From time to time a politician would arrive on a tour of secondary schools and warn the boys against taking part in politics. They knew too well that almost every major political upheaval in West Africa since the Second World War had been engineered in part by secondary-school boys or those who had just left the secondary schools. Ultimately the Premier of the North himself, Alhaji the honourable Sir Ahmadu Bello, Sardauna of Sokoto, addressed an audience of students from every secondary school in the North on the need for discipline and self-control, an address which was circulated to every schoolboy in the country, translated into Hausa and English. Much good it did. As the Sardauna well knew, the members of the ruling class itself were the worst offenders. Presuming on their high connections, they left school compounds at will, drank, gambled, refused to obey the staff. In one provincial secondary school, where they conflicted with the Principal, it was the Principal himself who left.

We knew, ourselves, what power they had. 'Good Muslims,' observed Father Glynn bitterly, 'I like, and good Protestants, and good Catholics—but these bad ones—what am I to do with them?' We possessed two particularly fine specimens of a type which had infested every decadent empire in the Sudan since the fall of ancient Ghana. One was a Nupe who bore a name which was scattered throughout the political circles of the Northern capital. Musa was the particular responsibility of a member of the diplomatic corps and came to us straight from America. The Christian Missionary Society Secondary School in Zaria, who had known him before, had turned him down. He came to us, an amiable well-fed sixteen, happy in the assurance that Nigeria was his to command. Salihu was equally friendly, was longer in the limb, and mad. His father ran a great industrial corporation in Zaria, not to any great effect, and seemed to have one desire for his son, that he should be kept as far away as possible from him, and at as little expense. Unlike Musa's father, he could not put an ocean between them, but Vwang was sufficiently far off.

Salihu's dominant trait was *naïveté*. He was all wide-eyed wonder. 'Madam, have you yourself seen Boadicea's chariot in London?' He was extremely good-natured. 'Can you not see that madam is tired; she wishes to go and look after her children.' When our second child arrived he cycled out to the hospital, an illegal action had he bothered to think about it, and there addressed her with such gravity and concern you might have thought that he was the father. His madness he admitted. 'When I was a child, madam, I was mad.' It largely took the form of complete isolation from everyday affairs. He worked when he felt like it, came into class when it moved him, obeyed the school rules when it suited him, without the least intention to cause offence.

Musa was more consequential in his behaviour. He, too, saw no reason to give anyone offence, nor to do as anyone told him. Once he had explored his American experience in his essays—'and, you know, they refused even me, even me, a cup of coffee in this road house'—he had completed his school work and had no further contribution to make. With Salihu he sought what little night life Vwang had to offer. Supposedly practising Muslims, they wandered bleary and bloodshot around the compound in the evening redolent of tobacco. Alcohol, which was also forbidden by Muslim law, they consumed after dark or at the week-end. On several occasions their beds in the dormitories were found empty, and they would come on to the compound an hour or two later, all injured dignity that anyone should have missed them. Earnest correspondence with Kaduna and a visit from an embarrassed representative of the Resident in Jos were necessary before they could be admonished.

They were pathetic. Salihu's frequent letters to his father were never answered and it was apparent that he had been consigned to us to do as we wished. Both boys began every term in opulence, arriving by official car, expensively dressed, carrying transistors, wrist-watches, and cameras. They ended always in indigence, begging permission to make telephone calls to Kaduna, uncertain whether they would ever get home at all. Moreover, their conscience prodded them in the most peculiar ways. They got religion, not their own, but Catholicism. They acquired rosaries and sat in class with them round their necks. Salihu admired the 'pretty candles' on the altar during Mass, and came beseeching the priests to baptise him. They refused the frightening prospect of having converted the lunatic son of a prominent Muslim dignitary. 'Then, father, teach me a prayer.' Father Sheehan handed over the missal, open as it happened at the prayers for the dead, and told him to get on with that. Salihu went off with it gratified that his soul had been saved.

They left the compound unconverted, to everybody's relief, and without anything to show for five years spent at Vwang, except a period of peace for their fathers. Presumably somewhere in the North they have acquired a niche where they can dissipate themselves without too much trouble for their relations, or wasting too much of their community's taxes. As far as the school was concerned, they were what the Northern Nigerian Government stood for.

The Muslim boys were outsiders in the school community, almost as much as the Ibos. Eighty per cent of the boys came from the pagan societies of the Plateau and its outlying foothills, whose culture I had tried to explore in the classroom and, when I could, out in the villages. It was these boys, whose upbringing and experience were so different from my own, whose personality was most difficult to appreciate.

Of the qualities encouraged by their demanding environment, courage was the most evident, and the most easily appreciated. This courage was of the dogged enduring kind, evident at the end of a gruelling football match against larger, stronger and more skilled opponents, or during the longer athletic events at which they excelled. Perhaps it was most evident in the boys from the poorer hill tribes, in Peter Ayaka, an Egon from above Akwanga, who played two football matches with a torn ligament in his ankle, or Clement Sati from Pankshin, determined to run the mile with a pulled tendon in his heel, or Lucas Dangaana, our skinny little high jumper from Kagoro, who had acquired his athletic skill by jumping off moving trains.

Equally striking was their loyalty. This was, in the first place, given to their family, their clan, or their tribe. It could be extended to their form, their house, or to the school. This accounted in part for the dedication with which they took part in football and athletics. It also accounted for their trustworthiness. Outside their lessons they were almost totally unsupervised, yet even at the worst periods of school history work was done, essential chores completed, and the interest of the community in maintaining reasonable standards of discipline to prepare for examinations upheld. I believe that such identification with a larger group was essential to them. They had been brought up as closely integrated members of a small tribal group. To this group they owed the loyalties and affection which our culture normally associates with a monogamous family. The prospect of individual responsibility without communal support was difficult for most of the boys to entertain. Certainly those without a group from their own tribe to sustain them often found school life difficult.

In the end it was on their loyalty to their people that their personality was based. An insult to their tribe was probably the gravest injury that could be done to any of them. Gabriel Nongo, in his first year, had gone weeping to the Principal because his form-mates had used the insulting Hausa term 'Munchi' to describe his people, the Tiv. The low esteem in which the Ninzam were held blighted the whole school career of Jerome Magaje. The gravest criticism of the old School Certificate course was that it brought up against their ancestors the slur of slavery. It was a deep personal affront to all of them.

The deep morality associated with their tribal cultures entered into everything which they did in the school. It had left them with a deep religious sense, noticeable in every reference to their tribal cults, which went far deeper than the ludicrous religious instruction which they copied down from the blackboard. It provided them with a set of standards by which to judge the value of the books they read in the English lessons, an acid test of the real worth of anything we put in front of them. This loyalty to their own people, which could be extended to the school, to the Church, and to the State, was surely the root of the most enduring impression they left behind, their dignity, their integrity.

It was not, however, easy for them to adapt their loyalties to the new circumstances of either the school or of modern Nigeria. They were difficult boys to know. In a crisis their response was enigmatic, only occasionally expressed through an essay. The reasons for this had to do with the great cultural and linguistic gap across which they had to communicate, but I believe that another real and terrible difficulty existed here. It was not merely that communication outside their group on any but a superficial level was difficult. I believe that their deepest personal relationships with other human beings had been checked or retarded. Of all relationships, that between father and son was the deepest, and this had not always been allowed to develop; the love between mother and child had usually been cut off in early infancy; while that between mother and father, husband and wife, was hardly allowed to develop in the polygamous family. I knew that there were exceptions, but where they existed the consequence was obvious in the greater ease with which the boy coped with other people.

Other consequences followed from the boys' emotional development. There was little gentleness about them, though it did sometimes come to the surface. Their humour was normally harsh, their laughter metallic, their attitude to physical deformity or mental incapacity one of scorn. To those outside the group they were often callous. They admired the strong, the violent, and the brutal. In the history lessons it was Frederick the Great and Peter the Great who impressed them, not Washington or Abraham Lincoln. The ambition they all expressed for their country was that she should have more bombs, more aircraft, and more weapons.

There were also intellectual shortcomings. Though the boys were conscientious and perceptive in working out a problem, and well able to sort out the ethics of a situation in the English or the history lessons, they seemed to lack individual imagination, or the ability to follow up their own thoughts. I suspect that imagination and originality were not qualities which could be afforded by their small, poverty-stricken societies, fighting against odds even to stay alive. So deeply identified were they with these societies that any idea which threatened their values threatened to undermine the basis of the boys' personalities.

It was the misfits who best illustrated the boys' dilemma. There were those, such as Jerome Magaje, who received no support from their tribal traditions. The Ninzam were poor and remote, and might have had serf status in relation to some of their neighbours. They may have been humiliated by the Birom, who had been given homes in their area by a resettlement scheme. Jerome was for five years the only Ninzam in the school, and the reputation of his tribe obsessed him. As far as possible he withdrew from all social activity. He sat glumly in the front row, and opened his mouth reluctantly only when spoken to. He was grubby; his clothes were normally torn; and it took a great deal of pressure to make him wash regularly. He kept away from all social occasions, saying that he could not afford the clothes. He was extremely intelligent, though it took me a couple of terms to realise this. This was partly because of his handwriting, which looped, uncontrolled, unpunctuated, and out of alignment, over page after page, the perfect expression of his personality. Once deciphered his work was usually shrewd and quite well expressed. He waged a constant propaganda campaign against every other tribe in the school. The whole Plateau, he asserted, would starve to death without Ninzam yams; would freeze without Ninzam firewood; was populated by wasters. Put in charge of the group that was to investigate the agriculture of our area for the school magazine, he quarrelled with the Birom, who refused to work with him, and went on strike.

As time went on he seemed to become more unbalanced. He won his argument with Mark Dimka and received a new shirt, only to quarrel in the following term with his house master, whom he assaulted. The term after that Clement, his house captain, tried to satisfy Jerome's self-esteem by letting him share his cubicle at the end of the dormitory, only to be half-throttled one night when Jerome was in a particularly violent mood. Shortly after this Jerome fell ill with pneumonia and spent a fortnight at the Protestant hospital in Vwang. He returned, a convert, with 'not me, but Him in me' scribbled over the cover of his rough note book. We dealt with Stalin in a history period. He was overwhelmed, and took Isaac Deutcher's biography of Stalin home with him, where he read it from cover to cover. He then undoubtedly had a mission in life.

Vincent from Kagoro seemed similarly isolated. It was difficult to see how any community could ever have accepted him. He was a religious maniac. A striking figure in the back row of his form, he was stocky, swarthy, with a strongly boned, heavily nosed face, like that of a Red Indian. His voice was harsh and penetrating, and he exuded self-confidence. From his first year at school he announced his vocation to the priesthood. He was not encouraged by the priests, and instead became a founder member of the school praesidium of the Legion of Mary, a quaint little institution which laundered the vestments for Mass, catechised a few illiterate women in the village, did a little extra housework around the school, and other minor good works. In his fourth year we reached Luther in the history lessons. He was most impressed, as were several of the boys. For him new vistas opened up.

His way through school was marred by quarrels with everyone from the Principal down, which only strengthened his sense of inner purpose. Before he left he composed a sort of testament for the younger members of the Legion of Mary, couched in biblical terms, from 'One who has gone before you', exhorting them to be of good heart. As expected, he failed his G.C.E. exams. He then disappeared. One of the priests gloomily prophesied that he would soon be founding his own religion somewhere in the hills round Kagoro.

'wp'

It was fatal to a boy's development to be isolated from his tribal community. It was, however, equally fatal for a boy to occupy an unprivileged position within it. As in the case of Joseph it might very well have marked him for life before he ever entered the school. He was a Goemai, a member of the school's most powerful community, and the son of one of the many younger wives of the Long Koemai. When he arrived in the first year he appeared to be about twelve years old. He was, in fact, about nineteen. There was a bald patch on the top of his head, said to have been caused by the head loads he had been forced to carry for senior members of the compound. He grew hardly at all in the five years we knew him, and his face remained wizened and pursed up, a constant frown coming and going from his forehead. He mumbled incessantly to himself, became excited very easily, stuttered when he tried to answer a question, and was laughed at rather unpleasantly by the rest of his form. His written work was incoherent, and did not improve. He was always dirty, his clothes usually torn and untidy. He had no money to buy more. His fees were seldom paid. He had been trodden under foot in his own society, was a butt in the classroom, and would become an outcast again when he left school to fend for himself.

These were among the school tragedies, but there was something a little odd about some of the happiest boys. Innocent, for example, stood as high in the esteem of the Long Koemai as poor Joseph was low. He may even have had a claim to the succession. He was a good-natured and apparently brainless boy, who sprawled his long limbs across the back of the classroom with a broad and rather vacuous grin occupying his long face. He answered to the nick-name of 'Abdulla' or 'Caesar', but preferred the latter. He was very conscious of his importance and very lazy. From time to time he condescended to come out on the athletics track, where he would complete a lap or two, his long legs striding, and his white robes billowing out behind him, a broad grin on his face, to an accompaniment of laughter and applause. As the most eminent of the largest tribal group in the school, his prestige was considerable. In his form he seemed to be the constitutional monarch, not bothering to exercise his power, but fully aware of its existence.

Less august figures left a very similar impression. Thomas resembled Innocent in appearance, was equally good-natured, and equally self-confident. He regarded himself as the expert in all he did. As school centre-forward, who missed nineteen out of twenty shots, and was as likely to fall flat on his back or to lame another player as to win his side a goal, he was prepared to lecture the whole team on the theory and practice of football playing. He was an authority on discus throwing, always astonished that he never quite managed to win the event. He was the most popular orator in the school debating society, for one could never predict what he would be inspired to say next, so voluble and excited did he become. Equally pleased with himself was John, who had failed to become a priest. On holiday from the Junior Seminary he had once required that his missal should be carried reverently ahead of him, as became his priestly status. Now that he had left the seminary he still spoke like one set apart, and like Thomas, was extremely proud of his wide vocabulary and oratorical skill. All three of them were like great children, rather spoilt, and rather pleased with themselves, with no responsibilities, and no care for the future despite the fact they were certain to fail all their examinations. Innocent had certainly been spoilt in the Long Koemai's compound; Thomas had been looked after by a doting grandmother who had hidden him from a prying headmaster in a grain pot to prevent him being taken away from her to school; John's excessive pleasure in himself also included an uncomplicated interest in the functioning of his own bowels. It seemed as if, for them, the clock had stopped. They had ducked out of the stresses which had faced them as they grew older by remaining small children.

The same was probably true of Anthony, who took so much pleasure in playing with our own children. His development also appeared to have been arrested. Perhaps one day he would be like his father, who was a stocky mine-worker, self-confident, intelligent, and by Birom standards quite well paid. He drank every penny that he received. At the end of each month there was commonly a race to extract Anthony's school fees before his father swallowed them. Both Anthony and his father appeared to live in the present, disregarding the unpleasant possibilities that the future might have in store for them.

Apart from Jerome and, perhaps, Anthony, all the boys so far mentioned were not outstandingly intelligent. Had they been so they may have reacted more positively to the problems that faced them. Even the most intelligent suffered from the burdens of their situation. Several of the calmest and most assiduous workers concealed a history of deprivation, which they could not prevent marking their personalities. James was from a remote area, a Mirriam, one of the poorest of the tribes who sent boys to the school. He was one of the most intelligent boys in his class, worked hard even by the standards of the other boys at the school, and was always near the top of his form. He was a most presentable boy, who took great care over his personal appearance, was well-spoken and courteous, in every way a model pupil. He had only one close friend, a boy from his own area in an older form, who was equally quiet and hard-working. Although he was an excellent worker, he took little active part in lessons, and tried to avoid attention. He had worked hard for his education. He must have been possessed of a passion to better himself, for with no encouragement from his family he had taught himself to write, with no other aid than a piece of chalk and a fragment of slate set into the side of his hut. His father, who was well able to, had refused to pay his secondary-school fees. Every year or two there was a crisis. Without any money to pay for his education, James would refuse to come to school. When others offered to pay he refused to let them do so. For weeks he would remain in his village, his ambition and his family pride in the deepest conflict. Eventually the parish priest or one of his colleagues would bring about some sort of compromise, and James would return unobtrusively to his place in class. Conscientiously and impassively he continued to work.

Poverty was always deeply resented. 'Hate me not because I am poor,' Gabriel Zi had written rather histrionically. His fees were hardly ever paid. Clement Sati was equally conscious of the poverty of his family, and was touchy and withdrawn because of it. With him, however, and one or two others, there was a rebellion. He had started his education in defiance of his father, abandoning the goats to attend the junior primary, and being thrashed for it each time he did so. In the end his older brother had agreed to forgo his chance of education and let Clement take it up instead. Here was an instance in which a boy had set himself against authority in his tribe. There was, however, no fundamental break. Clement was still intensely proud of his tribe, accepted its traditions, and was glad to talk and write about them, but he became increasingly independent in his opinions. He was the only boy whom I heard speak about women with any gentleness or understanding. 'We must respect them,' he said when he was in his third year, 'for the pain they have to suffer when they bear a child.' He was one of the most forthright and uncompromising in his expression of anger. I particularly remember his expression of shame and disgust about the poor treatment given to the athletics team sent to represent the Northern Region in the Federal Sports the year after he left. He was one of the few who would occasionally try to analyse his personal feelings, to explain in his case why he was so touchy, made so few friends, and lost his temper so easily. There was no doubt, he said, that this was the result of being poor. He felt it, and hated it when other boys seemed to notice it.

Such detachment was seldom achieved. Aloysius Shilong was probably the most rebellious of the boys I had to teach. He came in the first place from a rebellious and belligerent tribe. It had successfully resisted change since before the colonial era, and he was pleased to relate in class how a neighbouring village had once killed a District Officer. Aloysius's only regret was that he did not come from the village. He must have been an unusual boy, for at an early age, perhaps when he was about eleven or twelve, he had dared to challenge the elders of his village, claiming to disbelieve tribal traditions. He had been taken into the ju-ju hut, where he had been shown a gourd which appeared to speak. He was only half convinced. Aloysius had challenged all the assumptions made by his tribal religion. He was equally vehement in his challenge to the beliefs offered by the missionaries. In his fourth year, in a lesson on Communism and Christianity, he broke into the discussion with a passionate denunciation of religion, and a statement of disbelief in the existence of a God. This was a remarkable intellectual and emotional achievement. Few boys gained quite such freedom and individuality.

Few boys made so evident a rebellion. Tough and self-contained, they kept themselves to themselves, and made their own judgements on the European civilisation that was presented to them in class. They were interested and usually non-committal. They had all benefited, as they had also suffered, from their early childhood. They had all enjoyed, and often disliked, their experience of Western education. They had remained loyal to the standards of their people, and waited for their time at school to come to an end.

Make we take things easy. In some years we go become better people. We go live in high well decorated houses, ride in luxurious cars, wear better clothes, and wak better chop, and marry de earth's beauties.

By 1965 the boys were leaving school. Far more than we had expected wanted to go back to their own people. They went to the Agricultural College at Zaria, where they would be trained to become Agricultural Officers, advising the peasants on how to improve their yield, use new machinery, fertiliser, insecticide, new strains of seed and so on. Eventually they hoped to borrow money from the Government, obtain land from the chief, and set themselves up to make a fortune by selling cash crops to Jos and Bukuru. Others found posts in firms and Government departments where they would become part of the urban lower middle class. The most fortunate were those who went on to study for their Advanced Levels. It was they who would go to university, reach the upper grades of the civil service, and join the ruling élite of the new Africa.

They came back occasionally to report. Some had gone down to the Emergency Science School in Lagos, set up to train those doctors and engineers which the country so badly needed. They attended mass lectures, crowded out the laboratories, and lived without supervision. Others went to secondary schools in the North. Clement wrote from Kaduna, where he could get no proper training for the mile, and where he spent all his Advanced Level history lessons copying down notes. Gabriel Salla was complaining of the heat on the Upper Benue, where the whole school appeared to sleep out of doors during the sweltering nights. Innocent was down at Okenne, where the library was inadequate, far worse than the one my wife had set up at Vwang. Nobody seemed particularly happy. I enquired of one of them which of all these schools was the best. He looked thoughtful, and then said casually: 'This is.'

How far had we been able to help the boys? Within the limits of the school situation we had probably succeeded well enough. All those boys who were capable of it passed their School Certificate examinations, and that was what the school had been established for. I am in no position to say what other good had been done. There was a sense of corporate pride felt by most of the boys. For its size and poverty the school's achievements were considerable—exam results better than all but half a dozen of the wealthiest and oldest establishments in Northern Nigeria, one of the best football teams, and one of the best athletics teams in that enormous region, and a school life which, while hardly luxurious, was at least decent and self-respecting. The boys were well turned out, polite, and alert. The buildings were clean and decently painted, the strawboard in the classrooms carrying evidence of work done in all the subjects, Constance's library well stocked and well used. The compound was tidy and now planted with hundreds of trees, for which Father Glynn had a passion. He planted them everywhere in straight lines, for which his tidy mind also had a passion, and every evening he and his two dogs set out to see that they were watered and attendant pests removed. The dining-room tables were now covered with clean plastic cloths, and the stewards at last wore uniforms which they were obliged to wash regularly. The food was adequate, the boys worked conscientiously, and the staff was happy.

St Jerome's College is, in our opinion, a good school doing sound educational work at a high level of professional competence . . . We hope that St Jerome's will long continue to educate the boys of Plateau Province with the wisdom and humanity that it does now.

Even the inspectors liked us.

Father Glynn had established the nucleus of a good school. He had gained, without the use of any force, a moral authority on which the school depended. While he had, as was essential in an African school, placed the day-to-day supervision of school affairs in the hands of the boys, he retained his position of ultimate power and arbitration. Even within the limited concepts of school life defined by the exam system and the precedent of the English grammar schools we had the foundations to build on. There were the human resources within the Plateau to build up a secondary school three or four times its present size, could we only overcome the low standards achieved by most of the primary schools. We longed for a sixth form in which we could complete the intellectual training we had set afoot in the earlier years of school life.

Leaving aside the concepts of European education, there was no reason why the school could not have developed its function as a link between the conservative, traditional worlds of Shendam, Pankshin, Kwa, Kabwir, and the rest, and the new world of Jos and the Nigerian cities into which the boys were moving. This was certainly a function of its teaching, to interpret the new world, while it attempted to investigate and preserve the old.

There were the multitude of personal and social problems the school might have helped to solve. At that time pastoral responsibility was carried out on a rather random basis. There was little organised attempt to make contact with the boys' homes. In five years Constance and I met the families of eleven of the children we taught, and these either because they were wealthy enough to visit the school or because they happened to live particularly close by. The priests met a great many more, rather by chance than policy, because they were stationed on one of the missions during the holidays. It is difficult to judge what difficulties there may have been in making regular contact with the boys' families, but many problems might have been clarified had we been able to do so. We might even have been able to save Mathew Zatiyok's life.

There were the problems the boys faced when they left school. These were straightforward enough when they went on to further education, to the agricultural college, or to another school, but the school did little to help in any other situation. The network of family relationships took over. Somebody had a relation in the Treasury at Kaduna, so all sorts of unlikely people ended up in the Revenue Department. Somebody else wanted to do forestry, but no relation from his tribe was there, so he left within three months. Another proposed to go into the Police Force, but his elder brother was a constable already, and a bitter family quarrel was in prospect if the boy took a commission. For totally obscure reasons the prison service interested several school-leavers. Some just disappeared. There was no careers adviser, nor any advice to give. I tried to do the job myself once, wrote to every firm and department I could think of, got about six replies back, none of them very helpful, interviewed all the school-leavers, a process they very much enjoyed, and failed to organise a single job.

There were also the constitutional problems of the school to be faced. The boys' people ought to have had a more positive part to play in the running of the school. The local dignitaries who served on the board of governors were supernumerary to the annual meetings. Their potential power only became evident when pressure was applied to collect fees, or to discipline a difficult pupil. One would very much have liked to know what these people really wanted from the school, remembering, of course, that their appreciation of the school's function was as limited in its own way as was our own. Where did they expect the children to go when they finished school? What problems did they find when the children returned to their homes at the end of term, or at the end of their school careers? What suggestions might they have had to make about school organisation, about discipline, about the facilities we provided?

We would also have welcomed a greater measure of interest, even of intervention, from the Central Government. It was otherwise far too easy for a school in Africa to become the plaything of local interest, political or religious.

It was this which was the school's undoing. The school belonged to the Prefect. The priests were his priests. The lay staff were under contract to him. The Government grant on which the school depended reached us through his good offices. So poor were we that the school had to rely on him for the occasional subsidy. His were the buildings, and his the siting of the merest latrine seat. At the end of 1964 he appointed an education secretary with great ideas about the staffing problems of the province. He moved Father Sheehan at once. When we asked that we be allowed to return to the school when our contracts expired six months hence, we were told that all this had been arranged. Twelve Irish teachers had been engaged for the following school year and we would not be needed. In any case, said the Prefect, the idea in future was to be quite different. No one would be appointed to a particular school; there would be a pool of teachers to be shifted from one school to another as exigencies required. We pointed out, correctly enough, that not a single contract had been signed, and that hardly any of the twelve teachers could be expected to arrive. Hardly any did. The only one we met was a nervous wreck when she arrived, and half out of her mind when she was sent home two months later. We further pointed out, exerting superhuman self-control, that the Prefect's scheme, or his education secretary's, was calculated to ruin the morale, the very survival of his schools.

'That may be, that may be, Mr Elliott. Ye'll know better than I, better than I. What? Cigarette, Mr Elliott?'

So the school was ruined. Within six months it had lost half its graduate staff, and with it all their experience. Any ideas Father Glynn may have had for expanding it were firmly trodden on. The school was cut down to size, relegated to something the Prefect could control.

We had been proud of our work. After five years' teaching we were beginning to know the country and some of the children.

We had made our first home there, and three babies had been born to us. Sarah, the third, had just arrived. By that time the senior boys had left and no one on the compound had been longer at the school than ourselves. Constance had built up the library book by book. I had run my athletics team, edited the magazines, and produced the school play. Rather arrogantly, I felt that I had learnt to teach history and English as well as anyone in the country. I would walk through the compound after lights out on my duty days, checking everyone into bed, seeing that no one was still up in one of the locker rooms for a night's illegal work. I felt a native of the place. I knew every stone and blade of grass. It was hard to envisage the school without us there.

Just before we finally left I had to go to the convent at Zawan. I had a carbuncle on the back of my neck and Sister Thomas More was treating it. Like most of her treatments, it was drastic and effective. A large syringe full of penicillin was pumped into my upper arm, which felt rigid as a poker. Now Sister Thomas More was due to apply a poultice, which she did with great gusto and effect in her little clinic. 'And there, Mr Elliott, that came out just right—a treat—got it just at the right time.' She bandaged the relieved part, giving a lecture as she did so on the correct treatment of boils and carbuncles, and we went out on to the verandah in front of her surgery.

A rather fat woman was there holding a baby on her hip. As Sister Thomas talked about carbuncles and boils, I glanced at the baby incuriously. Then I could not look away. Something was wrong with the child. It was larger than our youngest daughter, Sarah, but bonier, its face a skull. The limbs I could hardly see, for it was wrapped in a cotton cloth. I could not understand why a baby so tiny could be so emaciated. Finally I asked.

'How old is that child there, Sister?'

'He'll be three, perhaps four now, Mr Elliott.' She spoke in Hausa to the woman, who said something off-hand without looking at the child. 'Four, Mr Elliott, just.'

'Months, Sister?' The child seemed a little large for that age.

'Years, Mr Elliott, years.' I was astounded, for he was a mere bundle in his cotton wrapper. I could not look away from the child, as old as my son, almost as small as my tiniest daughter. His head lolled. His eyes, enormous eyes, focused on nothing. His mouth was slightly open.

'Is he retarded, Sister, or something?'

'Oh, not that, Mr Elliott.' Sister Thomas spoke again to the woman, who replied again off-handedly in Hausa. She did not look at the baby, who was held carelessly, slightly away from her, against her right hip, as if it did not belong to her.

'His mother died, ye know, Mr Elliott, soon after he was born. That's his father's other wife there.'

'But what's wrong with him, Sister?'

'O-oh! He's not that well looked after, ye know. They bring him in here from time to time—cough, diarrhoea—ye know. I put him right. A few months later they'll bring him back.'

'Won't he ever get better?'

'They'll not look after him, ye see. He's not their own. It often happens.'

I could not take my eyes from that silent baby. With what strength all mine bawled, with what exuberance they chattered and laughed.

'Sister, is he dying?'

'Surely, Mr Elliott. He'll die soon.'

I looked at the baby, dying. What help was there I could give him? What help had I ever given? I remembered a week after I had first arrived in Vwang that little boy, Mathias, with the tin trunk and the bandaged leg, ill, tired, turned away with no help for his suffering. I remembered the sick children in the dust at Kuru two years before. I turned away and let the baby die. My mind would not comprehend such suffering, and I understood that I could never entirely comprehend the minds of boys to whom it had been a part of all their daily life.

We left the country three months later.

17
Epilogue

We should have been grateful to the Prefect and his education secretary. They had saved our children from seeing murder committed on our very doorstep. In January 1966, five months after we had left, the Sardauna was assassinated. As the anti-tank shells blasted his house apart he fled to his harem, where he died sheltering among his women, his body left, according to one report, lying among the ruins for the Kaduna mob to poke at. It was a pathetic end for one who was in so many ways a great man, perhaps the last of the great Muslim potentates of the Sudan. I was reading *Julius Caesar* when I heard the news. Ahmadu Bello had been too like Caesar, in his abilities, in his power, in his weaknesses, and in his death. On him, for all his shortcomings, the welfare of the State had depended. Now he was dead.

> Blood and destruction shall be so in use
> And dreadful objects so familiar
> That mothers shall but smile when they behold
> Their infants quartered with the hands of war,
> All pity chok'd with custom of fell deeds;
> And Caesar's spirit, ranging for revenge,
> With Até by his side come hot from hell,
> Shall in these confines with a monarch's voice
> Cry 'Havoc!' and let slip the dogs of war,
> That this foul deed shall smell above the earth
> With carrion men groaning for burial.

My prophecy to a startled second form seemed somewhat foolish, for nothing happened. 'Three premiers dead in an evening, and not a dog barks. What a country.'

It must have seemed to the conspirators, and to the majority of

Nigerians, as if a troublesome boil had been lanced. But the very bloodstream of Nigerian political life had been infected by tribal, religious, and cultural arrogance, by greed, violence, and selfishness, by the wealth and ostentation of a few, and the poverty, frustration, and envy of the majority. The Federation had long been sick. Now it seemed mortally ill, racked by one convulsion after another. General Ironsi's life, spared by his officers, was lost at the hands of Northern mutineers a few months later. In a fever of public apprehension rumours of plots and pogroms moved backwards and forwards across the Federation.

The Ibos were said to have been planning the destruction of Northern troops, and were then preparing to take revenge for Ironsi's death. In their turn Northern soldiers and their officers were believed to be planning their own coup. As the rainy season passed the Northern hatred and fear of the Ibos rose bitterly. From Enugu the Eastern Governor, Colonel Ojukwu, urged his people home. The heavily loaded refugee trains began their movement south, and the lorries overloaded with fugitives churned their way over the treacherous rain-soaked roads towards Makurdi, the Eastern frontier and safety.

By the beginning of September Jos was full of rumours. The emirs were supposed to have held a meeting up in Bauchi. Strangers from the North were arriving in the town. A few days later wireless reports told of riots in the Eastern Region, and of Hausa corpses being brought up by train from the South. On Wednesday night, all over the North, as if in concert, the mobs and the troops moved in upon the unarmed Ibo, killing all they found. It went on all that day, all through Thursday, and into Friday. Then, when it was finished, they went to the mosques to pray. Thirty thousand dead is now the popular guess for that three days' work, with a possible error of up to ten thousand in any direction, for after a time the authorities, such as were left, gave up counting. The municipal labourers in Jos stopped the count after burying the first thousand. As many must have died in Bukuru. In Vwang the junior staff quarters across the road from our bungalow were devastated. Forty-eight corpses were thrown into the streets, so much offal to be disposed of. In many cases the Ibo seem to have given themselves up to the slaughter like sheep. Strong men allowed themselves to be beaten to death by mobs of youths. Nowhere does there seem to have been any organised resistance.

There was no refuge and no mercy. Those who fled from the towns to seek refuge in the pagan villages were cut down there. The murderers occupied the very convents, even Zawan itself, and slaughtered their victims as they came for shelter. In the maternity hospital in Jos men and women were cut down shrieking at the German doctor's door. The wards were entered, and a child lying sick in one of them was taken out by a soldier and shot. The police lorries trundled the streets packing away the wounded and the mutilated.

The country was overwhelmed by the violence. Soldiers ran amok; men in authority of every nation panicked; the heads of great firms forbade their people to shelter their Ibo employees. Others did their duty. The police in Zaria and Jos turned their compounds into refugee camps. In Jos the American Sudan International Mission, the ancient Bible belt foes of the Irish priesthood, set up a field hospital at the police station, where some aid could be given to the wounded, the sick, and the dying. The other missions joined them there, distributing bread to the refugees. 'At last,' intoned an American missionary as he and an Irish priest handed out half loaves, 'breaking bread together.' An airlift was organised by the European community which flew out over a thousand, some of them, I was told, so wounded that it was difficult to understand why they should wish to go on living.

Individuals risked or even gave their lives. A Hausa steward put himself in danger from his own people to hide an Ibo servant in his employer's roof. The chief at Kagoro, one who supported the American Protestants, risked his position and his life to fill his compound with fugitives so that they might be sent down by train to the South.

Above all I was told of Patrick Chukwu, the headmaster of the little primary school on the Vwang compound. His reputation was not a good one, and before we had left the country he had spent a good deal of time going through our books to see if we had any about sex which we wanted to sell. We were not impressed by him, for he was noisy, loud-mouthed, and vulgar. He was one of the three who were marked down to die in Vwang. The other two, George Onokwei the contractor, and Mr Ezebuiro the Director of the Vet., escaped. He, the most harmless of them, died. He had sent his wife and children south, but had stayed, like so many of the victims, to clear up a few business affairs. He knew he was doomed when he went to confession at the Fathers' House. He was offered shelter in the roof, where Isaac the steward was already hiding. He refused it, saying that they would come to seek him even there, and went out, knowingly, to his death.

Our boys escaped. Even Athanasius, working at Maiduguri, where five out of every six Ibos died, made his way to safety. Some of the others got on to the very last train before the pogrom started. From the mission's schools most of them were lorried southward a few days before the massacres. Only one child died, a little boy in the third form at St Murumba's. Even now I find it difficult to comprehend why anyone should wish to kill a child of fourteen, the one who was taken from his hospital bed. I recall now the names of children I knew, like Athanasius, or the little boys my wife taught, Charles, Claver, who always liked to spell his name Clever, Remigius, and many others, and I cannot understand why anyone should ever have wished to kill them. Yet I suppose it was only an everyday killing, one of the figures in the newspaper every morning, an incident in modern history.

The Nigeria we knew was ruined. Out of those ruins some new construction may be built. Already Jos has been declared the capital of a new Middle Belt state which is to reach down to the Benue, but few of the boys we taught will survive to run it. Many must surely be dead already. Young men like Athanasius will surely have taken up arms for their people. Others like Clement, from whose country Colonel Gowon came, must surely have enlisted in the Federal army. And if they live, what memories they will have. For five years we were concerned in the founding of a new nation. This book might have recorded something of the people who should have built it. It may still be so, but if they have failed it has become only a memorial to the dead.

A few weeks before we left we stood on the hills over at Diu. It was the place where the Birom still buried their dead in graves, whose shafts were marked with broken pots. On that hill we stood by an old and grubby compound, the last of the buildings whose ruins covered the near-by hills. The walls were reinforced by lines of stones and their bases were supported with small boulders. Dolorite grinders lay about the ground outside. The skulls of dead animals were fixed in the clay by the entrance, framing the frontal bone of a duiker, the totem of that clan. With one of the boys we looked northwards towards the next range of hills about two miles away. 'Those are our enemies,' said a boy. 'We often fought them in the past with arrows.'

> Tim, Tim, Tim,
> The strongest on the battlefield
> Have brought home the captives' heads.
> Now let us rejoice!
> Now let us play with the heads!
> Let them be angry who fled.

In the fields opposite the school I had sat near one of the compounds while some of the boys spoke to an old farmer. He remembered the old days. There was a look-out, then, constantly, on the top of Diuti, the crag we could see from our school windows. It had been debatable land between the Birom and the Rukuba; bush country covered the whole territory where the Vet., the school, and the farmland now lay, used only for the annual hunt. Into this rough country the Birom settlers cut out their fields. Through the bush crept the Rukuba. The skulls of their victims were heaped in the fields till the flesh rotted and they bleached in the sun, then they were stored in a cave. The last attack had been fifty years before. In those days the five-mile journey to Zawan could not be undertaken alone. The world then was limited to Vwang, near which salt was obtained, and to Zawan and Du, which smelted iron.

It was a way of life: the constant menace of the enemy creeping through the thorn bushes, the weapons always carried to the fields, the poisoned arrow, the short stabbing sword of the Birom, the bleeding trophy, the heads thrown down by the triumphant home-coming raiders, the ritual cannibalism, the dances that repeated past triumphs before an admiring posterity. Now the spears are out again. The skulls of the Ibo who fled to those villages for shelter must now lie bleaching in the open fields.

> On my journey to Mangu, Nbamu,
> I tried to cross a river, Nbamu,
> Which snatched away my brother, Nbamu,
> To the land of my enemies, Nbamu.
> 'What colour was your brother?' said the foe.
> 'Don't ask me the colour,' I said to him.
> > 'He was found with a spear in his chest,
> > You have murdered my brother,' I said to him.
> > 'Come and look at my spear,' said the foe.
> > 'Mine differs from the one in his chest.'